# FREEDOM TWICE LOST

## Arlene Krieger

CLASSIC DAY
PUBLISHING

Seattle, Washington
Portland, Oregon
Denver, Colorado
Vancouver, B.C.
Scottsdale, Arizona
Minneapolis, Minnesota

ISBN: 1-59404-046-X
Library of Congress Control Number: 2004114299

Printed in the United States of America

For additional copies or information contact:
Classic Day Publishing, LLC
2100 Westlake Ave. North, Suite 106
Seattle, WA 98109
www.classicdaypublishing.com
Email: info@classicdaypublishing.com

Design: David Marty Design
Editor: Deb Wolf

Classic Day Publishing, LLC
2100 Westlake Ave. North, Suite 106
Seattle, WA 98109
www.classicdaypublishing.com
Email: info@classicdaypublishing.com

DEDICATED TO
ROBERTO MIRANDA'S
DREAM OF BEING UNITED
WITH HIS FAMILY.

# TABLE OF CONTENTS

# FOREWORD

The book was compiled through a series of taped interviews with Roberto Miranda, research at the Clark County Court House, and interviews with friends. Names of close friends have been changed to protect their requested privacy.

# FREEDOM
# TWICE LOST

Maria Teresa lay in the birthing bed at the local medical center contemplating the birth of her next child. Staring at the fly infested ceiling, she prayed silently that this birth would go quickly, with little pain. There was no money for medicine or the state hospital, and if complications ensued, but this thought she quickly erased from her mind. She knew if problems occurred death was a firm possibility. Too many of her childhood friends had died giving birth at the local medical centers or had the sudden death of a child. Twisting her head with each wrenching contraction, she concentrated on good thoughts on how healthy and happy the baby and she would be. Her deeply bronzed skin, now dripping with perspiration, began signaling the arrival of her second child. "Push," demanded the nurse, as she maneuvered her hands in place to aid the arrival of the newborn. With weighty breathing and profound determination, Roberto Herandez was born June 5,1943, as the steamy summer afternoon sun crawled into the dimly lit room. Cradled in his mother's arms, Maria thanked God for a safe delivery, adding another prayer for the sustained wellbeing of both her and the new infant.

Proud that he had again impregnated his wife, Nmacelnio, Teresa's husband, smiled as he reached down kissing his wife's damp feverish brow. "This child," he proclaimed, "Will be someone special. Everyone will know my son. He will make a difference in the world. You'll see." The tiny curtained cubicle seemed overwhelmingly claustrophobic as husband, nurse and the new child crowded Teresa's space.

"I can't breathe," she whispered. "Please I can't breathe!" Retreating, the nurse quickly returned filling an empty paper cup with tepid water, and brought it to the new mother's lips. Slowly she consumed the contents, then Teresa closed eyes falling into a deep slumber.

Barking quick commands, the ward nurse hustled Teresa's husband out of the room, explaining that his wife needed rest. The nurse would see the baby was comfortable and would take care of the newborn for his first feeding. "She is exhausted, give her time," the nurse prudently reminded.

Not one to argue when it came to women's affairs, the dutiful husband kissed his wife, then clutching her hand tightly he thanked her for giving him a son, and departed the dingy birthing room. He knew there was no money for home nurses; his wife would be on her own as soon as she left the confines of the medical center. Caressing the newborn, the elated father walked proudly out of the room. His firm body stood erect, his moistened mouth in a joyous smile as he announced to the husbands in the waiting area, "I have a son, a beautiful son." This moment of ecstasy would soon be splintered as he hastily walked back to the worksite. Unable to extend his lunch hour, fearing loss of wages, he calculated his return trip factoring in the seven minutes left of this memorable hour. Energized by the birth, Nmacelnio rehearsed the announcement he would make to his co-workers; "I have a son. A beautiful healthy son."

Teresa slept as much as the nursing staff allowed, for she knew all too soon she would endure the arduous quarter mile walk home. Worry and prayer was all the energy she had the time for. For years, she had hidden her Catholic faith under the mattress. A rosary and a silver cross. Overt religious practice was outlawed under the Communist regime. Castro had closed every church. Fearing reprisals, Teresa worshipped Jesus surreptitiously, not even allowing her children to watch her in prayer. It was in this moment she needed to believe that her Lord would aid her and hew new son, and that her daily prayers for a healthy child would be answered.

Although the nurses had coaxed her into taking several short strolls down the crowded hall, the long walk home seemed unfeasible. After the birth of her first baby she had struggled to reach the flat. This time she was older, her body was not in the condition it had once been, and the simple walk seemed an insurmountable journey. Closing her eyes, she drifted into a deep sleep dreaming for the strength to get her and the newborn home safely.

The next morning, a blissful Nmacelino arrived at the center carrying a tiny bouquet of summer flowers picked along the short route. Announcing himself to the receptionist, she beckoned him over to the desk, explaining that his wife would be released the next morning. Acknowledging the grimace upon his face, the receptionist waved her hand at the processing center, "You see all these women? They, too are waiting to give birth, we need the beds. Your wife and son are fine; they will be strong enough to leave tomorrow. Now please don't argue. Too many others are in need." The joy of the moment had been shattered with the reality that his wife and son had to depart so quickly. Four years earlier, he recalled, the clinic had allowed a week stay. Now, with so much poverty, and so few funds, patients were whisked out quickly.

Greeting his sleepy wife, he proudly handed her the bright bouquet, gently kissing her forehead. "Tomorrow is the big day, coming home," he declared. Surveying his spouse for signs of disapproval, all she revealed was a sly smile, and a loving grasp of his callused hand.

"We will be just fine," she assured him, "You will see. Our son, Roberto, he is special, he will be a fine young man." Knowing how to bolster her husband's fearful mood was a gift she had unraveled from Nmacelnio's mother. Recalling the conversation, the words of her mother-in-law would unlock the secret to a loving and strong marriage, "Look into his eyes. Look deep into the blackness of his iris. For there lie the thoughts of his heart. Learn to read his eyes, and you will have a love and a marriage that will endure."

Interrupted by the plump, young, mulatto nurse, the visit was abruptly ended. Stealing a short kiss, he pecked his wife on the neck, squeezed her shoulders and set off for another day at the construction site. His well-chiseled arms became limp as he brushed by the attending nurse. "Rest," he warned his wife, "That Roberto will be a handful." Painfully aware the walk home the following day would be a gruesome effort for both mother and child, he knew he would have to come up with a plan. And that night, upon his return from work, the idea was waiting for him at the doorstep of the flat: a hand truck used to haul groceries from the marketplace. Perfect, he thought. Rummaging through the closet, he located a blanket that would serve to cushion the wooden bottom. He would treat Teresa like a princess; he would haughtily load his family up and parade them through the streets of Havana.

As dusk arrived, Nmacelnio appeared at the center toting a borrowed wagon; ashamed he couldn't offer a better form of transportation but proud he had located something. Escorting his wife and son out of their dingy confines into the soft breezes of the tropical climate, Teresa gathered strength breathing the air, then jubilation as her husband pointed to the blanketed cart. Swollen with pride, Nmacelino announced this was their transportation home. "No need to walk when you can be carried through the village in this cart." The relief reflected in Teresa's smile was proof of her sublime faith in her husband's ability to take care of the family. As she silently prayed, she knew as long as she and Nmacelnio would be married he would always take care of her. Sitting in the rustic cart she felt overwhelmingly secure. "See," she smiled at Roberto. "Your daddy will always take care of us. Now we go home to meet your sister, Myrna. I know she is going to love you."

The short trip took longer than expected as neighbors emerged from their tiny bungalows to wish them well, showering them with congratulations. Opening the front door of their tiny home, both husband and wife were surprised as Myrna came rushing to meet them, then gestured to the white wicker bassinet announcing, "Presents from the neighbors!" Tears welled up in Teresa's eyes as her daughter pointed to the powder blue layette spread across the room. Most of the clothing and blankets were hand-me-downs, but freshly cleaned, perfuming the room with the smell of lilac and talcum powder. Again, Teresa withdrew into silent prayer thanking her Lord for the gift of life and the donations generously given by the neighbors.

Settling in for the first night home, the family was visited by a constant stream of well wishers, who dropped off additional gifts of food, toys, and clothing, honoring the birth of their second child. Teresa's eyes fell on the corner of the room, watching her first son peacefully sleeping while in the opposite corner, their first daughter sat quietly consumed by a comic book. The fidgeting infant in his bassinet would be different. She too sensed Roberto was a special child, that he would do great things.

Teresa's chest tightened as the small home became smaller

with each child. The one room slowly began closing in on her. "How will we make ends meet?" she asked her husband. "Just look at our home, dirt floors, no toilets, no privacy, how long can we survive like this?"

But worry was part of being a parent, and Teresa feared there would be many a sleepless night with her newborn. Their cramped flat was a block and a half from the baseball stadium, and when the team hosted games, the ruckus could be heard for blocks. If the Havana team won, the streets resounded in wild jubilant cheering followed by a late evening procession of half drunk men littering the streets with empty glass beer bottles. If the team lost, the parade was simply quieter; men chucking the same bottles of beer, but with less enthusiasm. Roberto would have to endure these late night intrusions of his sleep, as did Myrna, the oldest child. Perhaps this was an omen. Perhaps Roberto would grow to become a famous baseball player. Perhaps this was God's plan. Faith. Teresa replaced her worries and looked to God's plan then fell promptly asleep.

Being the center of attention was short lived for Roberto as his parents quickly added two children to the blossoming family: Maria Teresa, [Cuchy ] and Nmacelino. Cuchy received her comical nick-name from a popular Mexican movie. "I want to name her myself," proudly expressed Roberto to his reticent mother. " Remember the movie you took me to see? How funny and pretty the actress was? I thought it would be great having a sister named after a famous movie star." Reflecting on Roberto's excitement, shaking her head in agreement, the nick name replaced the birth name. Nmacelino, the last child, was given his father's traditional Spanish namesake. It was in this tiny one room flat the Miranda family lived; the toilets and the shower were a few paces directly outside the front door, and were shared with the immediate neighbors living next to and across from them. The simple task of eating was complicated with ice blocks serving as the only form of refrigeration, and a small outdoor charcoal barbecue pit serving as the only form of preparing hot foods. They lived in utter poverty; the dearth of food was unbearable at times, as constant hunger stalked the home.

At that time, in Cuba, it wasn't easy for a poor family to get a refrigerator, but they did have electricity. When Castro came into power, so many people became poor, and lost jobs, there was no money to pay for things. The Cuban dollar could only be used to purchase food, clothing and bare necessities, no one was allowed to use the Cuban dollar to purchase imported goods. Anything the family wanted to buy that wasn't produced in the country could only be purchased with American dollars. No country in the world accepted the Cuban dollar. It had no value.

Despite their destitute life style, Roberto reminisced about happy times spent with his mother and sisters. One of his fondest memories was the yearly carnival. The streets were filled with vibrant parades. People dressed in exotic costumes. There was food, games, and loads of pulsating Latino music. It was truly a joyous event. His brothers and sisters standing at the edge of the parade route would whistle and cheer, catching trinkets thrown by the clowns and street dancers. There were long Conga dance lines with loud trumpets playing, and flamboyantly costumed dancers singing zealously. "This is a so much fun, I love the music and the costumes," Roberto would tell his mom.

Making money was almost an impossibility when he was very young, but when the American ships entered the Havana port, he learned how to beg for coins from the tourists. His friends had taught him how to say, "Can you spare some change for my family," which worked wonders in opening up the pocketbooks of rich, heartfelt Americans, especially during prosperous periods.

Then there were times that were not so happy. When his mother would get angry at Roberto, she would threaten to dress him in girl's clothing, and boy, would that make him mad. Teresa knew how to get her second child to behave. She knew he would never want to wear girl's clothing, he was too macho for that humiliation. The oldest sister was born when money was more plentiful and was blessed with a much more extensive wardrobe than the second child, so the punishment was easy for Teresa to administer.

All the children attended the local elementary school, which was only four blocks from home. Because of overcrowding, the school had two shifts; morning and afternoon. The four children attended classes from 7:00am to 11:00am each day, returning home for lunch. Roberto was a street kid, never enjoying school. When his older sister, Myrna, would drop him off at school, he would wait until she had entered her classroom, then he would sneak out of school and play with the kids on the streets. He wanted to be with the kids on the street, but most of the time they were fighting. Afternoons were spent on homework and ball playing. The brothers loved playing baseball, often dreaming they would be one of the famous players on the Havana team. Since birth they had been enticed and entertained by the cheering crowds up the street, and as they grew, they sharpened their skills in preparation for this dream. Street ball was the favorite pastime of all the young boys in the village, keeping them from getting caught up in more dangerous forms of activities such as stealing and drugs.

Pointing to his ankle, Roberto proudly showed off a scar, a battle wound from a spike entrenched in his leg during the heat of play. Standing erect he swung at a curve ball with all his might, sending it halfway down the street. A homerun! he anticipated as he hurriedly rounded the bases. But the fielder was just as intense in getting this little squirt out, and with an outstretched arm the savvy street boy grabbed the loose ball making an accurate throw to home plate. Sliding into the base, the catcher and he collided. Angry, Roberto retaliated for this injury, soundly beating up the offending friend. Unfortunately, Teresa had been a witness to the squabble, and with great disapproval, marched onto the makeshift playing field paddling her son in full view of the neighborhood. Mortified, Roberto realized he had better change his ways, or suffer the wrath of severe punishment.

There was no doubt that Roberto had ball playing on his mind much more than schoolwork. Another incident occurred when the baseball went over the side of a house, so he decided he would climb over the roof to retrieve the only ball his friends had available. Much to his chagrin, the roof was in such poor condition that he fell through an unprotected opening and he landed squarely in the neighbor's living room. All he could recall was waking up in a hospital with his mother and sister starring at him. He knew he was in big trouble, but his mother smiled and said everything was going to be okay.

After this incident, Myrna carefully checked in on Roberto at school, making sure he stayed in the classroom and completed his studies. Everyday so much work, he thought, he wasn't the smart one. That was Myrna. She helped her younger brother with his homework. She had all the brains in the family, the only one who attended a private college. Her dreams were to become a doctor, but she married instead. What a shame, lamented her family, she would have been a great doctor, she was so smart, but she fell in love and got married, that was the end of her possible medical career.

In addition to playing baseball, Roberto's second great love was watching the game. Many childhood afternoons and evenings were spent in the bleacher section of the baseball stadium cheering the Havana team. Luckily, one of his comrades had located an entranceway allowing them to creep into the games undetected by the ticket takers.

Amazing his family, Roberto completed elementary school, but not high school. His fondest memories were of the pretty girls in his classes. Back then he was considered very handsome, and had many girlfriends. He used to point out a girl and say to his pals, she was one of his girlfriends, but he didn't know her name. They would all laugh at him. But sure enough a week or two later, he would be holding her hand or talking to her, and then his doubting friends would see she was truly his girlfriend.

In Havana the parents were very old-fashioned when it came to courting. When Roberto called on his dates, the parents would come to the front door and tell him to stay away and not to come calling again. But when the family approved of him as a possible suitor, the couple was chaperoned by a parent or close relative. This made kissing and handholding impossible, but people were traditional and protective of their daughters. The old people wanted respect.

In spite of the accepted traditional courting practices, Roberto managed to act on his fantasies by spawning children with lovers Madtha Sorocco, and Barbara Judith Martinez. He had three grown children, that he is aware of, Robertico from Madtha and Barbara and Milagros from Barbara. He often ruminates about them although he hasn't seen them since infanthood. He was very young then, and very wild. He loved the girls and they loved him back, maybe too much. He hasn't had any contact with the children. He doesn't know where they are or what they are doing. He lived life by taking chances, he never looked back. Sometimes he thought there might have been another child, but he didn't know where. He was very sexual, and the women thought very handsome. For him it was easy to find lovers.

Once he was in love and she broke his heart. He did not want to talk about her, or reveal her name. The last time he talked about her was in 1971. All the women who had entered his life brought love and happiness, this was the first time a woman had crushed his ego. If he were to marry this would have been his choice. Up until this mysterious woman had entered his life, love was wrapped around sexual pleasure. Barely out of teenage years the infinite passion of true love blinded him. Never had he experienced the euphoria that being in love meant. The forlorn longing, churning stomach, and ever present smile defined his behavior. Looking after her own welfare, his girlfriend saw no future in a poor street boy living in a single hut with a huge family. Still a teenager, she knew he had a lot of growing up to do before they could marry His reputation as a lover, already fostering three offspring further fueled her rapid departure.

The sedentary life of marriage escaped this young man who aspired to find life's meaning within the political arena. Mending a broken heart, he sought a more challenging life in the changing government. Fellow street fighters grew up channeling their energy in the same direction. Although their actions were reminiscent of earlier street play, their motivations were not. Together they rallied against the changing tide of government. The loving passionate young man, had found another passion, fighting the incoming Castro regime.

# A FAMILY
# IN TROUBLE

As Teresa's four children grew rapidly, and the household needs became more demanding, she obtained a job as a maid, cooking and cleaning for a wealthy family. It was around this time that Nmenclio began his weekend binge drinking. Loving Teresa had consequences, more children. As the tiny flat bulged with each new infant, he became meaner growing impatient at the least bit of misbehavior. Nmenclio felt the walls closing in on him with the cry of each new child. He was overwhelmed. Although his job was steady, it paid for only the bare necessities. He was frustrated and sought to put the blame on the intolerable conditions elsewhere. When the Friday afternoon paychecks were handed out, he would quickly turn it into cash, then head for the local bar and brothel. After hours of carousing, he returned to the flat, and instigated fights with his wife. The routine continued for months, with a plethora of nasty and violent incidences, a few sending Teresa back to the local medical center where nurses tended to wounds from the drunken beatings. As the poundings escalated, they began to include Myrna, which Roberto found intolerable. There was no outside help or support groups; as the beatings grew worse and worse, extending to more family members, Teresa found herself in a hopeless situation.

With the six of them sleeping in one room, there was no privacy, nowhere to run or hide from the brutal beatings of a drunken husband. The two sisters sharing a cot, and the two brothers sleeping on the floor, used every inch of space in the tiny flat; at times, the walls seemed as though they would come crashing down on Teresa. The infidelities and drunken outbursts of her husband were impossible to hide from the children. Despite both parents working, the children's empty stomachs grumbled most nights as she kissed them goodnight. Teresa felt she had no choice but to put up with the violent behavior, otherwise the children would be even worse off than they already were. It took two parents working to be able to offer the family even the scantest of life's necessities.

Her nightly prayers of hope and happiness were transforming into desperate outcries. Where was her Lord when she needed him? Teresa often thought that Castro's closing of all the churches had in fact closed Jesus' blessings on her family and Cuba. All the love she had to give to her four children wasn't enough. They needed food, clothing, and education to survive. So worried for the need of basic necessities, she spent little time reflecting on her husband's brutal treatment. All energy was poured into caring and providing for the family. Fondling her rosary, she asked Jesus to give her the strength needed to get through each day.

The brutal scenes played out in Roberto's mind, causing many sleepless nights. He began plotting his retaliation against his father. Roberto's physical prowess had been honed on the streets, his fists were ready for confrontation. Street smart, Roberto wasn't about to initiate a fight he couldn't win. Being the oldest son, he felt as if he were the head of the household, and therefore responsible for avenging both his mother and his siblings. Summoning all his courage, he approached his father threatening him if he touched his mother or siblings in a violent manner. There would be ramifications. Stepping outside the flat, father and son began a violent fight, bashing, punching and kicking. Raising his fists, Roberto dealt the first blow knocking the wind out of his dad. Then a left hook sent the son screaming onto the dirt with pain. Glancing up, Nmenclio caught Teresa's eyes filled with tears as she silently stood in the doorway. Waiting to see if his son was alive, the father bent down grabbing Roberto by his shoulders. Steadying himself, Roberto caught his breath, grabbed his father's arm, and staggered up. Then with all his might he punched his dad in the chest and knocked him backwards. Hitting his  head on the edge of a trashcan, the father lay unconscious. Crying hysterically, Teresa grabbed her son, gently carried him back to the solar, and tended to his wounds, while the neighbors flagged down a police car which quickly removed his father to the local jail.

Deciding he needed a change of atmosphere, Roberto packed a bag and moved into his grandmother's home, where he would be safe, better fed, and loved. His father was not opposed to this arrangement, as it left him the freedom to continue his abuse on his wife and sisters without fear of another reprisal from his son. The grandparents were financially comfortable, living in a hacienda style home in the rural countryside. The trip would take two hours on the bus, as the only road was filled with potholes from late afternoon downpours. Loaning money and dabbling in construction allowed the grandparents a richer life style with luxuries their grandson only dreamed of having. His doting grandparents showered him with attention, teaching him music, finances, enhancing his reading and writing skills. But mostly they taught him about love, and the art of congenial family relations.

The grandparents had made numerous overtures over the last

several years, but Teresa's husband balked at every gift. Not only did Nmacelnio view it an intrusion, but considered their presents demeaning to his manhood and his ability to provide for the family. With the birth of each child, Nmenclio had less to do with his in-laws. Perhaps it was jealousy, thought Teresa, as she hid their gifts in the homes of neighbors.

One day, Sofia, Roberto's grandma, prepared rice and sardines, but her grandson balked at the fish, stating he hated eating the wiggly things, and that he was allergic. Persisting on tasting the gourmet preparation the dutiful grandson acquiesced. Leaving the plate partially empty satisfied his obligation, but the allergic reaction had begun instantaneously. Grabbing his grandmother, he pointed to his tongue as he gasped frantically for air. Distraught, she pulled him into her arms, dragged him into the van, and drove wildly to the local hospital. Screaming loudly to the nurses, Sophia accompanied her sick grandson into the emergency room. "Its all my fault," she cried "I should have listened to him, I should not have pushed him into eating the fish." Crying from guilt, she hastily explained the nature of his illness, while the nurses worked at a rapid pace to prevent his throat from completely closing up. The severity of his illness mandated a long stay in the hospital as the staff worked relentlessly to combat the reaction, massaging his heart back to a steady rhythm.

Each morning Sofia would come to visit her grandson before she set off to the office, but one day Roberto noticed a redness in her eyes, and a somber mood. Kissing him gently on the forehead, she whispered that his father would be coming in a day or two to take him back to his home. "I love you, but I must also respect your father's wishes, especially since he blames me for all of this." Gathering his hands, she kissed him again, and promised to take care of him in the future.

Besieged with fear of retuning back to a household filled with fighting and hate, Roberto dressed, packed up his few possessions and fled the hospital. This time he didn't return to his home, but went back to the streets and his comrades in Havana. Periodically he would check up on his mom and siblings, but most of the time he kept his distance. Homeless, he stayed alive by hard work, and by using the skills he had gleaned from both his parents and grandparents. He did housework, sold bottles, shined shoes, pushed fruit carts. He did anything and everything. Using most of the money for living expenses, he dutifully dropped off a portion of his income each week to his mom.

"Such a good boy," Teresa sighed, reaching out to kiss her son. "You always take care of us. You never forget your mother. I wish you would come home to live. I hate the place where you are living. It's a homeless shelter and you are not homeless. It's dangerous, that place. Please think about coming home."

Reflecting on the austere rooms filled with the sounds of drunks and the wails of drug addicts tempted him to return home, but the brutality of his father dominated his decision to stay away.

Taking his mom's hand, he promised to visit soon, but he couldn't specify when. He had to try to make it on his own. He told her he needed time to experiment with different ideas. Excited, he described a new friend. "Professor Albani is teaching me to play music, just like grandpa, and I love it. Maybe I will become a famous trumpet player or drummer."

"Just come home anytime," she told him. "This is your home and I love you."

Then one rueful day his father destroyed the house. It was a Friday afternoon and he had used his paycheck to purchase bottles of rum. Arriving at the flat completely drunk, Nmacelnio was angered at the sight of Roberto. He took a knife and cut Roberto in the arm. He retracted the weapon and turned on his mother, stopping just short of murder. Myrna called the police, and the cops took Nmacelnio away.

After the shock of the fight scene had subsided, the household was secretly relieved; the family would be safe from the weekly brutalities inflicted by a drunken father and husband. Again, Teresa prayed that her family would have the food needed to survive. Now there was one less breadwinner in the family. Again, Roberto took charge of the household, landing a decent paying position at the local post office. He and Myrna felt both guilty and responsible for their father's incarceration, believing they had burdened their dad with more than he was capable of handling.

Replacing the second paycheck was most paramount in his mind. He was fortunate to obtain a job as a mail carrier, a job he held for two and one half years. It was hard work, with the sun so hot upon his face, and there were so many houses to deliver to. But he did it. He got paid once a month. As soon he received the paycheck he would cash it and give his mother most of the money.

Tired of the treacherous heat, Roberto grabbed the opportunity to become a city bus driver. In spite of lengthy hours, the vast part of the day was spent in an air-conditioned bus chauffeuring the locals from the ocean to the inner city of Havana. Once in a while, a tourist would put extra change in his hand, but the majority of the time the bus was filled with Cuban minimum wage passengers. A clean uniform added importance to his job, serving as strong motivation to keep the comfortable position as bus drive for several years. The route had come to be routine, perhaps even mundane, as he set out each morning in his pressed and authoritative looking uniform. He was proud of his job, never taking the responsibilities of transporting his fellow countrymen lightly.

The morning breezes cooled the air as Roberto deftly wound the large bulky bus along the rugged road from the ocean to the heart of the city. Although there were fewer cars than normal, numerous construction trucks passed the bus both coming and going to the ocean shore. He persistently panned the road, he was a cautious driver, never in a rush to make a schedule; safety was the overriding goal. Abruptly, he heard the hum of a truck, but the speed at which it was moving was faster than anticipated. An explosion of engines ignited, as fire broke out instantaneously, and the two vehicles met on a head-on collision. Metal flew violently into the air. There were cries of children and mothers fiercely seeking survival, as dark gray smoke engulfed the interior of the bus. Passengers were tossed inside the burning inferno, as the heat grew more intense. Roberto's head had been knocked against the windshield. His scalp bled profusely from the savage glass blown into the driver's seat, his chest gushed with blood from the force of the flying glass. Yet he collected his thoughts, and opened up the door. He dragged out as many passengers as his strength could muster. Passers-by quickly came to the aid, calling ambulances and administrating to the causalities.

Disorientated, Roberto awoke to the bustling sounds of an emergency room. He looked at the bandages, noticing an I-V, and breathing device on his nose, "What happened?" he mumbled.

"You are a fortunate man," answered the doctor, "You are lucky to have survived the crash. Many others didn't make it. Your injuries are extensive. We will have you here for a while."

Receding into a semi-comatose state, it was several days before he learned the gravity of the accident: eight people dead, several serious injuries, and one fortunate bus driver who would survive. The three-week stay in the hospital allowed his wounds to heal, but the nightmares couldn't be cured. Scarred both physically and emotionally, he never returned to bus driving.

# CONSEQUENCES OF DEMONSTRATION

Although other jobs kept him busy, he never gave up the street life. His friends, now grown, had transformed from scrappy fighters to fighters with a cause — to oust Castro. Channeling their pent up energies, Roberto, along with his friends, collected weapons, guns, explosives, and ammunition, and began scheming demonstrations to overthrow the Communist regime. Rallies began peacefully enough as the band of street fighters gathered strength in numbers as well as ammunition. The altercations escalated violently, until one day, guns began blazing while protestors screamed. "Death to communism." Suddenly a bomb exploded, scattering the crowd in a thousand directions. Shrieks of terror filled the teeming streets as both civilians and military dashed for safety. Castro's police gathered up the bloodied fighters, throwing them in paddy wagons sending them to the political jails or off to the sugar cane fields. Luckily Roberto had escaped the crowds, hiding in an alleyway.

The young militants wanted Batista back in charge. There was food on the table, jobs, and money in the cookie jar during the leader's reign. Welcoming the Americans, and the money they lavishly deposited throughout the tiny country gave Cuba a sound financial base. Between the tourist industry, and exports of cigars, rum and sugar cane, young men and women were able to make a decent living. Castro destroyed everything.

Unharmed yet undeterred, Roberto promised revenge on those who took his friends. The bloody scene set the stage for his unabashed resolve to avenge his lifelong buddies. Freedom was the simple goal; they were ninety miles away from a country where everyone had freedom. This basic human need was worth fighting for, perhaps, even losing your life for. He continued prowling the streets, meeting with political allies sharing the same dream. Next time, he promised himself, he would go to the demonstrations armed, and ready for war.

Assembling in clandestine locations, the band of protestors planned the next altercation. Bubbling with anger, excitement, and anticipation, they shared a vow of strong resistance by becoming martyrs for the plight of freedom. Taking the streets, they gathered strength as small numbers of young men and women joined in the prodigious march up the village square. Fortified with opposing weaponry, Castro's army ambushed the band of dissidents, carrying many off to jail. This time Roberto was not so lucky. Brandishing a small pistol, he managed to fire off several shots, but was subdued by police, and carried off to jail where he spent the next four years of his life paying penance for opposing the Communist regime.

The Cuban prison was not a comfortable place. Hardly any food, the dirt floors teaming with insects, hot, no sanitation to speak of, and then the guards sent the inmates to the sugarcane fields to work as slaves. But he survived the four years. One day, the police just came to the jail and released Roberto. They took him off to the sugar cane fields and made him work there all day long in the hot sun. It was free labor, that was how the country survived. So the slaves cut the sugar cane for free, then made it into rum, and that made the money for the country to run.

Roberto's incarceration was political, but many other prisoners were arrested and convicted of murder; the death sentence was their punishment. The police put a prisoner in jail and in one week he was taken outside and shot. Boom! Just like that, and one's life was gone. Cuba is a country not to be arrested for killing, as justice is handled swiftly, without recourse.

Roberto fought against the political scene because Castro killed people, he killed a lot of people. This was information that Americans did not know. Each person lived out their lives, and one day someone was killed, and no one knew why. That person was just gone. Cuba was not like other countries, there was no free local newspapers, people in the country did not know what was going on, they read only what the government told the papers to print, not what was really happening. Gramma, the communist newspaper, was printed at the whim of the government, reporting only approved articles, with no mention of political anti-government rallies, or any behavior that would undermine the goal of the regime.

Upon his return home, the police were relentless, arresting Roberto for no reason, other than to badger and bully him. Defaming Castro's government would prove to lead to a life of constant harassment by the henchmen serving the Communist party. The police knocked upon Teresa's door almost daily, intimidating and frightening her and her children. This was when Teresa began begging her son to leave Cuba and find a better life, one that was free from the torments and tortures of the Communist police.

A childhood friend had confided to Roberto that his family had located a small motorboat, and was planning to sail to the United States; this would be a golden opportunity to safely escape. He wasn't ready to leave his family. Although everyday was a living hell evading the police, his family, the only thing he valued, was in Havana, and he unselfishly could not leave them, after all he was the man in the family. Duty to his family took precedent over anything else, even his political convictions. Had he followed his friend to America he would have been in a much better position. At that time, Cubans had relocated there were many more economic opportunities.

From a high vantage point he could clearly view the constant reminder of what freedom meant; the façade of Guantanamo Bay, home of an American base. This monument to freedom loomed as unattainable. There were six checkpoints where everyone had to present papers or some formal document in order to get through all the checkpoints. It was impossible. One of his friends had tried to use this as a way to escape for political asylum, and he was refused by the U.S. military base, sent back and put in a Cuban jail for years. No one wanted to be in a Cuban jail, especially if seeking political refuge. The guards treated the inmates very badly. The existence of this military base was inherited and accepted by Castro, allowing the Americans the right to the piece of property, provided none of Castro's countrymen used this as a device to escape the island. Even though the base was close enough to walk to, it would not accept locals. It was too dangerous to try. The Cuban guards were armed and would shoot anyone who tried to run. And there ended any possibility for freedom

In April 1980 a Cuban man, with six passengers in tow, revved up the engine of his car and crashed it through the gates of the Peruvian embassy. A brawl commenced, resulting in a security guard being shot. Mortified, Castro asked all Cuban security guards to abandon their duties, allowing anyone who did not wish to remain in the country to depart at will. What ensued shocked even the most jaded Communistic leader A large group of over 10,000, Cubans rushed into the Peruvian embassy, and demanded political asylum. Word of the insurrection hit the streets like wildfire, as thousands jammed into the tiny embassy. Hearing the screams from the street Teresa searched out her son. "Now is the time to leave," she pleaded. "Please do not let this opportunity go by. This time you will be safe." Pointing to the chaos on the streets, "You will be just one of the thousands in the crowd."

There was no time to think. Freedom was all he desired. Wrapping his arms tightly around his mother, he kissed her good by. He never looked back

The press had a field day snapping photos of children, pregnant mothers, and young men all living without food, water, or toilets in exchange for life as free humans. Several thousand were airlifted to Puerto Rico. But the onslaught of citizens was so immense, the Cuban leader announced he would open up the port at Mariel, giving the fleeing masses alternative forms of transportation.

Caught up in the roaming crowd, Roberto found himself at the door of the embassy. Surrounded by throngs of fellow countrymen they pounded on the thick metal gates begging for asylum. Miraculously, the gates swung open allowing the asylum seekers to filter in. Lying on the embassy floor, Roberto dreamed of the freedoms he would experience. He could go where he wanted, buy what he wanted, love who he wanted, read, eat, listen, breathe what he wanted. For once he would not have to answer to a government for the simplest of life's needs; he could choose his destiny. Thoughts ran bittersweet as he mentally balanced what he would be giving up as he parted his childhood home. Pondering the reality that might be months or years before he would ever see his family, his own children, or the love of his life, he fortified his reverie with hopes he could pave the path for the others to follow. Once he landed a job, he would send money home. He would bring all his loved ones legitimately to the states, and they would all live together, but better, happier, free, with food in their bellies, clothes on their backs, and a decent place to live. America was the golden land of opportunity. He would make his life a success. He would show the communists that a free life was a better life.

Teresa had unselfishly encouraged her son to take the chance and go. As foreign sounding voices announced the seaport had been cleared for the asylum seekers to leave Cuba, Roberto took off all his clothes except his underwear. He boarded a small fishing vessel that would take him to freedom — America. He truly believed by shedding his clothes, he would be shedding his past. Although metaphoric in nature, it was his way of showing he wanted a new beginning. He wanted a new life filled with hope and prosperity. These were the only valuables he would bring to America.

# LANDING
# ON FREE SOIL

Roberto, now 37 years old, became one of over 125,000 refugees to escape Cuba seeking a better life — one filled with freedom. This grand exodus was named the "Mariel Boat lift." He remembered the Cuban guards standing at the edge of the docks heckling the crowd, throwing rocks and cursing, as they boarded the boats. Not only did civilians flee the tiny island, but additionally, Castro benevolently threw open the gates of the prisons, the hospitals, and the centers for the mentally ill. Cordially inviting all the indigent, sick, and prosecuted citizens of his fine country to leave. The dictator cleaned house of all citizenry he deemed unfit to remain in his country.

There were numerous safe departures, but on this day God did not make the warm gulf seas friendly. As Roberto settled in a corner of the fishing vessel for the seventeen hour ride, it was easy to become distracted by the needs of others: young children, infants, mothers and elderly people needed strength and help in surviving the arduous journey. Without food, water, toilets, or clothing, the small band of asylum seekers would be forced to conjure up strength from within their souls in order to bear the vicissitudes of the journey. Infants wailed, mothers prayed, elderly clung to the sturdiest piece of ship; children smiled or cried as the boat slowly tipped from side to side as it left the weathered wooden dock.

Sounds of waves lapping up the sides of the ship defined the first taste of freedom for the passengers tucked inside the hold.

Momentarily, Roberto was distracted by the voluminous clouds passing above. Looking up at the azure blue sky, he began playing out a metaphor in his eye's view — the clouds, so free to come and go, crossing vast expanses of earth. Why can't we as humans be just as free? How do we as humans justify the nature of our existence when simple clouds are free to roam the earth, yet our lives are kept in bondage by a few armed men? Does coming to America mean we travelers on this ship will taste the freedom the clouds have? Will the forces of nature give us the opportunity to share in what seems to be so acceptable? Will our choices be based upon our wants and needs, rather than the dictates of a few military men? The air, so clean, warm and pure, heightened his senses, opening up his mind to the possibilities that lay ahead.

Turning to a crying infant, he offered the mother a hand while she tended to her two older frightened children. The wet diaper, fraught with a pungent odor, signaled the need for a quick change. Smiling, they exchanged duties, the mother changing the infant, while Roberto hastily clutched the arms of her sobbing children. Throwing the soiled diaper overboard relieved many passengers sitting downwind. As the trip progressed, so did the warm Caribbean winds, the seas churning with foaming whitecaps slapping against the bow of the fishing boat, forcing the travelers to find sturdier points to cling on. The smiling faces now scowled in fear, but for many, seasickness overwhelmed their terrified state. Children's demeanor escalated from unrest to fright. With many screaming, and crying profusely, it was all the mothers could do to quiet their young. The noise from the sea drowned out the sea captain's warning to hang tough, the ride ahead would be rough.

Without food, water or toilet facilities, the trip proved impossibly grueling. When a passenger had to pee, they were forced do it overboard. The women who needed privacy, were surrounded by several other women who created a makeshift lavatory. They picked a spot, and when they had to go, they created privacy by standing in a circle.

Roberto was an excellent swimmer, spending hot summer days at an inlet near the docks, where he learned how to dive for shells and coins. Many island boys realized it was lucrative to learn how to swim, as they found pocket change diving for money thrown overboard by wealthy cruise ship travelers. But the seas ahead of him were stronger than any he had ever encountered. His confidence disintegrated when he realized how far the ship was out to sea, and the impossibility of swimming to the safety of shore. Gathering strength, he kept replaying a self-made mantra — he would survive, he would survive.

There were times when the reality, the finality of life was unbearable. When things were seen, when circumstances allowed people to see what should be unseen, to hear sounds that were not intended for the ears of a passerby, to feel the wretched sense of the impact death had upon humanity. For so many believers schooled with the sense of God in the psyche guiding and explaining, or minimally allowing the mind to cope with the unimaginable, our hero had nothing to appeal to when he, and the passengers on that boat witnessed the ravages that empowered the nature of the ocean to unleash.

In the distance, perhaps one hundred meters away, another fishing boat, filled with fellow Cubans escaping to the coast of the America, began to rock wildly. A huge wave, bigger than anyone had noticed washed over the edge of tiny vessel, and caused it to capsize. Fifty bodies were flung over the ship into the rolling seas. They were screaming mercilessly. The horror was witnessed by all the terrified passengers on Roberto's ship, as they cried and begged the captain to redirect their boat toward the drowning victims. Heads bobbing, arms flaying, shrieks, and bodies floating in the curls of the treacherous waves were all that could be detected from the remnants of the ship.

"No," replied the captain, "Our tiny ship is already overloaded, and if we take additional passengers, we will capsize as well. Just look at the wild seas. We still have many miles to go. No, God will have to take care of those souls now. Look behind us. There are huge waves. I can't turn the ship into those waves." Holding the wheel with renewed determination to safely route his passengers to shore, he steadfastly aligned the boat to meet the oncoming waves with the skills of an expert seaman. He would not be deterred from his duty of bringing the ship safely into the dock of an American port. He had been entrusted with a flock of asylum seekers, and they were all the ship could hold. No more, he rationalized to himself. Better they should survive, then pluck the dying passengers and destroy the hopes and dreams of his entire ship.

Roberto's eyes welled up with tears as he tried to cope with the tragedy of his fellow countrymen dying before his eyes. He had never been witness to death, so many at one time. Recoiling from the scene, he could remember fights, brutal street scenes, but never ever had he seen cold-blooded death of the purely innocent. There were women, infants, young children, a group just like the one on his ship. They did nothing to deserve this untimely demise. Nothing, nothing, he could think up could make sense of this catastrophe. Reaching inside his soul, he could find no answer, no rationale for the instant death of so many harmless beautiful people. The only thought ravaging his mind was that freedom was so powerful that many had to die so others could enjoy the life America had to offer. Unlike the few elders on the boat, who had been privy to the solace the Catholic faith could offer, he had no God to help him cope with the horrific fatalities. As a few pulled out hidden rosaries and jeweled crosses, pleading to Jesus for salvation, Roberto had no one, nor nothing to turn to. All resolve had to come from himself. Through devoted prayer, they begged God for both mercy on the drowning souls as well as mercy upon the themselves.

Those clinging to their symbols found peace, as their Lord saw fit to allow the tiny overcrowded ship to anchor into the port at Key West. The seas had died down, and the captain proudly yelled, "Land. The port is in sight." Mustering strength, the weary band produced anticipatory smiles, focusing all eyes at the front of the boat to view the sight of free land, the first vestiges of the American shore. Slowly the motor died down, as the captain expertly docked the boat at the pier delegated expressly for the incoming refugees. One by one, each jumped off the wavering boat onto the soil of freedom. The motley group was met by affable Cubans who escorted them to a holding area where they received water, food, clothing, and shelter. The local community had already received the first wave of asylum seekers, and was told another group was on the way. Roberto was in the second group of escapees. Anxious, perhaps scared, the group scattered into diverse areas of the military camp where their needs could be evaluated. "So this is what freedom looks like," Roberto thought. "Kind, everyone was kind, and caring." The immigrants were given food and water, even though they didn't ask. They were given a place to sleep. He wondered what he must do in return.

Spanish interpreters thoroughly explained to the asylum seekers that they would remain in the encampment until a sponsor could be located. Then each would be sent to live in the sponsor's home. The encampment wasn't bad. The immigrants were free to come and go as they wished, but at night they had to return to military base and sleep. Roberto spent his days wandering the narrow crowded streets of Key West, a sleepy port town, which bustled with snowbirds escaping their northern homes in the winter months. Quaint plantation white-washed buildings lined the streets, as did boutique eateries and souvenir shops. This upscale resort was home to many cruisers, and catered to middle and upper class families who wanted to sail to more exotic ports in less conventional types of ships. The harbor was replete with entertainers, musicians, and vendors selling local crafts. There was always something to see, which kept Roberto amused during the warm humid days, as he waited patiently for a sponsor to materialize. His constant thought was, "At least I am free," which served as the basis for his continued survival. He had food, clothing, water, and shelter, more than he had back home; the necessities had been benevolently given to him by a free government, and for this he was appreciative and profoundly thankful.

Life could be seen as a level of comparison, or at times, a trade off. Giving up family and loved ones who offered support, were the sacrifices the asylum seeker was willing to make in order to aspire to his dreams of freedom. To wake up, to smell the air, walk where you decided to walk, eat what you chose, say what you wanted, read what you desired, was Roberto's passion — his destiny. Even though he never tasted complete liberty, he desired it, and now, although his days rambled on without purpose, he had achieved his destiny; to live as a free man. He asked for little, as he had lived with so little.

An immigrant in a strange land, he was reticent to form deep bonds with his countrymen as the holding area was a transient home, and everyone he met would shortly be transferred to another location. America was a huge place, thousands of miles long and wide, and any chance for developing an intense relationship would be destroyed the moment a sponsor had been found. The landmass was so large, it would prove to be a remote possibility anyone he befriended would be sent to the same location. Thus he sheltered himself from establishing deep relationships with men, and especially women. Laughing to himself, he was cognizant that he had left at least three children in Cuba, and he was in no position to plant the seed of another child.

# SETTLING IN

Six months had passed in aimless, but free, living conditions, when a Wisconsin farmer contacted the camp and offered a sponsorship. Now, Roberto, close to forty, the aging immigrant had few years remaining for heavy manual labor, but he gladly accepted the challenge. Gathering his few possessions, and bidding his compact group of countrymen goodbye, he boarded a bus headed to a rural farm in the midwestern state. Grasping the bus ticket, he humbly presented it to the mulatto bus driver, who thanked him, then pointed to the empty seats, and motioned him to take a place. Luckily, the driver was bilingual, fully comprehending the plight of the refugees, as he had played chauffeur for hundreds of Latinos over the past several months.

After what seemed like a hundred hours of travel, Roberto arrived at a mid-sized rural farm set in bucolic central Wisconsin. The warm sunny morning was comforting as his new sponsor introduced himself, then bid Roberto welcome to his expansive dairy farm. Smith Jackson, a tall robust farmer sporting the quintessential ruddy outdoor complexion, joyously welcomed his newest employee. Giving Roberto a sturdy handshake, he escorted him to the oversized worn truck, threw his belongings into the back bed, turned over the engine and bolted out of the parking lot. Driving through what appeared to be endless fields of corn, they finally arrived at the dairy farm. Afraid to say the wrong words, each man sat in silence the duration of the short trip. Flipping on the turn signal, Smith headed down a gravel road lined with tall evergreens and an assortment of walnut and fruit trees. Twitching his nose, the immigrant smelled manure for the first time in many years. There was no doubt that cows were lazily grazing in the thousand-acre farm. The promise of a better life came to fruition as he sauntered through the various fields and pastures of the rich farmland.

"I have never worked on a farm before," admitted Roberto, "I have never even touched a cow." Ironically, he recalled the farm his relatives owned on the far end of Cuba. He hated going there, and hated the harsh work of cutting the sugar cane. Suddenly, he was shaken with worries of his inability to handle the job. But his fears were allayed as his host promised to train him in the art of farming, explaining that most of it was just plain hard physical labor; gratifying at times, frustrating at other times. Helping to deliver milk and feeding the masses of the city was a rewarding career. The time and energy spent would benefit hundreds of people. Shaking his head in agreement, although comprehending little English, Roberto's hopes were high — he had finally found a home and a job he could be proud to hold.

Settling into the small cabin, he unpacked the few possessions donated from the military, and began life as a farmhand. His sponsor was patient, kind, and generous, but frustrated with the language barrier. The two communicated through hand gestures, almost as if they were deaf, but this worked well, as Roberto quickly became adept in milking and caring for the large herd of milking cows. "The smell was awful. I never smelled anything like that before," he humorously admitted to his boss. The work was hard, and Roberto got up very very early 4:00am. He cleaned the cow's teats, then put on the milking machines. There was never a day off. The cows had to be milked every day. He didn't mind the work, though, it kept him busy, but he didn't have any friends, no one to talk to, and no women. There were days when he didn't have the strength to take a shower or eat. He only wanted to sleep.

Life was filled with the relentless work on the farm. He remembered driving the tractor, feeding the cows, cleaning the stalls, and preparing the milking machines. Gazing down at his rugged hands, toughened by austere farm life, he reflected on the hard fact that freedom came with a price. Few alternatives were available to a Spanish speaking middle-aged single man fresh off the flotilla. He earnestly tried making each day meaningful, accepting whatever tasks were required.

He continued working for several months until the first snowflake glazed his cheek. Roberto wildly screamed, "I am going to die." The sponsor rushed to assist the hysterical wavering farmhand. In broken English, Roberto explained that snow would kill him and he had to leave. Puzzled, the owner assured him the snow would not kill him, that it was beautiful but harmless, and his own children loved to play in it. "No," screamed Roberto. "Every time I see snow, everyone dies. I can't live in the snow. It will kill me. In Cuba, we saw lots of movies with snow, and everyone ends up dead. I can't stay here anymore." That evening Roberto consulted with another farm hand inquiring what part of America had warm weather, where he could be guaranteed never to have to endure a snowstorm: Las Vegas, Nevada, he was told.

The very next morning, Roberto packed his meager belongings, placed his earnings in several pockets, thanked the sponsor for his support, and boarded the next bus heading directly southwest. Growing up in a warm climate, the bitter Wisconsin winter proved too harsh for his blood. He hated being cold all the time, and even when dressed in endless layers of wool, he found himself constantly shivering. His intuition hinted he would find a better life in the warm sunny streets of the exciting and booming town of Las Vegas, a town that never slept. Work would be readily available, and the climate would be comfortable. Closing his eyes for the long journey, he dreamed about the beginning of his second winter season in the states. Had he remained in Wisconsin, there would be several months before his hands and feet would ever feel warm. He was getting up in years, and wanted an easier existence.

After another lengthy bus ride, he finally arrived in sunny warm Sin City. Although it was December, the air was dry, and the rays of the sun caressed his copper face, and welcomed him to a new life. If nothing else, this transplanted Cuban could come and go as he wished; freedom allowed his fickle mind to choose his own destiny. "This is a great country," he silently professed, " Any place I want to go I can go, just get on a bus." Grabbing his satchel, he headed for the center of town. He located an inexpensive older motel in the northern downtown, known to locals as the Strasophere section. Paying two weeks rent, he unlocked the musty room, took a long soothing shower, plopped on the soft mattress, and fell promptly asleep for the remainder of the day. Exhausted, he dreamed of his new life. There was a substantial Cuban population in Las Vegas, perhaps he would find another love, even a wife. Perhaps he would be blessed with many good friends, and a decent job. With the unknown occupying his mind, he focused on the positive, living for the moment, seeking the fruits American life had to offer. Often tormented with nightmares of his boat ride, he felt his life was blessed with good fortune, even though he had few material possessions. He was alive, while so many had perished. He would make everyday count, would live for the moment, would relish all that life had to offer. After all, he rationalized, he could have died along with the others.

Walking through the brightly lit streets, he began searching for a job, something simple that would pay the rent and afford him a few necessities. In 1981, he obtained a dishwasher job at the Frontier Casino, one of the older hotels dotting the strip. Without comprehension of the English language, limited education, and few skills, opportunities for better paying positions were severely limited. Grabbing the first job, he surmised it was possible to work his way up the ladder. Starting at the bottom meant there was only one way to go. He was sure after many successful months at any job, he could slowly move into higher paying positions.

Immersed in work, his confidence was boosted by allowing an influx of acquaintances and friends to enrich his life. "To be called a friend, is a person who really cares about you, who will help you, to respect you no matter who you are," he explained to a fellow worker. Without family, his entire social life evolved around a new group of Cubans who replaced the emptiness in his heart. Every evening he would rendezvous at a park just north of his motel, where he would socialize with fellow countrymen. The wooden benches were occupied by men and women, all seeking friendship and ties to their mother country. Those acquaintances guided him, advised him, and helped him find a small apartment where he could live freely and peacefully. This section of the population bonded closely, sharing so many common experiences, family ties, and common friends. They relied on each other to share news from home, changes in the political or economic scene, improvements in living conditions, and ways to smuggle American dollars undetected into the country. Many did as Roberto, mailing portions of their weekly paychecks back home in hopes of enhancing the lives of their families, or expediting a way out of the country. The heavily patrolled park represented a haven where transplanted

Cubans could freely and safely communicate with each other without fear of reprisals or harassment.

Living for the moment was the only way Roberto could approach life; without a bank account, he purchased all his needs with cash, stuffing the extra cash in shoes or drawers. He didn't trust banks, fearing if it was robbed, he would loose everything. If he put money in the bank, he might not be able to take it out when he needed it. If he wanted a television set, he would just go and pay for it with cash, there was no need to put the money in the bank. In Cuba no one robbed a bank. The money in the Cuban banks was no good, as it could only be spent in Cuba. The police would catch the robber right away. Everyone knew how much money each had. Everyone knew the money earned from every job. If a family had extra spending money, the police easily deducted who the robbed the bank.

A simple life with few luxuries satisfied Roberto's needs. More importantly, he felt compelled to send all extra money home to his family, where the American dollar could purchase washing machines, refrigerators, and television sets. The rewards of his work were the ability to give his family greatly desired necessities, plentiful and cheap in America, but unavailable to the poor working household in Cuba. He felt as if he were the head of the household again, even though his home was thousands of miles away. His love for his family, especially Teresa, could be exhibited in giving them prized possessions the Cuban dollar was unable to purchase. Placing the cash in a simple white envelope, surrounded by copious letters of American life, he proudly dropped it in the mail slot.

# ESTABLISHING
# RELATIONSHIPS

Days became months, as the routine of work and friends developed into a stable life. The strenuous job left little energy for negative thoughts or altercations. Because of the modest dingy apartment, the vast majority of his social life was spent interacting at the local park. The abundant warm weather coupled with Latino music was conducive for sharing a beer or soda with friends at the local bar. Conversation flowed easily since everyone understood Spanish, it wasn't necessary to interpret conversations or wait for frustrating and lengthy translated explanations. Often the local police would walk the rotunda after dusk making sure the populace was under control, secure from violent activities. In addition to the serene Cuban socializing, this well lit public park also played host to local gangs, often congregating after midnight. This poverty stricken portion of the downtown became an eyesore for the mayor, who felt great pressure to clean it up. Perhaps more raucous than necessary, the uniformed bicyclists cast glances fraught with skepticism as they observed the activities of the locals. Although most ignored the police, Roberto's past paranoia caught up with him, causing him to feel circumspect for any minor action that he might commit. Measuring every word and gesture, he closely guarded himself so as not be misinterpreted by some overzealous cop.

There, amongst the crowd, a beautiful young woman caught his immediate attention, her enticing smile caught his eye, and finally his heart. Mustering up all his macho energy, Roberto advanced toward the thin, dark skinned woman, and opened the way for a flirtatious conversation. Approachable, this woman had spotted him on several evenings, studying his broad build and handsome face, admiring his carriage and the pride emitting from his tall stature. Their conversations began with histories of life and lost loves. Little time was spent on trivia their worlds were too grueling to pretend life was simple or easy. One evening Teresa, his new found friend, arrived in the park earlier than usual with a young child. "Roberto," she introduced, "This is my daughter." Startled, the suitor took the revelation in stride, grabbing the child's hand and offering up a ride on the swings.

"You know, I have three children of my own back in Cuba," he admitted. "I love them, even though I do not see them. Now I can love your little girl. There is plenty of room in my heart. She is so pretty, just like her mother."

Although this seemed to cause a ripple in the relationship, it wasn't reason to enough to deter his love. Afraid of another mouth to feed, he worried the child may not have everything she needed. He continued doting on this needy young Cuban woman. It may have been love, or simply passion, but his time with Teresa became dominant in his daily life. As he scrubbed pots or chopped ten heads of celery, he daydreamed of time spent with her. "Perhaps I may get married, and she may be the right one. I don't want to make a mistake with this woman. This time I think I am ready to commit," thought Roberto. Teresa and her daughter were living with a man named Feranando, a local Cuban whose reputation was circumspect. "No need to worry," Teresa warned Roberto. "He just allows me and my daughter a temporary refuge until I make enough money to move out. But now, it's hard for me to find a high enough paying job to survive on my own. He was kind. He took us in. But I told him as soon as I could I would move out and repay him for the rent."

# HERE IS WHERE THE NIGHTMARE STARTS

Arriving at the park Roberto began his routine of greeting old friends, and introducing himself to newcomers. By now, he had met most of the people who gathered nightly, but this evening a new face appeared. A man, slight of stature, who's skin color marked him of Mulatto descent, introduced himself as Fernando. His new friend's strong dark piercing eyes seemed to reach the core of Roberto's soul, as Fernando's tongue flooded with words of distress and hurt. The two began conversing almost nightly. There seemed endless topics for discussion and for a while, those two were companions until it became painfully clear that Roberto's new friend was homosexual. Fernando had lived at the opposite end of Cuba, where the sugar cane fields were abundant. In the beginning they were good friends but then Roberto found out his friend was not a macho man and that he lived with another man. Roberto didn't like him anymore. He could put up with two men sharing an apartment, but not the same bed. That was not how Roberto was raised. Men do not sleep together, it's not right. He could not have a friend who would do such a thing. Obviously this began the tension in their relationship, one that Roberto wanted to end quickly. Fearing association with a homosexual would make him a marked man, he immediately sought avenues to sever the bonds. Although

Fernando had a live-in lover, Roberto's macho pride would be destroyed if anyone thought that he too was of that persuasion.

When Roberto was born, his mother said, "I have a son a wonderful son, I don't have a girl, I have a son." His mom, had expected him to act like a man, not like a little girl. She was proud of her child. She said Roberto was the head of the household after his father went to jail. He had to be a man his mother could be proud of. If Roberto had Fernando as his friend then people would say that guy must be gay too. Why else would they talk to each other?

What Roberto didn't realize was that Fernando had sought him out. The young Cuban woman, Teresa, sharing his apartment had described her new acquaintance in such animated detail Fernando was curious. As Fernando's comfort in their friendship developed, he made the fatal mistake of revealing his sexual preference. This was a topic they had never discussed. It was at this juncture that Roberto blasted out his blatant disdain for homosexuals. This outcry created a rift in their relationship. Changing their friendship to animosity, and eventually hate.

One evening, Roberto arrived at the park later than usual. Dusk had fallen and the desert air began changing from searing heat to mildly warm. The rare northern winds cooled off the asphalt, creating a luxurious balmy blend of a luminous twilight atmosphere. Serenity was abruptly disrupted as Roberto spied his girlfriend seated on a bench. Holding her forehead in her hands, he heard her softly crying. Reaching for a tissue, he dried her eyes, and immediately demanded to know the explanation for these rare tears. "He hit me," she reluctantly admitted. Turning her blackened eye up at Roberto, she explained the circumstances inside the turbulent apartment. "Fernando is not such a good guy," she admitted. "I stay with him because I have little money and no where else to go. But the apartment is not safe. He makes his money selling drugs. People come and go day and night. They do things that are not right. That are illegal. Last night, there was a loud banging at the door. Two big Latinos appeared, demanding to see Fernando. Terrified, I let them into the apartment. The men stormed into Fernando's bedroom catching him having sex with his boyfriend. After insults and more yelling the two departed. I was scared, and then the baby started crying. Mad, Fernando walked into the living room and began yelling at me. He was angry I had let the two men into the apartment without asking him first. Then he hit me. I will leave as soon as I can get enough money."

"Fernando, that gay guy hit you," yelled Roberto. Angry and heartsick, he vowed to himself and to Teresa, he would make things right. He would protect her and her young daughter.

A couple of days later, he saw Fernando loitering at the rotunda. Gathering up his courage, he approached the young Cuban. "Look, my friend told me what you did to her. Next time," Roberto promised, "you will feel the same pain because it will be me and you."

Storming off, muttering to himself, Roberto realized changes had to be made in order for both he and his girlfriend to live in peace and safety. No rationale was given for the beating; money, sex, drugs, or perhaps just an unbridled temper could have perpetrated the violent behavior. No way was he going to stick around and watch this happen again. Next time the child could be the brunt of Fernando's vicious attacks — one that the child may not survive. Although Roberto and Teresa's love was strong, they had not made a lasting commitment to each other. What was paramount in Roberto's heart was the abuse of a young woman and the possible threat to her child. Roberto could barely support himself, let alone a girlfriend and her child. There was no way they could live together.

Childhood memories of Roberto's father beating up his mom, himself and his sisters and brothers bubbled to the surface of his mind. Living with an abusive father, Roberto knew the damage that could be inflicted. He worried about Teresa, and her child. He had lived through household violence. He knew the permanent scars it caused. Roberto's worry overtook love. He was more concerned for the safety of Teresa and her child then their sexual relationship. In his own way, he felt like a knight in shining armor. Protecting the two became the basis of their relationship.

Replaying the scene of drowning children in the Mexican Gulf, Roberto vowed he would never allow another human to die if he had the power to save them. He would extract a promise from his girlfriend to move out. Even with limited funds, he would help her. She was drowning and he was her only lifeline. About a month after the revelation occurred, Roberto walked to Fernando's apartment and confronted him with the problems the beating had caused his girlfriend. Apparently, the physical damage done to Teresa was greater than either had realized, causing a chronic and persistent set of pains rushing through her back, and severe migraines due to a concussion. Roberto picked Fernando off the ground by his neck and he threatened, "Never hit my friend again."

This was the first time he had ever fought with a fellow countryman. Cubans fighting within themselves was a rarity in the select ghetto. So obsessed with mere survival, no one had the time or the inclination to be at each other's throats. But this was unacceptable. The community supported each other, Roberto desperately thought. Naïve, he was unaware of the great number of homosexual Cubans who had banded together in a tight knit subculture within the Cuban community. Life in Las Vegas became too hard; too many problems, Cubans against Cubans, some even started killing each other.

The police, who had been kind but vigilant, had changed their demeanor, becoming more suspicious of all of the Cubans in the community. They were seeking out the violent individuals causing crime. People started saying all the Cubans were criminals, putting all of them in one classification. It was as if the entire city was suspicious of all Cubans.

There were problems in the poverty stricken ghetto, and Roberto wanted no part of the violence and the drugs permeating the darker side of the population, especially when it came to Fernando. Fernando had other enemies, one being a dark skinned Mexican named Manuel Torres whose hate simmered from surmised sexual encounters with Manuel's current girlfriend. One evening Manuel found himself outside Fernando's apartment. Knocking on the door, he let himself in. Finding Fernando and Rosita (Manuel's girlfriend) on the bed together ignited an anger so fierce that Manuel could only settle it with force. He had no patience to learn the truth, what he saw was not in fact the truth. Manuel only guessed at the truth. Fernando kept his sexual preference well hidden. Few knew his true inclinations, and he intended to keep it that way. Manuel's girlfriend came to see Fernando seeking out drugs. Because of the tiny size of the apartment, the only private place was his bedroom. The only piece of furniture was the bed. The compromising situation witnessed by Manuel was misguided. Rosita knew Fernando was gay, but she knew she could easily purchase drugs. Fernando had a reputation of keeping his business dealings quiet. She trusted him.

The late afternoon sun shed a fusion of hazy light on a fight that broke out between Manuel Torres and Fernando at the back parking lot of a local casino. Several witnesses observed the brawl, overhearing threatening remarks by the miffed and humiliated Fernando. Punches to the gut, and jabs to the groin left both men throbbing with pain. Neither had used fists as a way to settle personal disputes, but macho sexual prowess was at stake and both sought to rectify their pride. Manuel needed to prove to Rosita he would not allow another man to tread on his sexual territory. Fernando needed to prove that he was indeed a heterosexual, willing to fight over a woman he had never loved. This stand off was simply a show of two conflicting egos.

Gossip spread faster than lightning in the cloistered Cuban community as remnants of the fight were told and retold. Speculation on the reasons for the fight ran from sexual indiscretion, to drugs, to thievery. Roberto knew drugs were involved in the fight. Teresa had explained that to him clearly. Those countrymen were disreputable and Roberto distanced himself from those types. He had had enough political problems in Cuba. He was living in a free society, his rowdy protesting days far behind him; just a simple life, without confrontations and political unrest was all he sought. Staying as far away from Fernando was a goal he intended to keep. Although his passion for Teresa was strong, he would avoid the apartment, promising himself only to meet her in a public area, or the privacy of his own apartment. Replaying an open-air brawl was the last scene he envisioned, he did not one to be the recipient of Fernando's violent blows in public or in private.

# THE MURDER

Dusk turned to nightfall and another cloudless evening enveloped the Las Vegas starlit skies. Hearing a knock at the door, Manuel Torres pushed himself off the sofa, checked his watch, wondering if he had forgotten an appointment. He tucked in his crumbled shirt, zipped up his faded jeans, and proceeded to open the front door. "Who is it?" Manuel questioned, but there was no response. Shrugging his shoulders with curiosity, he readily opened the front door. Surprised by his visitor, he was immediately pushed aside as the intruder harshly slammed the door. Screams viciously emanated from this familiar face, as the violence of the intruder escalated. Turning over the kitchen table, the visitor began wildly dancing around the apartment. Then the first stab of the shiny steel blade hit Manuel, and another, and another, until all the air had been sucked out of his lungs, and his heart stopped beating. Eyes dilated, he saw his killer throw glassware, pull the plug on his television, and grab his throbbing wrist ripping his watch off.

Outside the quiet streets boasted little activity except for an occasional pedestrian, bicyclists, and assorted scattered cars. The erratic movement of two silhouettes inside the apartment, caught the eye of a local out for an afternoon stroll. Although the screams were drowned out from the noisy blare of Spanish music from passing convertibles, there was no doubt trouble was brewing inside the dark stucco apartment. In spite of being curious, the person continued walking looking back every few moments to detect anything unusual. On the third twist of the neck, the observer saw a thin darker skinned male hurriedly leaving the apartment carrying a television in his arms. Suspicion was immediately replaced with fear as the passerby quickened his footsteps into a slow even jog.

On Sunday morning Manuel often had friends stop over for coffee, or to perhaps make small drug transactions. Callers at all hours of the day were not an unusual occurrence in this cloistered Spanish area of town. "Hey," yelled out an acquaintance. "Open up the door, I thought we had an appointment." Noticing the door was slightly ajar, he gently pushed it open, shocked at the sight of his friend lying listless on the bloodstained carpet. Terrified, the visitor bolted out the door, located the first public phone, and anonymously called the police. His hands trembled as he hung up the phone. Hastily, the acquaintance headed to a safer part of town. With a string of minor arrests, ending up in convictions and stints at the county lock-up, the witness kept to himself. After the last time he had been in jail, he guaranteed himself never to return. Keeping his nose clean, and out of trouble was his goal. "No," he told himself. "I do not want any part of this." And he ran as fast and as far as he could to escape the horrific scene. This man became the secret witness.

Reaching his tiny apartment in eastern mid-town, the witness phoned his friend Emmett Anderson. "I have to tell someone what I saw," the witness shouted. "I do not know what to do, I do not want to become involved. Maybe you can think of something. I want to stay out of this. I trust you to tell the police what has happened." After a lengthy description of the fight scene, the secret witness felt absolved and cleansed. His conscience was clean.

Ironically, one of Roberto's friends in the community was

Emmett Anderson, who became a crucial character in the events that unfolded after the violent death of Manuel Torres. Emmett's sworn voluntary statement to police would point blame to one man, exonerating another. In a lengthy interview with the police Mr.Anderson described the following incidences.

"About 7:30am, I was driving home on Cleveland Avenue when Fernando flagged me down and asked me to drive a stick shift blue and white pick-up because his friends could not drive a stick shift. The friend was a black mulatto American, with short dark hair, 6'1", weighing around 240 pounds. I did not know his name. I took my car home and walked back to where Fernando was. I told Fernando I would drive his truck while Fernando and this other man drove the blue truck. I saw this man had a set of keys to the vehicle. I drove Fernando's pick-up truck to an alley behind Cincinnati Street, where Valentin, a good friend of mine, lived. I asked Fernando what he was going to do with two trucks, and he said he was going to sell one. I noticed a pair of sunshades on the dash. Then Fernando and the Mulatto locked the blue pick-up and left in Fernando's truck. I walked home to my apartment on Cleveland Street. I turned on the news and I saw a report of a murder nearby and a mention was made about a stolen pick-up truck. The description matched the truck Fernando had driven to Valentin's apartment building. I then called a friend who had been the observant passerby, the secret witness, and told him all about this incident. The police came by later, looking for Fernando. It was about a week later I saw Fernando in the park and again I called the secret witness."

The next day, at their usual park meeting place, Emmett, Roberto, and several other Cubans were chatting and joking when Fernando came speeding by in a dented Ford truck. Spotting Valentino Franco, Fernando beckoned for him to come to the truck, as there was something important on his mind.

After a few moments, Valentino returned to the group, ashen and shaken. Incredulously, he retold the conversation that Fernando had admitted killing this Mexican guy, Manuel Torres, the same man who had head-lined the news. This guy, Manuel, had been sleeping with Fernando's lover, and Fernando decided to get even. "I don't want to know nothing about this conversation, I would stay away from that guy. Don't get involved. It's very serious in this country," warned Roberto, "I am leaving from this state. I don't like it anymore. Too many problems, and the police all the time will stop you in the park. They know who everyone is in the park, who is Cuban, and they don't like you. This murder is too close. It scares me."

Valentin elaborated that he had seen Fernando Cabrera on Sunday, August 9, drive up in a red truck, with his shirt, pants and boots blood-stained. "Fernando told me he killed a man to rob him and that he wanted me to help him with the stolen things. I saw a stereo, guitar, television, electric stove, and other items in the back of Fernando's truck. He asked me to keep the stuff at my house until he could sell it."

Although Emmett had already notified police, he had not relayed this information to his comrades. Matters of this nature were best kept as quiet as possible. He didn't want to be the one who fingered the possible killer, and he didn't want to be a snitch and lose his close ties in the community, so he remained silent, listening and reacting to the shock of the revelation. Now, he wasn't the only one who carried the secret of this murder.

Frightened, Roberto felt compelled to leave Las Vegas. Although he had strong feelings for his girlfriend, after his years of persecution in Communist life, he decided to pack up his belongings and move to the Cuban section of Los Angles where the police wouldn't be scrutinizing every move. Valentin's description of Fernando's crime terrified him. Even though

Valentin was but a casual friend, he did not want to be privy to inside information related to an outrageous, heinous crime. Distancing himself from local the Cuban population would prove to be the best thing for him. Making a fresh start with more conservative people would make his life easier and much happier. During evening conversations at the local gathering park, Roberto was able to find a couple of useful contacts in California. Thus, upon his arrival he would have a safe place to stay, and support to help him find a job.

Returning to his meager apartment, he informed the landlord he was leaving, then methodically assembled his possessions in a tattered duffle bag and prepared to depart the next day. The brilliant morning sun caused Roberto to squint his eyes as he rose for  another journey, adding a new chapter in his American life. As his head was cocooned in the folds of the pillow, he mused the brightness of the new day might alter his plans, that the clarity of a fresh day would shed logic on his decision to leave. But no, the problems in the community would not change; the overheard conversations would not bury themselves from his memory. Leaving the town was the only way he could cope with the problems. In Havana there was no means to escape problems, so one simply stayed and dealt, but here in America, he saw his chance to leave an emotionally unhealthy environment and seek something better. Even if Los Angles proved not to be a panacea, at least it would be different, and if he hated it there, he rationalized, then he could travel somewhere else. He was a free man in a free country and could go and come as he wished. Never having the chance to wanderlust, he was making up for lost experiences.

Monday he boarded the early morning bus to Los Angeles. He pulled out cryptic notes of names and addresses he had hastily jotted down, promising himself to contact those potential friends upon arrival. The uneventful five-hour bus ride abruptly ended as the driver opened the door, bringing the hot afternoon air filtering into the crowded aisle. "Final destination," yelled the pudgy unshaven driver, "Los Angles California, home of the movie stars and Disney Land. Have a nice stay." Vacating the crowded bus, Roberto made his way to the closest phone, called his contact, and began another bus trip across the city to the Cuban ghetto. Arriving at a congested street, he pulled out the address and began walking down the crowded pavement until he had reached his destination.

Roberto tentatively rang the doorbell. Two guys opened the door smiling, introducing themselves and the two Cuban women who lived in the three bedroom flat. It was so crowded, that he slept on the sofa or the floor. The filthy apartment had rats, and the old tenant building was not a safe place, but it cost little. While living in the Cuban ghetto, the familiar cooking smells of his country wafted up the halls permeating the flat with delicious memories of his mother's meals. At the street level, several family-owned cafes and bakeries lined the streets constantly filling the air with smells of Latino style cooking. Although this was comforting, the congested living arrangements were too reminiscent of his childhood, memories he did not want to relive. The beatings, the drunken behavior, were all too prevalent in his memory. He would force himself to remain in this overcrowded apartment until a better plan was attainable.

Although Roberto had applied for numerous jobs, desperate for money, he began picking apples in the nearby orchards. Waking up before sunrise he dressed in layers, taking care to bring his cap each day so he would have a clear view of the fruit at the top of the trees. As he climbed the thick tree branches, the sun often unexpectedly blinded him, causing him to nearly plummet off the rickety wooden ladders. He quickly discovered his hat was the best defense from losing his balance and tumbling to the earth. Although the drudgery was exhausting, Spanish was the common language in the fields, and conversations flowed easily. Lunch break was the highlight of the day. The field workers gathered around long wooden picnic tables and discussed the weather, food, or the dispositions of the fruit trees. They philosophized and predicted how long the work would last based upon the fickleness of nature. Would rain come or would too much rain come? Would the sun prove so hot as to destroy the crops, or would flocks of birds arrive too soon from the north devouring the apples before the laborers had a proper chance to salvage the crops? As Roberto silently listened to the workers' rhetoric, he thought of the irony. Still working as a field hand, as in Cuba, but the circumstances were much different in a free country. Here, he was paid for his work, adequate time and place was offered for meals and ample toiletry facilities were available, conversations were open, and uncensored by the foreman.

Living from day to day, his life was simple; he asked for little, just to live quietly and freely. "I never look to the future, just live life from day to day," he would tell his roommates. When there were apples to pick, he had work, but when the crops were depleted, he was left without any income. He would just sit in a local bar and watch and wait. Maybe something would turn up, he would hope, but mostly he did very little. He looked at people who walked around the bars. Miserably unhappy, he was unable to find work. He spouted, "If I don't have any money to pay the rent, then I will just sleep in the street. I am not one of those people who must to work all the time, but without work I can not survive. I could live on the streets, but here in America I believe anything is possible." Although puzzled, the Mexican sharing the beer, cocked his thick neck in disbelief. This was a human being who asked for little, and demanded little out of life.

He was not the typical aggressive immigrant, whose expectation level was so high as it would never be met. Live and let live, was the mantra of Roberto's simple style. Although his convictions never aroused other migrant workers to act, they looked at him as a sage with advice that was worthwhile. Many afternoon lunches were spent in animated Spanish discussing Roberto's philosophy of life.

The rumbling in his stomach, served as a constant reminder of his inability to find work. As the late fall set-in, the need for day laborers had shrunk. No one was looking for cheap help. Roberto was hungry. Glancing at the date on the front page of the local Hispanic newspaper, he noted it had been three days since he had eaten a real meal. He could not reach into garbage pails where he might have to compete with the rats and mice, nor would he stand in line at the welfare office and ask for a hand-out. He walked into a small corner grocery store and gazed at the abundance of food. "All this food, Roberto thought. "Yet I can't eat any of it. I have no money." Without thinking, he grabbed an apple and a candy bar, and left the store without paying. The clerk at the cash register saw Roberto steal the food and promptly called the local police. It was Roberto's unlucky day. The police were parked directly outside the store sipping the free coffee the manager routinely gave them. Caught with food, Roberto didn't argue. But, petty larceny was noted on his record, making him officially a criminal.

Los Angles was not his ideal place. It was too big and too crowded. Everything was too spread out. It took several bus rides to go from place to place, and it was more expensive to live there. For ten months, he lived in the crammed flat, promising himself he would leave as soon as the first opportunity arose. Although he might have convinced fellow field workers he did not feel compelled to work, the reality of ghetto poverty and despair set in as a rampant cancerous growth. Looking to escape drugs and violence and poverty, he continued searching for employment and a better life.

It was late afternoon as the orange-colored September sun began setting over the Pacific Ocean. Agitated, he plucked the car keys from his corduroy vest. He aspired to change his sour mood by watching the sunset at the edge of the ocean; this he knew, would calm him, clearing his mind for decisions. Inserting the key, he listened for the sound of the four cylinder motor purring. He was relieved, as he knew the used Chevy would make it to the Santa Monica Pier. With a third of a tank of gas, the car would easily manage the round trip, unless there was a huge unexpected back-up on the interstate. Signaling, he eased the aging car onto the busy highway, as he cautiously checked the rearview mirror for impatient aggressive drivers. Because of the dearth of highways in Havana, the tragic bus accident, and lack of professional training, he drove like "a little old lady." Fearful of high speeds, he rarely held the car over forty miles per hour, irritating the most courteous of California's drivers. Glancing at the rearview mirror for the tenth time, he noticed a police car tailing him. This was not unusual, as cop cars often followed slower cars in between emergency calls. He ignored it. Continuing crawling down the interstate the cop car kept dogging him then suddenly flashed his lights signaling Roberto to pull over. He saw the officer with his gun pointed directly at his throbbing heart. "Oh boy, this isn't good at all," he screamed. Remaining in the car, he witnessed another three police cars arriving with sirens blaring, two in front and another behind. He was completely surrounded. As the officers stepped out of their vehicles all armed, pointing their pistols in his direction, terror rushed through his veins as if someone had immersed him in a bath of ice-cubes.

"Please get out of the car," the gaunt officer demanded. "Put your hands on the car and spread your legs while I check for weapons." A second cop repeated the command as he acted as a reinforcement further frightening the Cuban suspect. After harshly patting him down, they demanded he lay on the ground. Then they cuffed him, put him in the back of the patrol car, and speeded quickly to the nearest police station.

Hysterical, Roberto pleaded with the officers. "I am not selling drugs. What is going on? Did I do something wrong, or what? Why are you handcuffing me? "

The shorter cop replied," They are looking for you in Las Vegas."

"Las Vegas?' Robert stammered. "I didn't do anything in Las Vegas."

Ignoring his response, the cops notified him that they would be sending him back to Las Vegas. That a man was killed and that he was to be sent back for questioning.

An instant state of shock set in. If his rights were read, no one would ever know as Roberto all but collapsed from the trauma of the situation. Undaunted, the policemen shoved him into the waiting patrol car, and left the Chevy at the shoulder of the eight-lane highway where it was confiscated within hours of the arrest. That was the last time Roberto would ever see his beloved car, the first one he ever owned.

With lights flaring and sirens blasting he was driven to the police station, where he was officially notified that he was wanted by the state of Nevada for the murder of a man. "What." shrieked the cuffed suspect. "I didn't kill anyone! No way! No problem to go to Las Vegas, I want to clear my name!" Booked and finger-printed, he was escorted to a private jail cell, where he spent a sleepless night in terror and torment.

Early the next morning, he was escorted into a waiting police car, and driven to a small airport where an officer handcuffed him to the seat of a tiny propeller plane. This was the first time

Roberto had ever flown; terrified, every fiber of every nerve was standing on end as the tiny plane lifted off the ground. Whatever meals had been consumed in the past hours were splattered upon his slept-in denims as he heaved his guts. Disgusted, the attending officers mopped up his pants, bringing fresh water to his parched lips. Embarrassed, he readily admitted this was his first flight; he was scared to death.

After what seemed an eternity, the pilot loudly announced they would be landing shortly, and cautioned the passengers to fasten all seat belts tightly. As the prop plane began its descent, it tipped from side to side, the wings gyrating up and down, compensating for strong erratic southern winds making their way through the Santa Anna Mountains. Roberto squeezed his moist eyes shut.

"Oh!" he screamed, "I am going to die. We are all going to die."

"Shut up," commanded the cop, "We are not going to die. I have made this trip a hundred times, and as you can see I am very much alive. Stop your belly-aching and act like a man."

With those words of sobering advice, the tires hit the tarmac, screeching toward a small battalion of state police vehicles. Escorted out of the plane by two tall armed guards, he was placed in the backseat of a patrol car, as the tiny parade sped toward the center of Las Vegas destined for the county jail. The captive was sure as soon as he arrived, they would see a terrible mistake had been made, that Roberto Miranda was not the person they were looking for, a meaningless excuse would be articulated, and he would be humbly and apologetically sent home. But the police were like hungry dogs that had grabbed onto a large meat bone and they refused to let go.

"You have been brought here because you killed somebody," the officers strongly pronounced.

"I never killed anybody, I do not know what you are talking about," screamed Roberto.

The police took the suspect's ubiquitous headshots, refinger printed, cuffed him, ordering him to a holding area until the judge was prepared to hear the case. As the hours crept slowly by, he paced with agitation. He had absolutely no concept of why he was arrested, why he was sitting helplessly in a jail cell, and what he was being charged with. Since departing Las Vegas over a year ago, he had no one to call locally, no one to come to his aid. He was more alone than he could ever have imagined, and terrified. He had lost touch from all of his friends, including Teresa. Losing patience, Teresa found an older Latino gentleman to take care of her and her young child. She never had another encounter with Roberto.

Because his command of the English language was weak, he was misinterpreting what was happening to him. He kept telling himself this was all a mistake, and when he would see the judge, he would be instantly cleared of whatever the police had accused him of. Closing his eyes to avoid the reality of the moment, he conjured up vivid images of his mother, and asked her to help him through this horrible time. Silently addressing her, he asked her why this was happening, pleading for advice and guidance. Please, he begged her, help me. I have no one else to turn to. Bowing his head, he cried for the first time since childhood. "Help me, please, someone help me," he shuddered.

"Pathetic," moaned. Roberto. "How could this situation have evolved? I am sad. I am a person without a sliver of sustenance, who has been accused of a capital crime. In this great land of freedom, how can a man, like myself, without good cause, be swept off the streets, deprived of all liberties, and accused of the most serious of all crimes; first-degree murder?"

All this was more than Roberto could accept. At times he thought he was dreaming, that he would wake up from a bad nightmare resulting from imbibing in too much tequila, or that he was losing his mind, or that he was hallucinating, or he had some rare disease that destroyed the brain. There was absolutely no way he could rationalize what was occurring; the arrest, the handcuffing, the plane ride, and the formal booking back in Las Vegas! "Mom, Teresa, I need you more than ever. Please help me."

That evening he wrote a letter to the man who was appointed to defend him, Mr. Tom Rigsby:

"I found out you are my attorney. I have to inform you that here, where I am being detained, I met the Cuban citizen, Valentin Franco. He told me you are defending him in court. He told me he knew about my situation, the same as many other Cubans who live here. He also told me that Fernando showed up at the park with his clothes full of blood and told him that he had just killed a man and he (Fernando) told him to take off his clothes. Fernando showed him what he had stolen, which he had in his truck. Valentin says that Fernando also came the next day to his house with a pick-up truck, where he observed Fernando removing a radio from the stolen truck and afterwards threw the rest of the stuff out of the vehicle onto the roof of the building where he lived. Valentin also told me that Fernando told him that the day Fernando was arrested, he accused me of stealing the truck and said at that time the reason for his fingerprints on the stolen truck was that he had seen me downtown, and that I told him I would give him a gold chain if he would take me or drive me to the truck. Who could think that if I do not know how to drive that type of vehicle, why would I steal it? What for? To sell it? Where? Without a title, knowing that everything here has to have a signed title by the owner in order to be able to sell it. Why would he say that I found him while he was walking when he always is riding in his truck? It is also very strange that this man is implicated in two crimes, and he was always innocent. Because he was accusing me of murder and robbery, when he was at the crime scene. I should tell you that Valentin Franco gave me his address and his telephone to be my witness. According to his words, he can identify the clothing that Fernando was wearing that day, as well as several stolen objects, which he knows where they are and that Fernando told him belonged to the deceased. I can assure you that everything I have said here is the truth. You can investigate if Fernando's fingerprints were found in the truck. You will realize this man has a great imagination, and he is playing with the law of this state of Nevada. Committing the crimes and then accusing others and that way he portrays himself as a defender of order and that way he can keep on acting anyway he feels like. That is the reason why I ask you to include Valentin Franco as one of my witnesses. Fernando also said in his statement in court that I wanted to return to the house again to pick up a glass that had my fingerprints, since I had asked for a glass of water. I ask myself, who did I ask a glass of water from, if Fernando stated that I and the dead man were the ones inside the house? How does Fernando know about the fingerprints on the glass unless he had put them there himself? If he says that he went in the house a long while after the killing, how could he know I asked for a glass of water? If I wanted to go back to the house to pick up the glass, why did I not take it when (according to Fernando) the crime was committed? Remember, Counselor, that I used to visit Fernando's house and there is a possibility that my fingerprints were taken in Fernando's house and that the next day when he went to pick up the truck he could have placed then there. Also please remember that relations between he and I were tense due to my ex-girlfriend and the arguments we had had frequently. I went to tell Pablo, Fernando's friend, about the murder, and I also remember that on that day, there were Fernando's brother and wife, and Pablo. I do not remember that day if I drank coffee, or if I drank something, but it is for sure that I did since every time I went to Pablo's house they gave me something. When it wasn't coffee, it was beer, or they would give me food. I do not know what to think of all of this, inasmuch as it has me all confused since I don't completely understand how it is possible that if a person has not been to a place how does his fingerprints show up? My nerves are wrecked; I can hardly control myself. I have seen several times in my country people who were fighting against the government and I am very afraid. It is your duty to investigate this. If you don't want to or can't because of the workload, you have to tell me and I will ask for another attorney. Remember that many people have been accused of things they didn't do. I know that I am innocent." Signed, Roberto Miranda.

Closing his eyes, he hoped the points made in the letter would establish his innocence and the court appointed lawyer would take the time to properly investigate all the evidence. He was being framed. There was no doubt in his mind, but he knew it would take some convincing to make Rigsby see the light. The letter would surely exonerate him from all the charges. Now, all his attorney had to do was to follow-up with the witnesses, and do some basic forensic testing and he would walk out of the stinking jail cell a free man. The cathartic sensation of writing down the story in detail eased his mind. A man of common sense would easily see the motives of Fernando, and the pieces of Torres' murder would be swiftly solved. The question tugging on Roberto's mind was why he had been targeted. Why was he the one being framed?

# HELP IS
# ON THE WAY

Locked alone in a dank, tiny holding cell, the guard's jingling keys woke Roberto out of a haunting stupor; a young man appeared announcing himself as the court appointed lawyer. "My name is Thomas Rigsby," he roughly stated. "And I am here to help you answer the charges." Young and inexperienced, this freshman assistant public defender was anxious to land a capital murder case. Barely a year out of a second tier law school, a case like this could catapult him to prestige within the legal community if he won over the jury. This would be the neophyte's first capital case, a new and exciting territory of law to traverse. Although the public defender's office was overburdened with cases, he promised Roberto an excellent and professional defense. Thomas' deep-set eyes, prematurely wrinkled temple, and closely cropped hair, gave the impression of a lawyer who took his work seriously. Unable to properly judge the attorney's skills, all the accused could do was simply accept whatever handouts the State of Nevada offered. With no source of income, limited English skills, and no close friends or family to serve as back up, this green defense lawyer was his sole resource. Roberto was in no position to question credentials, to ask for a more appropriate professional, or to alter legal procedures. He would just have to sit back and take what the free society of America offered.

Concentrating on the charges, trying to eke out any morsel of comprehension, Roberto overheard information which would thoroughly explain his incarceration: Fernando, the only enemy he had made in his short stay in Las Vegas, was a paid police informant. Yes, Fernando was the only person who he had ever challenged since his arrival to the states. There was great hatred between the two. This snitch for the police created a lie, and set him up. The conversation reverberated in Roberto's mind as he replayed the image of Fernando talking to Valentino Franco, telling him of the stabbing of a Mexican guy. The explanation for the murder finally revealed itself. Fernando's male lover was not pure of heart, he had sexual liaisons with a Mexican man named Manuel Torres. This was too much for the proud ego of Fernando to endure; he wanted to teach both his lover, and Manuel that cheating was unacceptable in the gay Cuban world. Fernando had committed the murder. Passion, motive, opportunity — all blatantly open for the most amateur trainee in the field of basic detective investigations to readily ascertain. It was simple to frame Roberto. He was a man without a spouse, no close family, no money, and limited ability to converse in the native tongue. He made an easy mark, a target. Besides, Fernando hated this macho man, who had been thoroughly disgusted by his homosexual life style. "How dare he pick me up by neck in front of Teresa and humiliate me," Fernando ranted. Revenge was an evil tool, and using his immunity as an undercover snitch, he implemented this to its fullest potential.

There had been a small gathering at Pablo's (Fernando's friend) apartment the night of the murder, of which Roberto had attended. A typical Saturday night socializing with a few Cuban friends meant plenty of rum laced with lime juice, freshly cooked rice and beans, and roasted sliced pork. Roberto left an empty plate and a thumbprint on a glass of water as evidence of his presence. This sole piece of evidence, the water glass, and the testimony of a paid state's witness encompassed the entire case against Miranda. Fernando was given complete immunity. "And when you have immunity, the prosecutor can't do anything to you. You can say whatever you want, do what you want, but the law can't touch you," Roberto later said.

Standing before the judge, the pathetic accused numbly listened to his fate dealt by the hands of the free American judicial system. "How free, how fair," he mutely contemplated, "how could all of this be happening to me? I did nothing wrong but try to help a friend find her way out of Fernando's apartment. This was a nightmare without an end in sight. Am I crazy, have I lost my mind, or is the rest of the world crazy? Has everyone lost their minds and any resemblance of good sense?"

"You will be held on two million dollars bail," the judge decreed as the gavel hit desk. "Until that time, or your trial commencement, you will be detained in the county jail." Without so much as a flutter of the eyelid, the judge was preparing for the next case.

It was as if someone had punched him in the stomach, causing him to lose all his breath and composure; he promptly fainted. Dragged off to a tiny cell, he woke up hours later as the desert sun was setting behind the cactus-filled hills. It was Fernando's hands that sealed Roberto's fate; a sole testimony by a paid informant pointed the finger to only one man. "I'm not ready to die, I can't die for a crime I did not commit. The fight is me against a million strangers, who want to blame someone for the crime. They don't know me, only that I am a stranger, and they do not believe me. I won't let other people kill me: I am innocent. I would rather kill myself." Lying in the dimly lit cell, his mind concentrated on how he would commit suicide. He had once been held in a jail cell, but not for a capital murder offence.

Although the trappings were familiar — the filthy mattress, stained urinal, tiny living space, bars on the inside — the charge for first degree murder was inconceivable. Murder. He was being charged for killing a man he never knew. Trembling with fear, his mind began retracing each step, placing time and people in positions who would act as alibis, witnesses, anything or anybody who would oppose the absurdity of the state's charges.

The District Attorney, Mr. Ferrraro had compiled an impressive set of witnesses against Roberto: Dr.Giles Green, Robert Leonard, David, Fernando Cabrera and Daniel Cabrera, Silveril Avila, and Roberto Escabo. The balance of the case seemed doomed from the beginning as witness for the defendant began with listing "none." Mr. Rigsby would be challenged to bring in a parade of credible witnesses.

Roberto was shocked at the tremendous amount of evidence the district attorney had amassed in such a short period of time, and the relative dearth of evidence his court appointed lawyer had compiled; the balance of power seemed to weigh in favor of the state. How could all this happen, so quickly and without facts floating to the surface?

The words written in letters by his mother echoed over and over: "If you are not guilty, don't ever say that you are. It is better they should kill you than you admit to a crime you did not commit. You are innocent, and you will not die. The truth will come out. Faith. You have to believe in yourself, and when you do others will believe in you too. You will not die." Teresa predicted her son's innocence and exoneration while held captive in Cuba. Writing endless letters fraught with encouragement and advice, she provided a lifeline for her son to cling to. Although his mother was thousands of miles away, her compassionate letters gave him hope and confidence. Stealthily holding onto those past haunting words of inspiration, Roberto would gather strength to face the rigors of the days looming ahead. His simple American life had been shattered; to live peacefully from day to day was all he had hoped for. Now his life would revolve around a matrix of legal dealings, more complex that he could have ever imagined.

Life in the tiny county lock-up was shared with three other inhabitants. There was no privacy when an inmate wanted to go to the bathroom. He had to hold a cover on top of himself, and the stench was unbearable. The sadistic treatment whittled down the last fragments of human dignity; an innocent man, having to suffer the indignities of the simple needs of toiletry. Incarcerated with only English speaking cellmates, loneliness became more pronounced as he feared for the sanctity of his life. The basic right of a single phone call was withheld, as the police informed him no long distance calls were allowed. Initially, he had no way of communicating directly with his family. Not a soul knew where he was or what he was doing. Bitter cries of anguish filled his chest as he tried desperately to hang on to his sanity. The simple pleasure of hearing his mother's voice was not allowed; he needed to talk to her, to listen to her words of wisdom and support. "Was America such a harsh country as to take this fundamental right away?" he brooded. America, the land of the free, had taken every bit of liberty away from an accused immigrant. Civility should have taken precedence in a free society, yet all these rights were denied him. The assumption of innocence appeared to be ignored by the district attorney, and his own lawyer.

Days of endless boredom passed; meals were served, and sleepless nights prevailed as he patiently waited to hear from his court appointed lawyer, Thomas Rigsby. Living in constant fear, he often paced the length of the tiny cell hoping to overhear some news or gossip from guards or other inmates. Dressed in prison garb, he felt marked as guilty. The jury would look at him and think that if he was dressed like a criminal then he must be a criminal. Why should he have to wear the clothing of a prison inmate, when he was not guilty and had not gone to trial? If he looked like a prisoner then people would believe that he was a prisoner — he did not want that to happen. But there was nothing he could do. All his worldly belongings had been taken from him, especially his beloved car. Sulking, Roberto reminisced about the demise of his first car, stranded at the shoulder of a highway. "What did the police do with it?" he thought. "What right had they to take it away from him?" Freedom, this was not a definition of freedom. Quite the contrary. This situation he had found himself submerged in was more the high jinks of an unfair government. Deeper and deeper his thoughts plunged until his knees buckled and he landed head first on the cement floor. Shaken, his cellmate grabbed his arm, and dragged him back to the cot. Unconscious, he slept for the balance of the afternoon until sunrise of the next morning.

"Miranda", a uniformed guard gruffly shouted, "Your lawyer is here". Unlatching the cell door, the prisoner was escorted down the narrow hall of the county jail to a private room where his lawyer was impatiently awaiting his arrival. Fidgeting with a broken pencil, Mr. Rigsby announced he had set up a lie detector test; it was scheduled for the next day, and he wanted to properly prepare his client. The lawyer explained that a Spanish interpreter would be available to explain the questions thoroughly, and there was no need to worry. "Its okay by me," agreed Roberto. " You will see that I am innocent, that I did not commit this crime. I am innocent, I am an innocent man, and I did not do what they say I did. I have witnesses who saw me, people who overheard that Fernando was the one who killed that Mexican guy. It was not me."

"Look," admonished Rigsby, "This is standard procedure in

the public defender's office. It will be fine. You have nothing to worry about. I will be back soon, and we will do this thing together. You must learn to take and heed my advice, and only answer questions that are asked you. Do not offer any additional information. Do not keep spouting off you are an innocent man."

The next day the guards escorted Roberto to the same private room where he took the lie detector test. As promised a young Spanish man was present ready to interpret anything that was asked. The detectives asked him all types of personal questions — about his family, friends, and finally if he had killed Manuel Torres. "NO, I did not kill that man," Roberto loudly pronounced. But all throughout he was scared. His hands were shaking and his face was dripping wet from perspiration. All those nervous physical responses were readily detectable. He was psychologically unprepared for the constant peppering. He truly thought they were going to kill him right then and there if they were unhappy with answers to the questions. In fact, he was never told what this test would be like, or the consequences. Harnessed to an elaborate unfamiliar contraption, he hallucinated that the machine would cause him great harm if he lied. But no shock or pain was endured. He had told only the truth.

Satisfied, the criminologist loosened all the wires, and an innocent man was walked back to a cramped county jail cell. Here he sat entombed in a cement cell waiting and waiting, as precious days of his life were slowly stolen by the state. The dullness of the days drove him to great despair and deep depression. He never exercised. The guards didn't want to be bothered with the extra chores. And there were so many rules, rules for every part of the day; when to eat, what to say, how to dress, how to speak to the guards, when to go to bed. Everything an inmate did was circumvented with strict rules, nothing was left for the inmates to think about except why they were imprisoned for their crimes, and when would their lawyers spring them to freedom.

Time floated by with no meaning or sense. One day, Roberto was beckoned back to the private conference room where his lawyer told him they would be facing the judge the next morning. He had brought a suit of clothes, and used, but shiny shoes to wear for this auspicious occasion. "I have to tell you," Thomas solemnly spoke, "The results of your lie detector test were not what we had hoped for."

"What do you mean?" questioned Roberto, "I told the truth, the only thing I know how to do. How could the test not be right?"

"Well, those experts who read it did not feel you were being completely honest," said the lawyer, "And this does not bode well with the judge."

With an armed guard the two were taken out of the county jail where Roberto was driven by a patrol car to the county courthouse, his lawyer following closely behind in a used Mercedes. Sitting squeamishly on the hard wooden benches outside the bustling courtroom, the two waited for the case to be called into the court. After what seemed an interminable about of time, another uniformed officer escorted them into the large prodigious courtroom. The rich wooden-paneled walls, towering ceiling lamps, highly polished oak floors, and large rectangular windows were vivid reminders of the purpose of the building — to set public records, to try and convict the guilty and to exonerate the innocent. Panning the room, Roberto deliberated on the fate he would receive from this room. Would justice be fairly dealt? Or would he be sent to an early and untimely death? Seated high in his chair the judge's black robes signaled the importance of his position and the decision he would be handing down. So many people doing so many different jobs. The court reporter, the lawyers, assistants, uniformed guards, secretaries and numerous observers sitting on benches behind the oblong front tables. This courtroom was not like the courts in Havana. Just the accused, the judge, and if the defendant had money, a lawyer. In and out of the courtroom, not like in America, where sentencing seemed to drag on eternally.

Roberto and Rigsby were not alone. This time the opposing party, the district attorney would be sitting at the adjacent table pleading the State of Nevada's case against Roberto Miranda. Taking in the complexity of the court scene reinforced the severe nature of the crime. A paneled room surrounded by pomp and circumstance of American law was drowning Roberto in utter fear. How was he, a simple Cuban going to convince all these people of his innocence? Could his lawyer perform a miracle? Was the court-appointed lawyer truly qualified? None of those questions could be answered, further enhancing Roberto's panic of his ability to cope with the dire situation. He had literally put his life in the hands of Thomas Rigsby, a young man but a year and a half out of law school, with no capital cases under his belt. Roberto would be the lawyer's first capital case, a guinea pig challenging the astute rhetoric of this attorney.

Roberto's borrowed suit and spit-shined shoes added a layer of credibility to his innocence, but underneath the defendant's shiny oak table, the trembling in his legs was matched by the strong beating of his heart. The court secretary announced the case, and all stood as the aging judge called out Roberto's name. Information was quietly relayed to the court reporter as documents were introduced and the district attorney pleaded the state's case. Numb, the defendant stood motionless as the court listened to the charges brought against him. It was surrealistic. This couldn't have been happening. The charges played over and over in Roberto's mind.

Scrutinizing the documents, the judge, pensively removed his glasses, looked the defendant squarely in the eye and announced the state had made a strong enough case to continue proceedings. A two million dollar bail would be required while trial preparations were made. "I don't have that kind of money," bellowed the defendant, "Where am I going to get that kind of money?"

The agitated lawyer pulled his client within close earshot, and explained that he would have to sit tight in the county jail He would try and have the bail reduced, but for capital murder cases of this kind, a large bail was always required. "Please," he begged his client. "Just be quiet and calm in the courtroom."

Roberto would have none of this. He strolled over to the prosecutor addressing the district attorney in earnest, "You know I did not do this crime. You have only one witness. Why do you keep doing this to me? You know I am innocent, that the man who said I did it is the man who killed the Mexican. I did not do this. You know I did not do this!" The guards rushed over to pull the pitiful defendant away, grabbing both arms, then hauling him out of the courtroom. Echoes of his wails could be heard as he was shuffled out the side door into a holding cell. Roberto overheard the judge's voice, "Keep your client under control," he warned, "Or he will not be allowed back into the courtroom."

Panic and fear set in like a sudden summer thunder storm. He was enveloped in a horror greater than any he had ever imagined. Not only was he going to die, but suffer every minute of every day until the bitter end. Silently, he pleaded for his mother to help him, guide him, hold him, comfort him; this was more than he could emotionally handle. Clutching his arms, he rocked himself inside the tiny holding cell. He stood catatonically for hours.

On June 13,1983, Rigsby and Roberto again stood before the court asking for a continuance as the seriousness of the case required additional time for preparation, and Rigsby was steeped in another case requiring much of his time. But Thomas Ferraro, District Attorney, fought against additional time, "Admittedly, the case is serious. Nevertheless, the defendant had one month to prepare for trial. Moreover, the defendant is represented by the public defender's office, and thus has more resources available than the average law firm. Further postponing the trial date may endanger the state's witnesses and increase the risk that others will abscond."

Listening intently, the judge ruled in favor of the State; a bad sign for the defense attorney whose time and resources were severely limited. The first witness had yet to be in place. At this juncture, there was no defense prepared by the public defender. Leaning over to consult with his lawyer, Roberto elaborated a list of names that would surely exonerate him.

"Be quiet," barked his lawyer. "Just let me handle this. I will be back to consult with you as soon as this proceeding is completed"

Angry, the defendant backed down, allowing his faith and trust in this man to do the job. Thomas was the professional, while Roberto knew nothing about law, especially American law, but he questioned the decision of the judge. It was not a fact that the public defender's office had a large pool of human resources. In fact, the underpaid, overworked attorneys had been overextended. There were many more clients than available lawyers, funding was not forthcoming to expand the work force to accommodate the needy poor. And a month, one single month, to put together a capital case seemed outrageously unfair. This scant amount of time hardly allowed for an intense investigation of any kind. "How would his lawyer pull this together?" wondered Roberto. Wrestling with the judge's decree put Roberto on edge.

He was shuddering with fear as the guards shuffled him out of the courtroom to the holding cell.

The evening sun was leisurely setting over the western mountain ridge as two county uniformed officers unlatched the cell bars, announcing Roberto would be transferred to the county jail. Picking up his pinstripe jacket, he stumbled out of the tiny holding cell into the brightly lit corridor. With an armed guard on either side, there was nothing he could do but listen and obey their rigid commands. "Where is my lawyer?" he asked. Neither guard answered. They simply pointed the direction, keeping up a quick pace out the long hallway to a side entrance. A patrol car was waiting, doors ajar, ready to receive the newly accused resident of the county jail. Without bail money, this was Roberto's only alternative. He had to make a jail cell his home until the trial was over. A glum prospect for an innocent man.

Holding his head, the officer pushed him into the back of the police car, slammed the door tightly, and then waved the driver to continue. Speeding out of the empty parking lot, the trip from the courthouse to the county lock-up seemed exceedingly short; this would be Roberto's last taste of the outside world for a long time. He wanted to savor every moment, see every tree, smell food cooking, watch the birds sail by, and see the last vestiges of the sun as it disappeared beyond the blush colored mountains. Tears welled in his eyes as the two officers took him into the jail, and presented him at the front desk where he began the process of signing papers and surrendering what little property he had acquired. After the usual humiliating searches, he was given prison garb and told to put it on while an attendant watched closely. And so began a lengthy adventure into the American penal system, where money talked and the poor sat in isolated cells without a fair chance for bail.

# THE ENCULTURATION
# OF JAIL LIFE

During endless empty hours lying in the sparse cell, Roberto contemplated why the court had bestowed him with such an inexperienced lawyer; Thomas' face was so youthful he hardly appeared as if he needed a shave. It was the mandate handed down from Morgan Harris, head of the public defender's office who sealed Roberto's fate. At that time, the public defender had established two policies that were to be adhered to: a failed lie detector test was proof positive a suspect was lying and therefore the defense should be minimal, and, two, the least experienced staff lawyers were assigned capital cases. This provided a spawning ground for lawyer-want-to-bes who wanted to grab the brass ring at important capital cases without having to endure years at private practice garnering the professional skills truly needed to properly try such cases. In essence, the public defender had created a fast track for aspiring attorneys to sink their teeth into significant cases without years of erudite practice. The least experienced lawyers had little back-up as the public defender's office had always been inundated with more cases than could be properly handled. The State of Nevada provided little money in the yearly fiscal budget for the needs of the poor. The huge expansion of the population during the last two decades of the century, created a much greater demand for social services than the budget allowed. People began slipping through the cracks, ignored and improperly attended to. The state would learn that it had taken bites too big to chew, and ramifications would occur from the callous and over-worked nature of the holders and wielders of power.

Roberto had a right to be frightened. With the quality of professionalism the state had offered, he would need a miracle from God to win over the jury. He had literally given his life over to a man whom he had to believe in, had to have the utmost trust in, to survive the wrenching ordeal. No mention was ever made to the client, the judge or the district attorney's office that defense strategy would be less than vigorous as a result from the outcome of a single lie detector test. How could an entire case rest upon the results of a test that were less than perfect, that were given in a foreign tongue? "There was an interrupter there," admitted Roberto, bitterly complaining to his cellmate. "But he could have been asking me anything. I don't even know if he was asking me the correct questions, and even if he was asking me the questions, he might have changed them around so I answered incorrectly. I don't know how anybody can say you did a crime from a bunch of needles on a machine. They should ask you, did you do the crime? I would say no a thousand times. That is what they should believe." Nodding his shaved head in agreement, the dark-skinned cellmate suggested that the police officers and detectives were much more anxious to pin the death on someone, anyone, rather than looking for the truth. Many hours were spent rehashing the questions and how they had been answered and asked during the crucial interview. Each time, Roberto came up blank, unable to cope with the concept he had failed the lie detector test, when in fact, he knew he had not lied.

Stewing in a tiny crowded jail cell, the uneventful days flowed from one to the next. Time had little meaning. Life outside the cell continued as usual but without his ability to live it. All of life's purpose began evaporating as the monotonous routine became the substance of living. He simply sat and waited: to hear from his lawyer, a friend, a relative, to hear from anyone who would have given meaning to the day. Endless hours were given away to idle thoughts. His life had lost all value. He did nothing, worked at nothing. His brain was growing dull and useless as the days were nothing but empty voids of human survival. Continual vacant days gave way to constant daydreaming, with suicidal thoughts slowly entering his mind as if clouds were dispelling the warmth from a sunny day. Without any stimulus to feed a worried mind, his thoughts began to darken. He felt as if he had fallen into a great abyss and had no way to crawl out. Looking up at the sky from the depths of the chasm, his mind played the scene of days turning into night. All he could do from the bottom of the pit was watch life pass by, he could no longer participate in existence. He had stopped being an actor in the game of reality.

Clutching his chest, there was a sensation of someone knocking the wind out of his body. He began shaking, his heart racing at lightning speeds, then he broke out in a rampant sweat from head to toe. Calling out for help, the guards ignored him. Begging did nothing to glean attention to the caretakers of the jail. After minutes of suffering, he collapsed onto his cot, closed his damp eyes, and fell promptly asleep. Roberto had just suffered through his first full-blown anxiety attack, a common side affect for jailed suspects. The arrest, and now his waiting for trial, had simply overwhelmed his emotional capacities. So daunted by the vicissitudes life had handed him, it seemed unbearable to live, every waking moment was shear torture. He simply was losing his capacity to accept what the courts had so pathetically unfairly handed down. The bold six-foot-two stature drooped.

His enormous oval brown eyes sunk deep into his skull. His wide smile ceased to exist; he had become a man without hope. The only thought he would cling to until his last breath was of his innocence. "No matter what they do me," he repeated over and over to the listless cellmates, "I am innocent and they know I am innocent. Everyone knows I did not murder anyone."

There was always a murmur in the background resolutely replying, "Sure you are innocent, Castro, just like the rest of us."

Roberto, a simple man with simple needs and desires, had been destroyed by an absurd set of circumstances wound so tightly and intricately within the legal community, he saw no chance at a way out. Not unlike a mouse caught in the most elaborate maze, at that moment, he did not have the ability to find his way out. He had entrusted his life to an attorney, a person he knew nothing about; his only option was to cooperate and give Thomas Rigsby all his trusting faith. A tugging from instincts knocked on Roberto's conscience and unconscious mind, spreading seeds of doubt as to the ability of this professional to tackle the colossal defense. Closing his eyes he felt the slowly receding pounding of his heart until it had stabilized to its regular rhythm. Clutching a worn tattered pillow, he rolled onto the cot and slept.

At the county lock-up Roberto had the companionship of one cellmate, who he conversed with on a limited basis, as his English was still poor. The jail provided a television set, lending endless hours of distraction and a chance to hear fluent English spoken. Books were also provided, in English, forcing Roberto to either learn the language or be void of all distractions. Without any alternatives, he delved into comprehending the mother language, spending most of his waking hours pursing learning how to read, speak and write. Bored, the cellmate aided in polishing Roberto's use of English, correcting both the written and spoken language, and he was pleasantly surprised at the speed Roberto was able to comprehend. "Maybe I will go to college when I get out of here," Roberto chuckled.

Each day the guards allowed the men out of their cells to exercise in a common courtyard. Roberto never went. He feared social interaction with the inmates. He didn't trust anyone, and would never let down his guard. Keeping to himself insured no one could hurt him, or that anything he would say might be misconstrued. Mulling over the precipitous relationship with Fernando, he was keenly aware of the fact he could never trust another human again; a snitch for the state, Fernando could and would say anything to protect himself from admitting to the murder, so he blatantly pointed a finger at a man he loathed. Roberto would never allow himself an entanglement that would put him at the mercy of another man. Keeping to himself would insure his safety and peace of mind. He would never confide in any of the inmates, would never even accept a free cigarette. He was worried, terrified, and completely disillusioned.

The only bright moments of jail life were the sporadic appearances of his lawyer, who would discuss the case, and assure him the public defender's office was working diligently on his defense. For a passing hour, sometimes as long as a day, Roberto would return to his cell renewed with a sense of hope and faith that he would shortly be a free man, completely exonerated from a crime he never committed. As each session would end, Rigsby would leave the jail a free man, while Roberto would return to a tiny dingy cell, where privacy and freedom were nonexistent.

Sleeping, shaking his head remorsefully, was how he spent a great part of each day. There was nowhere to go, just the television to watch, and he didn't want to talk all day to the guys in the jail, so he slept. "When you sleep", he admitted to Thomas. "You don't have to face the real world. You can dream and think

of better times, safe times, free times. So I sleep and sleep."
Using this gloomy scenario, Roberto hoped to elicit sympathy
from his lawyer.

A waste of a human life forced to sit and vegetate in a tiny
cell. An innocent man paying dues for a crime he didn't commit,
a crime someone else had committed. Money would get him out
of jail, and money would purchase the best defense. In the free
American society, he was trapped by the lack of funds. The only
thing stopping him from emerging from the confines of the jail
was money. Poverty was the only crime Roberto was guilty of and
that was not a punishable offense. As time slipped away, little
information had been forthcoming from his lawyers. Doting on
the reality that lack of funds probably translated into a lack of
energy and professionalism on the part of the public defender
was reason for great concern about receiving a fair trial. The reality that the state had appointed the cheapest legal representation
was a euphemism for the poorest defense. "What would motivate
this Rigsby to do a good job defending me if he was paid so little? America, the lawyers make lots of money. How would he
defend me with so little money?" Roberto badgered his cellmate.
It was an ongoing worry that would become paramount in his
mind. Fearing he might go completely crazy, he focused on the
sounds emulating from the television set as he listened impas-
sively to the babble of American sit-coms.

# THE TRIAL

The day before the trial commenced, Thomas Rigsby shuffled into the jail garnering a brief case and a package of clothing. Meeting in the brightly lit conference room, he handed his client a change of clothes that included used, but shiny shoes, and black socks. "You will wear this at the trial," he instructed, "You need to appear honorable and credible to the judge. Please remember not to say a word. You must just sit and listen. If you make noise, the judge will have you removed from the courtroom and that would further damage your case." With pleading eyes, Roberto knew he would have to take this advise to heart. He knew if he burst out, and created a scene it would make him look bad; he had watched enough American television and learned how to mimic proper behavior.

The initial arraignment took place, the following day, April 1,1982, case number 4063 in the District Court of Clark County Nevada. The official criminal complaint accused Roberto H. Miranda of murder, grand larceny and the use of a deadly weapon in commission of a crime between August 9,1981, and August 10,1981. Elaborating "that he did then and there without authority of law and with malice, willfully and feloniously kill Manuel Rodriguez Torres by stabbing at and into his body with a knife and did willfully with intent to deprive the owner steal and drive away a 1971 Chevrolet pick-up, and take personal property."

At 7:00 am the guard announced the inmate should get prepared. He was walked out of the musty cell, shepherded to a small brightly lit room where the guard pointed to the clothing in the bag, demanded him to strip, then stood there while the inmate carefully dressed into proper court room attire. Knocking on the heavy door, another guard announced that they were ready for the transfer. The bulky metal door opened quickly, while the two cautiously walked the defendant down a narrow hall to an awaiting van. Firmly locking him in the back seat, the seasoned driver whisked off to the county courthouse. If nothing, else the crisp morning air and the sight of a few passing clouds awakened Roberto's senses. Tasting some minor form of freedom gave him hope and dignity. His appearance was clean and somber, still handsome. He would hope his honest smile, his bright eyes, and strong posture would add to the credibility of his innocence. The short trip to the holding cell left little time for extended thoughts of freedom as he was rapidly escorted to the holding cell near the edge of the courtroom. This small cell was built expressively for prisoners waiting trial; its lack of amenities aligned with the consequences of a guilty man. An innocent man would be offered a space reflective of respect for human mind and body. He was not given the right to walk into the courtroom with his lawyer. Only those who had money and could pay the bail had that right. With deepest humiliation, the defendant would be ushered into the courtroom by an armed guard.

For the public defender, it was just another day at the job, but for Mr. Miranda, the accused, it was a day of judgment; would he live or die? Cloistered in the tiny jail cell he became more terrified as the minutes worn on. Pacing up and back in the tiny cell he waited to be called into the courtroom. Fearing he would lose total control, he diverted his mind to his family, and his mother, asking her for help, strength of spirit and hope. Not wanting to ruin the well-pressed creases in the borrowed suit, he continued pacing until the guard unlatched the cell door.

Quietly, yet solemnly, he slowly walked to the plaintiff's desk where Mr. Rigsby was patiently waiting his appearance. No smile, just a perfunctory handshake, and a weak, "Good morning." Seated in the hard sturdy wooden chairs, the attorney began explaining procedure, again reminding him not to say one word during the course of the trial, that he should look up at the jury, face them and be strong, show them he is not afraid, because, he was an innocent man. "Always look up. Don't look at the floor. That is a sign of a guilty man. Sit up straight," he advised. "Look the witnesses in the eye. Stare if you must, but show no sign of emotion. The jury looks at emotions as a sign of weakness or even guilt."

Glancing around the room, it was painfully obvious the defendant had no support of friends or family; similar to a wedding with the bride's and groom's families on opposite sides, here all the jury could see were supporting characters of the district attorney's office, none for the defendant. This worried both Roberto and his lawyer; the jury would see a man with no support, a loner, not a good point in a capital murder case. The accused family lived in Cuba, and his friends were in California. It had been several months since he had contact with any of his local Cuban comrades. They weren't even aware he was in town. Perhaps, when the trial hit the papers, some of his supporters would come to his side, but for now, he was utterly, shamelessly, and completely alone as any man can be. He could not recall when he had ever felt so alone; a single man with one lawyer facing a battalion of lawyers paid by the state. Granted, the district attorney's office paid little to their employees, but many were willing to work for comparably small salaries for the opportunity to work on high profile cases. So there was no lack of manpower to prosecute this innocent man, just a totally unbalanced tilt of both manpower and experienced attorneys. This point exacerbated his sensation of loneliness even further, creating relentless anxiety. For once being forced to remain mute would be easy. The terror running through his nerves deadened his tongue.

Low mummers filled the stately hall as all waited anxiously for the appearance of the judge. Unlike Cuban courts, there were numerous people who worked in the courtroom: an official court reporter, several guards, an assistant to the judge, a secretary, and of course endless prosecuting lawyers. The staff seemed to be at ease with the austerity of the environment, just another day for them. The routine of listening to the fate of another human being was commonplace.

Rigsby had explained that the trial would last at least one to three weeks. Such a long time, thought Roberto. In Cuba, if an accused was lucky enough to live to see the inside of a courtroom, the case was heard in one day, and guilty or innocent, one's fate was sealed within eight hours. Communist society had no time for beating around the bush. Decisions were made post haste with little decorum. Accused of capital crimes, a guilty person met death within a week of the judge's verdict. Cuban government had no elaborate system of appeals. Once a decision was made, the accused abided by the court's decision. The tiny island did not have room to house thousands of prisoners, so off to the gallows the guilty went, shot or hung, within days after an expeditious trial.

Although Roberto felt the American legal system far surpassed the lopsided Communistic laws, he had not been allowed the freedom to call home and notify close family and relatives. At every possible opportunity he begged and pleaded with guards and police officers to allow him his right to make one phone call.

His mother, he needed to tell her what had happened to him. He desperately needed her support and advise. But time and time again this simple and rightful demand was left unfulfilled. Sitting so isolated in the courtroom, he imaged a conversation with his mom. He saw her wide smile, her deep-set brown eyes wet with tears, her long thin fingers clutching his bicep. He felt her breath whispering words of wisdom and comfort. "They never would allow me to make the call home They say I can't make a long distance call," he hallucinated. His mother was the only person he needed to call. She needed to know what had happened to her son. Roberto desperately whined, "Nobody in my family knew where I was or what I was doing."

There was never a time when he wished more for the presence of his family. Not only did he need their unequivocal support, but he also needed to exhibit to the jury he had a family who supported and believed in him. The unbalanced exclusion of family and friends further accentuated the illusion of his life as a drifter, a worthless person. The jury would surreptitiously question why a man in his forties would be so alone. Where were his friends, his family, a spouse, perhaps a girlfriend? Without these overt signs of a person who had made commitments to relationships they would see him as asocial, a worthless part of society, just another wetback who was using their country to his advantage. And look how he ended up, the jury would surmise, killing another man. Roberto worried, he fretted, and he agonized over this surreal situation. Pinching himself, he brought his thoughts back to the reality of the austere hushed courtroom.

"All rise," announced the court secretary, as Judge Bixler made his initial appearance. Standing stiffly, Roberto, couldn't help but think this elderly, black judge may have a soft spot, that the judge being black would help his case. The judge's stern face narrowed as he cast his dark eyes onto the accused.

Furrowing his brow, he selected a group of documents and began silently reading as if no one existed in the room. Satisfied the charges had been correctly completed, he asked both lawyers if they were ready to try the case. A positive affirmation from both tables signaled the beginning of a long and turbulent presentation.

Opening statements were given by opposing attorneys, with Ferraro taking his time listing three offenses: murder and use of a deadly weapon in commission of a crime, grand larceny, and robbery and use of a deadly weapon in commission of a crime. "Ladies and gentlemen of the jury," he respectfully addressed, strategically placing his hand near his heart, "The state is asking for the death penalty. When such an atrocious crime such as this occurs, punishment should be in kind, and the death penalty would be the true penalty. Anything less undermines the seriousness of the nature of this case and the crimes committed by that man seated over there." Gesturing to the traumatized accused, the convincing district attorney was confident he would be victorious in winning the capital murder case.

The district attorney had been fastidious in doing his work. On April 15, 1982 a warrant was issued for Fernando Cabrera, with bail set at $25,000. So worried about the star witness, (Feranado) the prosecutor wanted a guarantee this man would show up at the trial and give plausible testimony. The warrant was based upon law premised upon the materiality of a witness:

If it appeared by affidavit that the testimony of a person who is material in any criminal investigation and impractical to secure his presence by subpoena, the magistrate may require him to give bail for his appearance as a witness. Thus a bench warrant was issued for Fernando. District Attorney Ferraro was fearful of the safety of this witness, asking for protective custody. No allowance for error could be tolerated. The case against Miranda was based primarily upon the testimony this witness would make, and he would do everything in his power to guarantee Fernando's timely appearance in court.

Robert Teuton, Deputy District Attorney, explained that, "It had become impractical to serve the subpoena as four attempts were made at four different addresses." Investigator James Togher learned from other people he had contacted that Fernando was avoiding service of the subpoena and in fact had planned on fleeing to Miami, Florida on April 14, 1982. Presently, Fernando was hiding out at a friend's apartment located at 21st Street and Freemont. Testifying under oath in a crowded courtroom, based upon a conjured up story that could not be collaborated by another soul, was not on Fernando's To Do list.

Searching relentlessly, the police finally caught up with Fernando, and escorted him to the local station house where he gave a statement of facts to police. "I drove Roberto to Manuel's home because he didn't own a car and didn't know how to drive a stick shift. He told me he needed to see this guy, that he owed him money for drugs. So I drove him there on that Saturday, and waited outside in my car. It seemed for quite a while. I got hot, so I entered the apartment, and I saw Roberto standing over Manuel, Roberto's shirt all bloody, the guy lying dead on the kitchen floor. I say to him, what are you doing? He answered, 'I am searching the house for drugs.' He said he had drugs here for me, but he tricked me. I don't see any drugs. Roberto, he tells me to take the television set, the stereo and the guy's watch. I did, I took all the stuff, and put it in the truck. And that's it. I was scared of Roberto. He killed a man and he was angry. He could have killed me too," explained Fernando.

All the elaborate protection had served the District Attorney well as his star witness took the stand and began the damning testimony against a man he hated: Roberto Miranda.

As the prosecutor peppered Fernando with questions, Fernando reiterated how Roberto had killed Manuel, how he had turned over tables rummaging through the apartment, then robbed him. The district attorney began questioning the witness: "What did the defendant tell you that night?" Fernando put his hand in the air blankly gesturing. He answered that he (Roberto) had gone there for drugs and that he had found none and he had been tricked. Roberto told me to help him search the place for drugs. Roberto said the deceased had tricked him, and that is why Roberto killed him. Manuel had told Roberto to come and buys drugs cheaply. Roberto said that he was sorry for killing the guy, but he had been tricked and he was angry. Roberto told me that he had come here for drugs, that there weren't any that Roberto and I should take this, as he pointed to the stereo and the television set, and the watch." Wringing his hands together, his forehead dripping with perspiration, fidgeting in the witness seat, Fernando had completed the testimony without a hitch. Measuring each step, he stolidly walked back to the gallery, mentally rehashing each word spoken. Smiling, to himself, his made-up story appeared credible to the jury, so credible that the public defender couldn't punch a plausible doubt in the libeled testimony. Of course the other two Cabrera brothers would back up his brother's statements. They wouldn't allow the state to send their brother to jail.

When questioned by the district attorney, David Cabrera, Fernando's brother, responded that it was a drug deal and Roberto had not paid him and that's why Roberto had killed him. Again, Thomas sat motionless in his seat, failing to challenge the credibility of the David Cabrera's statements. By this time his client was seething from the blatant acceptance of evidence. Tugging on Thomas's jacket sleeve, Roberto told him to challenge the statements, to ask for tangible proof. "Where is the physical proof that I was ever in the apartment? There is none. Ask him, I beg you ask him, where is that proof?"

"Shut-up," Thomas whispered angrily, "Just let me handle the case. Now sit quietly and don't make the judge angry."

Again, Roberto tugged on his lawyer's arm, reiterating for him to say something, question the witness, challenge the battery of lies. Make David and Fernando tell the truth. That Fernando was in fact the murderer. "Shut up," growled Thomas." Let me handle this."

Again the defendant quieted down, blindly allowing his lawyer to lead the way. It seemed an impossible task to remain riveted to the wooden chair when he should be on his feet lashing out at the outrageous set of lies perpetrated upon the jury.

On July 31,1982, the defendant did the unthinkable, and petitioned the court to dismiss counsel. So angry, disturbed, and distressed, Roberto had to make the judge see that his court-appointed attorney wasn't doing an adequate job. Sensing there was nothing to lose he filed the following document with the State of Nevada:

"Submitting the following arguments and points that counsel's failure to research the law, prepare and investigate the care and threaten defendant had denied the defendant effective and competent assistance of counsel. Under the sixth amendment of the constitution, all persons have a right to assistance of counsel. In this case, counsel was confronted with exculpatory (outside) evidence by the defendant that someone else had committed the crime, and that counsel acknowledged that he was aware another individual had committed the crime and failed to investigate such when counsel himself was aware who the other suspect was. This significance of the error on defense counsel was of enormous constitutional magnitude when viewed in the light of the salient fact that if counsel had properly and effectively investigated the case, defendant might not have been in a state of terror. Counsel's insistence to plead guilty amounted to a sophisticated form of mental coercion; the effect was recognized by the United States Supreme Court as adequate grounds for dismissal."

The judge, whose sympathies did not appear to side with the defendant, denied the change of counsel. Although the defendant's case was well presented, eloquent in format, logical in presentation, and tenaciously documented, Bixler could not see his way clear to appoint a new attorney, thereby extending the trial. Nor would he allow an immigrant, who spoke little English, to have the run of his courtroom. "No, the defendant should be thankful that he had an attorney paid for and provided by the good people of the State of Nevada. How dare he look a gift horse in the mouth, Just think of the justice he would be receiving had he committed those crimes in his own country," retorted the judge. Thus the trial would continue on without any breaks or disturbances. Glancing over his busy calendar, the judge didn't want to prolong proceedings. There were simply too many other cases to hear.

"Petition denied," resounded loudly in Roberto's ears. He could not utter another word, nor challenge the judge. Once again, his trusty attorney, now miffed and humiliated that the defendant should challenge his strategies and expertise, quelled his behavior. The trial continued.

As other witnesses were brought to the stand, little if any cross-examination was forthcoming from the defense lawyer. Dr. Green served as one of the best examples. Testifying from the autopsy results that the murder had to have taken place on Sunday, sometime between late morning and early afternoon, Rigsby never linked this fact with the fact that Fernando testified the murder had taken place on Saturday morning, one full day before it actually occurred. Making copious notes on a borrowed legal pad, Roberto's knee gyrated up and down, exasperating the anxiety fomenting every nerve ending.

Another collaboration with Dr. Green's testimony was the statement by a neighbor that she had seen the truck, owned by Manuel, gone from the house on that Saturday night, during the time of the alleged killing. This fact further refuted statements made by Fernando, yet Rigsby never cross-examined Fernando to dispel the lie.

The forensic specialist testified that one thumbprint had been lifted on a broken glass next to the deceased body. More damning evidence thought Roberto as he jarred his fingers into the hard mahogany table. Again grabbing his attorney's arm he whispered the invalidity of this testimony. "I don't know or understand how that can be, for I had never been inside the residence of the murdered man. If, as Fernando had previously testified against me, I had been to the apartment turning the place inside out for drugs, wouldn't the experts have found an abundance of prints and other tell tale signs of my presence? Matching hair, skin samples, shoe prints, saliva, my own blood?" questioned Roberto. Roberto begged his lawyer to question the witness, Rigsby again backed down, again reminded his client to be silent. The forensic specialist found absolutely no other evidence that Roberto had ever stepped foot into the deceased's apartment. The defendant's lawyer never questioned how a tiny thumb print could have been discovered yet no footprints, saliva, hair, or skin particles. Did Roberto simply fly into the apartment through the ceiling, place his thumb on a glass, and then fly back up to the ceiling and leave? All were pertinent questions that neither Rigsby, nor the judge, nor the jury had been supplied the answers to. Infuriated that no challenge had been made to the testimony, Roberto continued scribbling notes, then, frustrated, he began to stand. Grabbing his arm, Rigsby pulled his annoyed client back to the hard wooden seat, cupped his hand over Roberto's ear, and proceeded to admonish his impertinent behavior. The squabbling was easily overheard by surrounding employees and visitors; it was painfully obvious that the defendant had been dealt an unfair hand when the public defender's office selected Rigsby to head the case.

Looking up the pathetic defendant spied a condescending chagrin on the face of the court reporter that further served as an admonishment against improper outbursts. Roberto was laden with frustration. He wanted to testify, he wanted his day in court. "If the jury would hear my story," Roberto relented to Rigsby's dead ears, "They would know that Fernando and his brothers have lied. They would have no case at all."

To add fuel to the fire, Silveril Avila, and Roberto Escabo, both close friends of Fernando, testified they had seen Roberto with a blood-stained shirt. Both witnesses claimed Roberto had described the stolen items, and was in fact wearing Manuel's watch.

The sparseness of the defense was felt only by the defendant himself, as few witnesses were called to the stand to relate their story. Kimberly Franco's husband, in custody for another crime would prove to be the most damaging witness for the prosecution, if allowed to testify.

"The night of the murder," began Ms. Franco, "My husband and I were at the home of Pablo Garcia when Fernando came to the house with blood on him. I saw Fernando carrying a part of a stereo. He explained he had sold it to a man named Matraca who used to work at Caesar's Palace. When my husband and I were visiting Fernando's house shortly after I saw the same exact stereo. Although I thought it rather strange. I never said anything."

Listening to the damaging evidence, Roberto became more

confident that the jury would begin to understand who had committed the murder and why. His hopes were pinned on another important testimony, that of Emmett Anderson. The problem was that Emmett had gone to Florida, and was nowhere to be found within the time limitation set for trial. Therefore, all the defense could submit was the statement given to the police.

Astute, the district attorney objected to the statement as hearsay. The judge hastily agreed with this point of law, forbidding the injurious piece of evidence to be submitted on behalf of the defendant. Again, Mr. Rigsby sat back, unquestioningly accepting Bixler's decision. Looking over towards the prosecutor's table, Roberto spied a coy smile wrapped widely across opposing counsel's face. Ferraro's neatly pressed suit, and highly polished shoes, added to the cool confident stature of a man who was steam-rolling his opponent to the point of humiliation. Not wanting to appear overly confident, the smile instantly evaporated He replaced the tortoise shell glasses on the bridge of his angular nose giving the illusion of grave concentration.

Defense called upon Detective Maddock to explain the phone call he had received from a secret witness who had seen Fernando with the stolen property. Fernando was driving the deceased pick-up. The judge excluded the testimony, as inadmissible hearsay since the actual witness never appeared in the courtroom. Nodding his head, the detective stepped down from the stand. He gave a fleeting look at the defendant. Maddock's statements were of no value in the case. The judge's tolerance of evidence was short fused. He would not allow Maddock to divulge Emmett Anderson's damning statements.

Valentin's testimony on behalf of the defendant was at best sketchy: "Sunday evening, on August 9, I was in the park with Roberto and several other Cubans. Fernando drove up in a red pick-up truck and we could all see there was blood on his clothes. Fernando told us he had just killed a man and asked me to help him with the things that had been stolen. He asked me if I could store the stolen loot at my house and I said no" Gliding out of the witness stand, Valentin slipped out of the courtroom, sweating, happy that the ordeal was over.

"Defense calls Ramon Franco," the clerk echoed. A handsome, mulatto man appeared, took the oath, then twitched uncomfortably as Rigsby questioned him. "Please explain to the jury what you saw on that Sunday evening."

Stuttering unsurely, he elaborated, "I saw Fernando, and his pants were blood-stained. He said that he had just killed a man and he wanted to keep the loot at Mr. Garcia's house." That was the first last and only question he would be asked as he too stepped in a lively fashion out of the witness stand. Rather than prolong the questioning, Rigsby felt one simple sentence would preclude any room for error or contradiction of facts.

The defense's last witness, Fermin Ruiz, spoke in broken but recognizable English as he related his testimony." On August 8,1981, I saw Fernando near Valentin's house. He was standing outside, and he had a stereo, and there was blood on his clothing. Fernando told me he asked Valentin to keep some of the loot that he had stolen. The next day, I saw Fernando at the park in the dead man's truck and later in his own red pick-up."

Quickly running out of witnesses and objections, Thomas wrapped up his defense in a remarkable amount of time, keeping the promise to himself that he would never allow his client to sit on the witness stand. It wasn't that he feared what his client would say, but the embarrassment of cross-examination by a more formidable opponent kept him at bay. Not admitting that he was out maneuvered, or that he had put on anything less than an exemplary defense, his overconfidence allowed the case to end rapidly.

"There is enough doubt in the minds of the jury to set you free, but if you wish to plea bargain we could offer that," Thomas advised.

Again, Roberto begged to have his day in court. No, there was no way he would plead guilty for a crime he did not commit.

The summations of opposing attorneys were short and to the point. Rigsby, pointing to his client, who appeared as if he were already on a guillotine, alluded to a sense of fairness, reminding the jury that any doubt would mean they should not convict. They should, Rigsby said, search the evidence and come up with the conclusion that Roberto was in fact innocent. "It had been hard for me to stand up here, go through a trial. I would prefer to avoid the great responsibilities that I have, but I decided to be a lawyer. I believe in our advocacy system, I believe everyone needs a lawyer. Capital punishment historically was a punishment for blacks and poor. It really will be you, " he said, pointing both index fingers directly at the jury box, "who kills Mr. Miranda, just as if you were there to execute him yourselves. You will have to justify it for the rest of eternity. We cannot bring Manuel Torres back. Boy, if executing Roberto would, I would say, 'go to it', but it cannot of course. I think all the witnesses lied to a certain extent. Fernando's testimony, I don't know how you should consider it. In my mind it only created more questions. I am not a psychiatrist, but I wonder what type of society created Roberto. Surely the poverty the mistreatment of a nightmarish government like Cuba had something to do with it."

The accused could hardly believe his ears at the absurdity of the statements. It was as if had condemned all Cubans, as if all Cubans were poor, black, stupid and psychotic. He couldn't help but wonder where his lawyer received his credentials. Yes, he could reach the bar, but how in the hell did he pass the bar? This neophyte lawyer stood tall as he admitted his wavering belief in the testimonies given by witnesses under oath. The summation was a pathetic joke, reminding everyone, including the judge, of Rigsby's inexperience and ineptness, and blatant lack of confidence in his own client.

Standing a bit taller, strutting confidently, the district attorney, the lawyer representing "the people" pointed his finger at the accused. "There, ladies and gentlemen of the jury, is the man guilty of the most serious of all crimes, murder. A man is dead, Manual Torres, and somebody has got to pay for this crime. …When anyone takes the life of another human being as senselessly, especially as senselessly as it was in this case, that person must pay something. Depending upon what the circumstances are of the case, that payment should be death. Nothing could be more senseless than robbery. This Cuban who came over here on the flotilla, and hasn't been in this country too long, and in such a short period of time has amassed two convictions — murder and burglary. (The burglary conviction was based in California). That is all we know about Roberto Miranda's life. He certainly has a significant criminal history for the length of time he has been here. I do no want you to shy away from your responsibility if you determine that he shouldn't receive death because you think you can put him in prison for the rest of his life and that he will never get out. Everybody knows that people can be pardoned — look at Richard Nixon. But not just by the governor. It also includes actions by the State Board of Pardons. I believe that the state has proved beyond a shadow of doubt that the person who did this horrible crime sits before you, and he should be punished. I ask you to come back with a verdict of murder in the first degree. Anything less would take away from the serious nature of his actions."

Staring, ashen, Roberto's heart stood still. He felt like he couldn't breathe, that the very life was being sucked out of him in front of all these people. How did his life boil down to this moment? So many people gawking at him, inspecting him, judging him. Pinching himself, he truly thought he was in the middle of a nightmare where there was no way out. He felt dizzy, his head was on fire, and his nerves tingling, as sweat poured from his bow, dripping down his cheeks and neck. "Where are you mom? I need you. Please help me someone, anyone!" Concentrating on the closing statements of his defense attorney, the defendant asked why the speech was so brief, why he couldn't defend him as strongly as his opponent.

"Be quiet," Rigsby threatened nervously, "Or the judge will remove you from the courtroom and that would hardly impress the jury of your innocence."

"I am an innocent man," Roberto argued, "And that lawyer, he is making me look guilty. He is saying things that are not true. He just wants someone to pay for this crime and he doesn't care who. Please, I beg you. Let me have my say before the trial ends."

"No," Rigsby answered. "It's done, but at sentencing the judge will give you a chance to have your say."

"By then it will be too late. The decisions will be made," he argued.

Turning his face away from the jury, the defendant put his head in his hands. Unable to define his shock, he stared at the floor. Frustrated, angry, he held his temper, kept his behavior in check as the pundit of the people recited law, refuting the defense's case with panache and eloquence. "Someone has got to pay," burst into Roberto's mind. But that someone is not me."

Judge Bixler nodded his head to both attorneys, and then turned to the jury box. Removing his glasses, he gently stroked his neck and pondered the elaborate list of instructions.

"It my duty as judge to instruct you in the law that applies to this case. It is your duty as jurors to follow the instructions and to apply the rules of law to the facts as you find them from the evidence. You must not be concerned with the victim of any rule of law — regardless of an opinion you may have as to what the law ought to be. It would be a violation of your oath to base a verdict upon any other view of the law than that given in the instructions of the court. In this case there are three separate offenses: murder and use of a deadly weapon in commission of a crime, grand larceny, and robbery and use of a deadly weapon in commission of a crime. Each charge should be considered separately".

Judge Bixler continued the orders, which described in detail the degrees of murder beginning with capital punishment to second degree, and finally, manslaughter. As Roberto sat motionlessly he observed Ferraro with a dry smile on his face, already tasting a win. As the judge continued the elaborate instructions pertaining to murder, he wondered where the balance was. When was the judge going to discuss his innocence? Why were all those instructions based upon the presumption of guilt? As the court reporter, Ms. Gold, hurriedly pounded on the keys of her noiseless machine, he wondered what she and others were thinking. What was the reporter for the Review Journal thinking? Would he cast him as the evil murderer, or would he brush away the pontifications of the well-spoken district attorney, and see the simple truths? Looking around the silent room, he was overcome by the abundance of rhetoric that had taken place, and how common sense discourse could have taken such an unexpected turn against him Common sense and the application of simple logic would have exonerated him. The entire trial was a farce based upon a hungry prosecutor, and a public defender lacking in both basic skills and intellect. Where was justice? Clearly, there was none. But, the judge, shouldn't he have seen through this farce? He would have to be deaf and dumb not to have garnered the imbalance. Humans are not without their prejudices.

None among us can say we are perfect, yet a judge is ordained with the trust of the people and should posture himself with that demeanor. To do anything less would taint his credibility, swaying the jury to a verdict which would be less than fair. As the defendant sat miserably, he waited for a moment of justice, for the pronouncement from the lips of Bixler that, "The defendant is presumed to be innocent until the contrary is proved. This presumption places upon the State the burden of proving beyond a reasonable doubt every element of the crime charged. A reasonable doubt is one based on reason. It is not mere possible doubt but is such as would govern or control a person in the more weighty affairs of life. If the minds of the jurors, after the entire comparison and consideration of all the evidence are in such a condition that they can say they feel an abiding conviction of the truth of the charge, there is not a reasonable doubt. Doubt to be reasonable, must be actual and substantial, not mere possibility or speculation. If you have a reasonable doubt as to the guilt of the defendant, he is entitled to a verdict of not guilty." Removing his glasses, the judge panned the jury box looking for traces of puzzlement. Satisfied, he shuffled through his notes, plucking out several additional pages of instructions.

"Although you are to consider only the evidence on the case, you must bring to the consideration of the evidence your everyday common sense and judgment as reasonable men and women," continued the judge. " Thus you are not limited solely to what you see and hear as the witnesses testify. You may draw reasonable inferences from the evidence you feel as justified in the light of common experience, keeping in mind that such inferences should not be based on speculation or guess. A verdict may never be influenced by sympathy prejudice or public opinion. The verdict must be unanimous."

With that said, the clerk announced that the jury would

retire to commence the deliberations. As they silently filed out, their faces reflecting the somberness of the instructions, Roberto hoped they would take a piece of his heart with them. The parting words of the Judge Bixler left little room for a verdict in his favor. The word "doubt" and "reasonable" had many meanings. He could only hope those words would play in his favor, that those men and women would see the truth, would question the sketchy details, conflicting testimonies, and lopsided presentation of evidence. Would they see the Judge hadn't played by "fairness" rules. When Roberto had asked to defend himself it was through the lack of caring and investigation by the court appointed attorney. His defense was doomed from the beginning, having to accept handouts because he lacked the funds to hire the best defense. The State of Nevada could surely swell with pride on the credentials of Ferraro as he pranced around the courtroom continually objecting to most anything Rigsby would place into evidence. His legal prowess overshadowed his opponents by a country mile. A polished attorney, Ferraro exaggerated every move he made and every word he uttered. It was written on the stolid faces of the jury. Every time Mr. Ferraro stepped up to pitch, his audience was enamored. He had them in his confidence. The jury believing his every word. If Roberto, a man who barely spoke English, could detect such a compelling imbalance in the two attorneys, why couldn't the judge? Why didn't the judge offer a fairer balance? Was he that prejudiced, that obsessed with putting a Cuban man to death that he would shame and compromise the legal profession?

The bailiff ambled over to the defense table, and ushered Roberto back to the holding cell. "As soon as we get word from the judge," instructed Thomas, "you will return to the courtroom."

Standing up, the defendant looked into his attorney's dispassionate eyes, "I guess this is it then."

"Just wait and see. You can never predict how these things may turn out," Thomas positively, but gingerly, advised.

Once again Roberto found himself locked in a tiny cell, without a human soul to confide in or converse with. In every way he was locked away from the world; both physically and emotionally. As the clocked ticked loudly in his mind, he paced the distance of the cell, hoping to exercise his body into a needed sleep. He remembered when he was a child and had visited the zoo and seen the black cougars pace back and forth in a small cage surrounded by fat metal bars. He understood what freedom or lack of freedom meant. I am like one of those cougars at the zoo, he thought. Except they were luckier than him, they didn't have to worry about a death sentence.

# THE VERDICT

A ll rise," demanded the court secretary. The jury was seated, the courtroom was still as all waited anxiously for the last appearance of the presiding judge, the man who would deliver the Roberto's fate: life or death. No middle ground, no further room for negotiating, this was the deciding moment. Both numb and weak, Roberto was so filled with apprehension it was almost impossible for his trembling limbs to hold him up. The endless waiting, frustration and musing had boiled down to this prodigious time. The borrowed suit had lost its sharp creases; the white shirt yellowed from perspiration, the tie wrinkled from constant fondling.

Thomas Rigsby also exhibited signs of the ramifications of a weary trial. His wrinkled shirt and soiled tie signaled another sleepless night working on the case. He didn't want to lose; winning this case would be a huge feather in his cap. He could envision the headlines: "Young lawyer wins capital case. David takes on Goliath and scores victory for a poor pitiful Cuban immigrant. Brilliantly fought, this young lawyer had the makings of a supreme court judge." The neophyte needed this win to prove to the legal community his quality of professionalism. This case would catapult him up the public defender's ladder, and into the arms of a rich public firm, willing to pay six figures for successful courtroom strategies. In his mind's eye, he had fought the case to the best of his ability, using all his talents, wit, and finesse to arrive at the imminently announced verdict. No matter what, Rigsby truly believed he had put on a dazzling defense, one that any immigrant could be proud of. Yes, he reminded himself over and over, he had done a fine fine job, and whatever the verdict may be, he had done himself proud, that his client, should take the verdict like a man.

Dressed in authoritative black vestments, the judge settled his eyes on the defendant, staring blankly; he would not give away his thoughts. Like a seasoned poker player, the neutrality that was imposed upon this position wasn't always what it seemed. A look, a gesture, a sudden twist of the head, or wrinkling of the brow, emulated signals to the jury. "The plaintiff is guilty; just read my thoughts." Credibility could be won or lost based upon subliminal body language. As the verdict was read, Roberto now knew where he stood in the empty stare of the judge: GUILTY.

Reading the jury's findings sent loud mummers throughout the crowded courtroom as news reporters grabbed their notes and scurried out to report the verdict of the capital murder case. Annoyed by the frenetic burst of decorum, the judge banged the gavel. He demanded quiet and respect. Glancing over to the jury box, he quizzed each member, asking them to reiterate the verdict. Each in turn validated the guilty verdict in firm commitment, never turning an eye to the accused. Fully satisfied, the judge thanked each member for their duty and excused them from the jury box. "Sentencing will take place in one week. Until that time, Mr. Miranda will be remanded back to the county jail."

Already weak and frozen with disbelief, Roberto began hyperventilating until he was sure he would pass out. Snapping some life into his lungs, Roberto walked over to the prosecutor asking, "Can I talk to you? You know very well that I am not guilty. Why did you do this to me? " District Attorney Ferraro simply responded, "Talk to your attorney." A look of shame and humiliation swept the prosecutor's face. He had won the state's case. It was an easy one to win. The case was too one-sided. The prosecutor waited with anticipation for the defense lawyer to put on his case. He rehearsed objections to stifle Rigsby's questioning. He deliberated strategies to combat witnesses but none of this was needed. The public defender defended nothing. At times, it seemed incredulous that Thomas Rigsby ever passed the bar, let alone landed the grave responsibility to try a capital case. At times, the district attorney was surprised at the judge's reactions, or rather lack of reactions to statements made by witnesses. A bittersweet win for the district attorney's office; a battle with no contention. There was no pleasure in convicting a man when the defense was so pathetically weak and unresponsive. It was as if there was hardly any defense at all. At times, Ferraro felt like a bully, that the scale of justice was so inordinately tipped decidedly in his favor even before the trial began. His battalion of trial lawyers literally steamed rolled the meager defense of the solitary public defender. Justice was supposed to be blind, yet it was also supposed to be balanced, and in this case, there was no balance. Even, if a man was guilty as sin, recognized the victorious prosecutor, he deserved a quality defense, especially in a capital murder case. This defense was so paltry that at times he was embarrassed, wondering how the legal community could accept such inept practice. Perhaps he should have questioned his own ethics. Did he falter the public's faith by remaining silent, never altering the routine of the case to fit the impoverished defense of the plaintiff? Ignoring all signs of an inexperienced lawyer, he plowed ahead, never for a moment allowing his plan to be shaken from its strategy. He would put on the best and most convincing case possible. But in this instance, it meant putting an innocent man to death. He represented the state, and he would only represent the direct interests of the state. The judge was supposed to temper the case when it was painfully obvious the inferior quality of defense. Brushing aside his insecurities, the district attorney could always fall back on this rationale; passing the blame would allow him to sleep at night. Maybe the judge would be the sleepless one, he conjectured remorsefully.

# LIFE AS A CONVICTED FELON

Stiffly grabbing the accused by the arm, the bailiff prepared to take Roberto back to the holding cell until the county sent over a patrol car. Hunched over, hiding the cascading tears, the convicted was led through the hall adjacent to the courtroom where he would have ample time to mull over his fate. Glancing back for the last time, Roberto saw the prosecutor being slapped on the back by his fellow associates. He saw him shaking hands with the deceased's family, appearing highly celebratory. For one brief instant their eyes met as the accused forever seared his fate into the memory of the opposing attorney. "You have sent an innocent man off to jail. You have sent an innocent man to his death," Roberto protested.

As promised, the patrol car arrived within the hour. This time, he was escorted by two officers, while another two armed guards paraded behind. Now that he was officially found guilty, his behavior became more circumspect, and in the eyes of the law, more dangerous. He had been tried by a jury of his peers and pronounced guilty of the most heinous crime; murder. Secured in handcuffs, the two cars sped, with sirens blasting to the county jail. It seemed as though they were announcing a victory. The revelry resounded in the Cuban neighborhood that foreigners seeking refuge must pay the price if the law was broken. Entering this great free country gave no one the right to kill. Take notice of the man seated in back, now a convicted murderer. The state got him and now this man will pay dearly for his crime.

The county had made special provisions for his return, giving him a private cell. Disrobed from civilian clothes, prison garb would be all he might ever wear until his death. Lying on a rigid cot, he closed his eyes in hopes of sweeping away rancorous thoughts of the trial. "The judge was black and I believed he would help me. But he didn't. He tried to block out, deny me everything. There were a lot of denials. It seemed as though every time my lawyer objected, the judge denied him," Roberto mumbled in his sleep. The problem was, nobody was listening.

Closing his eyes, he mentally beat himself up for not testifying on his own behalf. Begging Thomas a chance to speak for himself, he trusted his advice, sitting out the case as if he were a bystander. Never uttering a word in self-defense, he sat day after day, consumed by weak and outright untruthful testimony. The state's snitch, Fernando, had complete immunity, yet he carried the secret; he was the killer. Turning over on his back Roberto stared directly up at the ceiling as he searched for answers to his dilemma. If he received the death penalty, life would be over in a matter of a few days, perhaps weeks. Poignantly recalling the speed at which the death penalty was administered in Cuba, he knew his days on earth were severely numbered. The death penalty, as practiced in his home country, was administered within a week of the decree; there were no appeals. What time he had left on earth he had to make count. Tomorrow he would again ask if he could call his family. He would beg, cry, and plead to have this last request answered.

Exhausted beyond sanity, he dreamed of facing the judge. "You got the power to kill me. Please spare me. I am innocent — you know that I am innocent. I had no motive, I owned no knife, there was hardly any physical evidence that I was ever in the apartment. You know I didn't kill that man. You know who killed that man. You know I am innocent, you know that I am an innocent man."

A week of this hell passed slowly until a guard appeared at the cell, he announced the trip back to the courthouse. Acquainted with the routine, Roberto held out his hands for the cuffs to be locked securely around his wrists, while another guard escorted him into the patrol car. No sirens this time, just an unhurried pace through the downtown until they reached the courthouse. Guns pulled, he was guided into the brightly lit hallway, and quickly locked into a holding cell until the case was called. Surprised by the unexpected appearance of Rigsby, who assured his client that no matter what the penalty, he would work on the appeal. That in fact, he had already begun the appeal process. Roberto could not respond; he had an empty gaze upon his face. The situation was too much for his psyche to digest.

What do you say to a man who was about to hear his fate? The lawyer was almost as speechless as his client. He could not pluck out the profound words he needed to assure his client that he would prevail. What exasperated the scene was the prominent trembling of Rigsby's hands, the noticeable twitch in his left eye, and the low timber in his voice. This was not the demeanor of a confident man. This professional was scared, not only for his client but himself. He found no reason to fault the case presentation, to place doubt on his expertise, to question the legal strategies, or motives. In his own mind's eye, he had performed with utmost care and precision. Rationalizing that he was simply outgunned and out-manned was enough grounds to soothe any guilt he might feel.

As lawyer and client stood shoulder to shoulder waiting for the judge's appearance, an overwhelming silence enveloped the staid room. The low sounds of breathing and anticipated arrival of the prominent appearance of the judge and the life or death decision he would hand down. "All rise," announced the bailiff.

Already standing, Miranda taut, as the judge took his leather chair, and slowly placed a pair of tortoise shell glasses firmly on his elongated nose. Turning to the court secretary, he received a small stack of papers, quickly reviewed them, then removed his glasses and stared directly into the face of the recently convicted. "The state has placed me with the responsibility of delivering the penalty of breaking the law," commenced the judge. "And in this particular case during the course of robbery you have been found guilty of murder in the first degree. The penalty," he continued, "is death. You will be remanded over to the state penitentiary in Carson City and at a date to be later established, will be executed." One could hear the sound of a feather landing on the highly polished wooden floors. Silence. Not a breath was taken as the judge evoked the unthinkable penalty: death by lethal injection.

It was that plain, that simple, and that quick. The judge did not mince words, nor take any unneeded time. It was just a simple pronouncement. "Do you wish to speak?" he offered.

An immeasurable stillness continued to cloak the room, as if someone had dimmed the lights, extracting all the brightness, and  the earth stopped rotating. Unable to breathe, let alone speak, the accused's legs gave way and Roberto slumped to the wooden floor. Rigsby, emotionally shaken by the pronouncement, was barely able to gather enough strength to come to his client's aid. Assistance fastidiously arrived as three armed guards gathered the crumpled man off the floor, and hoisted him over their shoulders. Apparently, this was not unusual behavior; both the judge and the courtroom personnel routinely handled these reactions to penalties conferred of such serious nature.  Placing

Roberto onto a hard wooden seat the room resumed its stillness as the judge patiently paused for him to regain composure.

"I am allowing you a final chance to have your say," barked the judge, as he fiddled with his glasses.

Thomas took his client by the shoulders, and whispered inaudible words of advice and encouragement. Shaking his head, he rose, turned stoically towards the judge. Roberto gathered his thoughts and embarked on his last and sole testimonial. "I am innocent, and you and everyone in this courtroom knows that I am innocent. I never killed anyone. I never had a reason to kill anyone, I never owned a knife, I was never at the home of the deceased, yet you decided my fate, based upon a witness who had complete immunity. I never, never killed that guy. The prosecutor knows I didn't kill that guy. If you put me to death, then I have no choice but to accept your decision, but you will never ever get me to admit to a crime I did not do. I am an innocent man, I did not kill anyone."

In Roberto's mind, the judge had set this decree against all Cubans. Immigrants could not come into the judge's town, commit murder, and then go unpunished. The death penalty would serve as a stern reminder that behavior acceptable in Cuba would not be tolerated in America. If Cubans murdered each other, it should be in their own country. The dispensing of the death penalty sent shock waves within the tightly knit community: criminal activity would not be tolerated. The death penalty was rarely used in the state of Nevada. The ghetto was constantly being monitored for drugs. Now further infiltration by spies and police would undoubtedly escalate. Fearing reprisals, local policing was beefed up; patrols and uniformed police made their presence known. Roberto saw himself as the recipient of hate and mistrust, of a fair and equal legal system tipped against foreigners. He sensed hatred for his skin color and culture. He believed his punishment was biased, ingrained by generations of Americans who mistrusted and loathed outsiders. Filled with contempt, he remained silent as justice was doled out.

"Are you finished?" asked the judge sternly exhibiting no visible signs of doubt or remorse.

"Yes," replied the convicted man.

With a nod of the head, he was removed from the courtroom by two armed guards, and returned to the holding cell. This time Rigsby accompanied his client to the holding cell and tried to calm him down, assuring him there was more work to be done on the case; that he would not forget. "I am not ready to die. No I can't die for a crime I never committed. When you are a stranger in a strange country the fight is you against one million people who want to kill you, and it doesn't matter if you are guilty or innocent. They want to see someone punished for this crime. I won't let these people kill me, first I would kill myself," Roberto mercilessly cried.

On September 9,1983, Judge Addeliar Guy issued the formal document stating that on April 27,1983, Roberto Miranda had entered a plea of not guilty and on September 9,1983, he had been found guilty by a trial jury for Murder in the First Degree. That execution on or about September 9,1983, Roberto would receive lethal gas. He commanded the Sheriff of Clark County to safely deliver the convicted to the warden in Carson City, where he would remain until execution.

Reading this formal document in open court served to validate the reality of the situation. Not only was he going to die, but he and the rest of the world knew the time and date of his demise. There appeared no options, no way out. His destiny had been signed, sealed, and soon it would be delivered.

Listening attentively, Rigsby reassured his client he would continue working on the case. So deeply bruised from the decree, mustering up animated conversation was short of impossible. His flawless case, all his hard work proved to be less than stellar as the product of his labor sat remorsefully behind bars. "I promise you," he again reiterated. "To continue working on your case." Turning to the guards, he asked to be released from the hallway. Picking up his burgundy leather satchel overflowing with legal papers and stained yellow note pads, he exited the jail, and his client's life.

Although Rigsby had numerous cases waiting for him at his office desk, the echo of his client's screams of innocence would forever haunt him, making it difficult if not impossible to concentrate on work for the balance of the day. He knew his arrival back to the office would not be a hero's welcome, as so many of his peers had received in past cases. Looks of sympathy, perhaps an, "I am so sorry," glance or furtive futile gestures of sympathy would be his welcoming. His client was handed the worst punishment the state could grant — the death penalty — and there were no concessions that would allow him a moment of celebration. His solitary option would be to immediately delve into an appeal, which meant spending a great deal of time in reflection of his defense, and an enormous amount of time investigating a valid basis to guarantee the death penalty be stopped. He knew he had only a limited amount of time, that there were other cases to be tried and hopefully won, and that he had to balance his work to accommodate as many clients as possible. These were not easy choices for a young man fresh out of law school. Life and death decisions were not covered inside the brick walls of the university, or as a matter of fact in any law college.

Although, he reminisced, several of his professors touched upon ethics and the awesome responsibility to the client, he was never prepared for the outcome of the death penalty. The powers he held in his tongue could decide the fate of a person's life. No, this was never covered in any course. It was at this moment he became painfully aware of the awesome power entrusted to him, and it frightened him, shaking his ego to the core, giving him pause, doubting his astuteness. Taking in one last glance around the empty courtroom, he buttoned his jacket, latched his over-stuffed satchel, and lumbered outside the building into the warmth of the late morning sun. This would prove to be a momentous day in his life and his career.

The convicted was later transferred back to the county jail, and the next morning he was taken to the state penitentiary located at Carson City, Nevada. It was here Roberto would spend time waiting until the date of the execution. Driving up to the large facility enclosed with the ubiquitous barbed wire fencing, reinforced the reality of his situation. "So this was where they bring me to die," he recited silently. Pausing briefly at the initial security check point, they headed to the main building where he would be officially greeted by the warden, then stripped, body searched and later indoctrinated into the endless rules of the facility. During the humiliation and the constant supervision, all Roberto could concentrate on was that this was the place he would die. That it didn't matter if he followed the rules or not, he was sentenced to die and it would be just a matter of a few days before all the life was thrust out of him. Just a few short days, and his life on earth would be ended. All this fuss about rules and regulations hardly seemed worth listening to. He would be long gone before he even had a chance to break any of the stringent directives.

Shaken down, destroyed emotionally, humiliated physically, he finally arrived at a tiny austere cell, reserved exclusively for death row inmates. A simple flat cot, and urinal were the only additions to the four bare walls and gray cement floor. It was as harsh and simple as one could possibly image while it still acknowledged the inhabitant of this space was in fact a human being. The people had spoken through the verdict: this was an evil man, a man who had killed another, and now his just reward was death. Only the bare necessities would be provided for. That was all this man deserved.

Plopping down on the rigid bed, Roberto stared up at the ceiling, and slowly moved his gaze around the darkened, undersized living quarters. The cot, a covered light fixture, a stained urinal, would be the only visual stimulus he would see until death. Closing his eyes, he wished for sleep to come quickly so he could once again slip into dreams of his family and home, washing away the reality of his imminent death. Clothed in prison garb, he was shivering with terror as he waited impatiently for sleep to arrive. Finally, as the sun nestled behind the western mountains, he escaped to a world filled with love and hope.

A sharp clanging, then a muffled ringing abruptly woke him from a ten-hour stupor. Still lying on his back, he sluggishly opened his eyes, he could see! He covered his chest with his hand to validate a heartbeat; he was still alive. He had made it through the night, and the state had not executed him. Sweat beaded on his brow as his legs swung over the side of the cot and onto the hard stained floor. Taking a cursory view around the cell, he remembered where he was, as recollections of the trial flooded his mind. He was put here to be executed. "Was today the day they will kill me?" he wondered. Standing up, he relieved himself into the discolored urinal, and pondered if this would be the last time he would ever pee. Every breath he took, every motion he made, every thought running through his head provoked visions of the last time.

The guard announced the morning delivery of breakfast, as he slid the tray underneath the cold steel bars. "Will this be my last meal?" He asked introspectively, grabbing the tray of food.

Surprising himself, he consumed every morsel on the plastic plate, eating greedily as this could be his last meal on earth

"When you are finished," explained the guard, "Just push the tray back underneath the bars and we will collect it. Don't want to leave a smelly mess for the rats to enjoy."

Retrenching back into his thoughts, he wanted to have final command of his life on earth. "I won't let the people kill me. I will kill myself first. I know I am an innocent man, and I will be executed very soon, but I won't let the state have the final say. I will have the final word. I will control my destiny, even if it means killing myself." With those weighty thoughts controlling his mind, he plotted his own death." I know how to get some blades to cut my skin. I know how to keep the razor to make it look like the blade is still on," he muttered.

Later that day, he was taken to the showers, given a small bar of soap, a clean yet stained white towel, and an inexpensive disposable razor. Although he was constantly watched, the guard dropped his gaze for an instant allowing Roberto to remove the blade and insert it into his buttocks. "Now I have a weapon with me. Not to hurt others, but to take my own life," he all but officially announced. Drying himself carefully, he dressed back into prison attire, and trailed the guards back to the solitary cell. Alone, he again reminded himself that this was his last shower. The warm water, and the fresh bar of soap felt invigorating, as a moment of contentment and reprieve was enjoyed. There was an appreciation that life could offer some fleeting moments of goodness garnered from the simple act of bathing. Wanting to live, but knowing he would soon die was not enough to deter the all consuming desire to commit suicide.

After the lunch trays had been gathered, and the endless afternoon in place, he unbuttoned his pants and waited for the right moment to extract the thin blade. Casting an eye to the hallway he searched for patrolling guards, the silence signaled freedom to begin his final act on earth. Holding the blade, he cut his left wrist, and then his right, dropped the blade to the floor, rolled on his back and stared up at the ceiling. The blood began trickling out of both of his arms, first warm, then turning ice cold as it hardened and spilled to the floor. He waited for death to arrive as the blood continued draining to the floor. He thought death would arrive spontaneously but he was wrong. Lying lifelessly on the bloodied cot, he was spotted by a passing guard who instantly took charge. Sounding an alarm, the bleeding man was taken to the infirmary where he was stripped, bandaged, and fed large quantities of water. For three days he was tied to a hospital bed, completely naked, while attendants nursed him back to health. Nobody talked to him. They did their jobs, giving him care needed to salvage his life, then left him alone. At the end of the fourth day he was returned to his cell with a stern warning not to try the act again. He was causing too much trouble and should concentrate on keeping his nose clean and paying strict attention to the rules or he would be severely punished. "Punished," laughed Roberto. "I am going to die within days, and you tell me to follow the rules?"

Annoyed death did not come as planned, he would have to begin again. Savvy, he knew the guards would be watching him closely, that the next attempt must be final and well planned. Pacing the width of the cement cell, he heard a voice call his name. "Who is that?" he responded.

"Your next door cell mate," responded a strange voice. "We all know that you tried to kill yourself," he spoke sympathetically.

"How do you know that?" responded the newest addition to death row.

"We know everything that goes on. We listen carefully. We hear the guards talk, I even gave up a cigarette so the guard would tell me how you are doing," continued the inmate.

"I just want to die. I am going to die very soon, and I want to be the one who takes my life, not some person who carries out the judge's decree. I want to have the final power over my life," he explained.

"You really want to kill yourself?" quizzed the inmate "If it means that much to you, we, the guy across from you, and me, well we can see to it that you have what you need. We will give you another razor, only the next time do it right, because they will know you got the blade from another person. Once you try to kill yourself with a razor, the guards aren't anxious to let you try again. You are handed an electric shaver. They always think they can out-smart the prisoners. Keep your eyes and ears open, and one of us will slide the blade underneath your bars."

"I don't know what to say, but thanks. Life is too unbearable, I know I will die any day, and ending it soon, on my own terms would be the last pleasure left to me on earth," he solemnly explained.

No names were exchanged, no additional conversation took place the balance of that afternoon. The promise of delivering a weapon to end his life was the only memory he would carry away. Closing his eyes he again slipped into a fitful sleep. In dreams he envisioned his mother, his sisters and brothers, the warm waters of the seas swaying from the rhythm of the trade winds. He tasted the salty cod, chewed on the bark of sugar cane, and imagined the faces of his children. In his imagination this was the only reality he would soon come to know. He spent little time reflecting on how his mother would react to his death. His father had died shortly after Roberto's arrival to America leaving one less person to mourn over his death. "I will join you in heaven, dad," promised Roberto. So absorbed by his own reaction to the sentence, he didn't dote on the feelings of others. After all, Roberto rationalized, this was his impending demise. He was ready for death. He begged for death to come swiftly, taking him away permanently into a contrived world of dreams where he would spend eternity.

The clatter on the cell doors announced the beginning of another routine prison day as the guards slid the breakfast trays underneath the bars. When the inmates were assured the coast was clear, one of them slid a razor blade across the floor into Roberto's cell. Soundlessly he lifted the weapon off the floor, unbuttoned his loosely fitted trousers, and hid it in a tiny padded corner of a pocket. It would stay concealed in this tiny space until his next shower. Zipping up his pants he lightly patted the pocket to make sure it wasn't bulging, not leaving any room for discovery. His weapon intact, so too would be his honor when he again would slit his wrists. This time, he promised himself, he would not fail. He would begin the process in the evening after supper had been cleaned up, and the majority of the guards had left for the day.

As the last meal of the day was cleared up and the evening routine of television watching began, Roberto contemplated his fate, rehearsing the proper way to slit his wrists. This time the blood had to flow quickly, draining the life from his organs in an expeditious and lethal manner. There was no room for error. The warden and the guards would make his life a living hell if he were to survive yet another attempt on his life. The prison officials were obsessed in carrying out the letter of the law. It was up to the prison to kill the inmates, not the whim of the inmates. If he succeeded, it would exemplify the lack of security and control the prison had over its population; this would not bode well for the renewal of the warden's contract. Once a suicide attempt was made, the inmate was watched closely, chided more often, and hazed more rigorously than the rest of the population. Aware of the dangers of failing, he contemplated the perfect moment to begin the ending of his life — that evening, he would put an end to the hell on earth he was living. He would join his father in eternity.

Waiting unwearyingly, he listened for sounds of guards making their routine rounds. Nothing. The deafening silence marked his chance to begin slicing through his old wounds. Extracting the blade from its cocooned pocket, he held it up to the light, carefully checking the lethal edge, and began slicing over the scars. This time he cut deeper until the pain could be felt from his head to ends of his pulsating fingertips. The left wrist cut, now the right wrist; deeper and deeper the blade lodged into the skin, cutting into the nerves and the muscles. Pain ran throughout his body like a shock of electricity causing him to bolt, screaming out in anguish. Angry he was unable to control his cries, he forced himself back on the cot and allowed the blood to seep directly down to the cold floor. As the excruciating pain rampaged his body, he concentrated on slowing down his heart rate and respirations. Death would come quickly. He would not fight the inevitable. He welcomed the release from the constant reminder of execution. Closing his eyes, a dullness fogged his mind as he began to cross the threshold from the living to the dead.

The sprightly sound of several footsteps jarred the convict from his semi-coma state as he was hoisted onto a gurney and rushed hastily back to the infirmary where a nurse was waiting with a plethora of bandages readied to apply on the gaping wounds. No one bothered to wake the doctor, who would be grumpy and intolerant of another attempt at self-destruction. Putting pressure on the dressings would prove enough first aid to stop the profuse bleeding, saving the inmate's life for the second time. No pain pills were offered, no antibiotics were provided, just basic first-aid was administered providing the body with enough care to sustain itself. Too groggy to fight, Roberto had no choice but to accept the care given by the perceptive nurse. "Second time," remarked the caregiver, "You don't seem to have much luck in doing yourself in. Why don't you just give up and let the state execute you as planned?"

In the morning he found himself tied to the bed and naked, just like the time before. A visit from the doctor was a further reminder he had failed miserably in his second attempt. The doctor did not mince words when he explained this was unacceptable practice, and that killing himself was not the answer. He had broken the law and had to abide by the penalty decreed by the state. "Your time will come when the state decides, not when you decide. You have been convicted. Now you must live by the laws set by the state," he reprimanded.

He remained tied to the bed for three days, and was ushered back to death row where the guards would be watching him closely. Opening the cell door, the guard gestured empathetically, "You will not succeed, as every movement you make will be scrutinized from this time forward." Afraid prison guards would harass him until he explained how he obtained the blade, he simply became mute, refusing to talk to anyone. "They will never beat it out of me," he silently proclaimed. "I will never give away the secret of how I got the blade." In truth he didn't know who had given the instrument. It appeared at the base of his cell, but he was unable to detect from which direction, or from which inmate. The repercussions in aiding a suicide were formidable. Life was hell. Adding insult to the unseemly existence would prove worse than hell. So, nobody talked. It was as if it had never happened.

Solitary confinement was a temporary solution, allowing endless hours of contemplation and plotting yet another, and hopefully final attempt to end his life. Any day, any moment they would come to get him. He would be executed in full view of hundreds of people. How undignified, the ultimate humiliation of a human life. If he had to die it would be with dignity and on his own terms. As the hours spun away he wondered if his lawyer would show up for the execution, who would pull the switch, what he would wear, what time of day. The darkness of the room caused his mind to run rampant over hideous thoughts of his impending death. Scouring the tiny room, there was no way he could possibly conceive of to kill himself. Every precaution had been taken; deprived of clothing, running water that might cause drowning, eating utensils which might be used as self-inflicted weapons, towels or blankets which could be used as a noose, he simply subsisted. His life boiled down to nothing more elaborate than that of a caged animal.

Lying on the barren floor, he made a solemn promise that if he survived the stint of solitary confinement, he would not fail on the next try. Two blundered attempts had taught him well. He knew what instruments were needed, the block of time required to slowly bleed to death and the routines of the guards. His only wish was to speak to his mother, to hear her comforting voice, listen to her wise thoughts and bathe in her love of him. Weeping, he dropped deeply into unconsciousness.

The clanging of metal keys inserted into the heavy lock signaled the end of his hell in solitary. Rising on unsteady legs, the guards took him to the showers, returning his prison garb freshly washed and pressed. Simple pleasures of bathing and wearing clothes became paramount. Basic human needs had been taken away. He lived the life of a caged animal, deprived of sound, fresh air, natural light, human interaction, clothing, and toiletry. Returning back to his death row cell was a major improvement. Lying on the cot, he could hear the sounds of his cellmates conversing, welcoming him back from the hellhole.

Again he begged them to help him end his life; he couldn't

stand not knowing which moment the guards would come, pluck him from his cell and execute him. Explaining that he wanted to be in control of his life, he cajoled his listeners into assisting him one last time. "I promise," he pleaded. "I will succeed the next time."

Listening with heavy hearts, a kinship had begun with the adjacent cellmates; obligations were committed to and honored. Yes they would help him, but all agreed this would be the final try. They didn't want to risk spending time in solitary. "Thank you," he weakly responded, "I will make this third try final."

The days passed in routine manner except Roberto's cell was patrolled more often and the guards spent more time chiding and threatening him. Each day in prison was a duplicate of the day before, and an exact precursor of the following day. Sense of time . escaped the life of the inmates. He merely existed. Without human relationships, his life had become subsistence to the point where he felt more animal than human. By taking his life, he would reestablish his humanity — animals do not commit suicide; they simply exist.

After the evening meal had been removed, his comrades told him to listen for the sound of heaven. He understood that to mean the weapon would be slid underneath the door that evening and to ready himself for its arrival. Lying on his back, he concentrated on a fool proof method that would ensure his quick demise. Guaranteeing no sounds would burst from uncontrolled vocal chords, he fashioned a gag for his mouth. Step by step, he reviewed errors made in the last two attempts, promising to correct past mistakes.

When no footsteps could be heard, when evening lights had been dimmed, when the night shift had passed several patrols, he made his final try. Putting the gag in his mouth, he extracted the blade and sliced through two sets of scar tissue, down to the very bone. Sweating profusely from the pain, he lie on his back, feeling the warm blood gushing out of his arms. Smiling, he knew this time he would die. He had done everything right. He was coming home to his dad, and on his terms. He could feel his heart beating faster trying to pump the thinning blood throughout his body. Closing his eyes, he anticipated death to be imminent. Telepathically he communicated with his mom. "Please forgive me. You know I did not kill anyone. I am an innocent man. I love you. I would never ever hurt you," he silently spoke.

It was early dawn when the guards spotted the unconscious inmate, immediately calling for a gurney, and hastily rushed him back to the infirmary. This time Roberto did not respond as quickly as before. His vital signs had continued on a downward progression; his body had been robbed of blood for such an extended period of time that improved vital signs were slow in coming. Shaking his head, the doctor was disgusted, and unsure of the patient's condition. Even if he would survive a third slashing so much blood had been lost, there was no prediction as to how his body would continue to function. "Wait and see," was the only advise he was willing to dispel. An IV was dripping in his veins, a thin sheet was draped over his naked body, and his legs and arms were tied to the bed, all in precaution to keep him alive. The warden did not welcome the publicity of an inmate taking his own life; it made him and the system look bad and inept. Instructing the doctor to do whatever it took to keep this man alive, he closely monitored Miranda's condition.

By the end of the second day, an improvement was forthcoming He had opened his eyes, his heart rate had returned to a regular beat, and all other vital signs had stabilized. Although not ready to return to his cell, he was able to stand up and consume liquids. Pulling up a chair the doctor began quizzing his patient about the three attempts. "Look," he explained. "You will never kill yourself if you continue doing this. Next time, put the blade here, on your neck." He pointed to the large artery running from his neck up to the base of his skull. "Cut deeply here. Cut into the large artery and I promise you will die before I can see you. Stop being a little baby and stop hurting yourself. You have a long way to go. Nobody is going to kill you until you finish all of your appeals, and believe me, anything can happen. Think about this. At least wait for your lawyer to finish all the appeals, then and only then you can do with your life whatever you wish to do."

Although Roberto's English was at a rudimentary stage, he fully understood the doctor's message. He had never realized there was an appeal system. Although his layer mentioned he would continue working on his case, he had no idea what that meant. Every day, death was imminent. He never realized there were alternatives to circumvent or postpone the inevitable. Lying in the infirmary, his thoughts reached out for the first sign of hope. Maybe, there was a chance someone would come to his rescue. Maybe he would not be executed if he could win an appeal. Maybe in front of another judge, he would have his day in court. He would be able to speak for himself, and maybe someone would finally listen to his story and believe the truth. There were a lot of maybes, but replacing these thoughts with death breathed life into the heart of a dead man.

This time, when the guards arrived, they returned the inmate directly back to his cell, no solitary confinement. He knew the doctor had intervened to lessen the warden's punishments. Extracting a promise from his patient not to attempt another try until all appeals had been exhausted, Roberto's situation had improved; the guards no longer hassled him as much.

But Roberto now had a lot of time on his hands, and perhaps a long life to live, and he wanted to do much more than vegetate, so he continued to study English. On death row, he did not know how to read or write English correctly. Whatever he wrote or spoke, he desperately needed people to understand him. He never went to school to learn English, what he knew came only through television a Spanish/English dictionary, and listening to the speech of other inmates. Little by little, the inmates taught him how to communicate, and how to write and speak English correctly. Because conversations had to end by early evening, the inmates conversed in sign language. He was the only Spanish guy on Death Row. Nobody spoke his language so it was very difficult for him to communicate. Learning English would make prison survival palatable, and prepared him for a future outside the walls. With a strong grasp of the language, he would be much better prepared when allowed back into the courtroom. With eloquent speech he would seem more believable, educated, and intelligent.

Roberto was smart enough to know he could extract information that would not only enhance his life, but prolong it. Studying law books and legal cases became an obsessively favorite pastime of the inmates, who would oftentimes call their lawyers with new information that would postpone or alter their cases. Another twinkle of hope was generated in Roberto's heart. Perhaps if he could conquer the language, and study the law, he could find a way out of death. Highly motivated, he became determined to immerse himself in comprehending the stuffy, intricate language of law. Although the prison routine never vacillated, the empty hours were filled with learning, hope, and petty gambling.

"We would get up for breakfast, eat, shower, then we would all go back to sleep. Our routine was to sleep during the day, and stay up all night long It was like we were bats. We did our living at night," he wrote his mother. Never offering an explanation, this was how the thirteen Death Row inmates lived. Perhaps it was to ignore the overabundance of day guards, perhaps it was to shun conventionality, or perhaps it was to further exemplify their indignation of inhumane treatment.

Life as he had lived it metamorphosed into a languid, meaningless routine, leaving him morose most of his waking hours. The bleakness of reality could be swept away through daydreams and sleep. He had been mercilessly plucked from society and tossed into a culture lacking all essentials of humanity. In sleep, he could escape reality fantasizing about love, family and friendship. For some of the inmates, their only reality was defined through dreams.

Nothing exciting ever happened. Life was as dull and purposeless as one could possibly imagine. Any new stimulus from the outside world was voraciously accepted, analyzed, and contemplated; a new book, letters from family and friends, new television or radio shows, or additional privileges based upon exemplary behavior. Anything fresh that could enrich their stoic lives added meaning to their feeble existence. These men represented the worst, the lowest form humanity society had created. They were an embarrassment, a potent sign of failure in a free and capitalist society. Hiding and destroying lawbreakers was society's answer. Shunning the evildoers by locking them away satisfied the populace into believing they were safe.

Occasionally the mundane hours were altered by the appearance of a visitor, usually the guilt-ridden trial lawyer. "If you are in prison, then you must have committed a crime. People see me and see a criminal, they don't see an innocent man," he complained to his lawyer during a rare visit. "Once incarcerated, it is difficult, if not impossible, to wipe away the stain of imprisonment. Everyone thinks you have a good lawyer," he chided Thomas. "So if you are found guilty, then you must have done the crime, and it's not true, not for me. I think now, people watch too much television and believe that the innocent always get off, but it's not true. In the courts, I could have a good chance if I would have had a fair judge But, look at me, I didn't get anything that was fair."

One morning, the warden entered the cellblock of Death Row, and addressed the inmates with the news they were to be transported up to Ely, a prison in northern Nevada. Because of limited space, all death row inmates would be relocated where more room was provided, and where it was more remote from the city. They were told to pack up all belongings and prepare to be moved soon. This was not good news. It meant they would be farther away from the courts, their friends, family, and lawyers. It was like someone was adding extra nails to a coffin to make sure the dead would not escape. The cellmates knew they had no choice but to accept the demands, so they did as ordered, packing and preparing to leave. Many scribbled out abbreviated notes to relatives so they could make plans on the next visitation day. A long ride would keep many away, but if there was a chance visitors would arrive, the inmates wanted them to know where they could be found. Ely was a tiny rural town in northern Nevada. The air would be cooler because of higher elevation, the summers more tolerable, but the remoteness and the isolation would impact their already empty lives, accentuating the purpose of their situation was inevitable death.

In society there are activists whose unabashed beliefs at the very least create controversy and at their very best engender change. Although the death penalty has numerous spokespersons, few of those individuals practice their art by becoming entrenched in a particular case. The Rising Son Ministry, A Christian Church, exemplified an extraordinary example of how faith and belief can help heal and sustain an innocent man. Not that the ministry is a vocal leader against the death penalty, but rather it promotes the healing of the heart and soul through Christian ministries.

Roberto had been raised in a Communist society where overt Christian practices were punished. Teresa, his mother, had kept all symbols and practices of Catholicism to herself. She never overtly practiced the faith in front of the children for fear of being caught by the police. She never discussed God, and the meaning it could bring. She was simply too fearful. The concept of God and Jesus was new to Roberto. He had never once turned to the Lord for help. He never knew who the Lord was or how some intangible being could make a difference in his life. Salvation of the heart and soul came through a barrage of letters written dutifully, unselfishly, and lovingly by the leaders of the Rising Sun Ministry. This outpouring of care brought a new dimension to the inmate's life. People were truly concerned about him and his hideous circumstances, people who didn't know him, never met him, had thrust their faith, energy, and time into his simple life. With each letter came hope, and an expansion of his faith in God. He learned the meaning of belief, and how to turn his bitterness into anticipation and trust in the future. "Someone will listen and some judge will set me free," became his mantra. "God will provide and God will prevail." That was how he would live out the years on Death Row. God forsaken years of his life, endless years of anticipating execution for a crime he never committed. "God if you are listening, my address is Ely Prison, Unit 3-A #17519, Box 1989, Ely, Nevada."

# THE APPEAL
# PROCESS

Lying on the rigid cot, Roberto reflected upon the doctor's words, "Don't harm yourself until all appeals had been exhausted." Taking this advice to heart was perhaps the best thing he had done, because his lawyer was plotting an appeal. Still tied to Thomas Rigsby, his faith continued. Letters describing the processes and arguments initially were slowly forthcoming, as Roberto's inquiring mind peppered him with incessant questions. Becoming a meager student of the law, he had gleaned enough rudimentary information about the appeals process as to constantly pester and badger his lawyer into performing expeditiously and affectively. In this remote location, Rigsby couldn't find the time for visits, but he kept reminding his client that out of sight was not out of mind, that he would continue to work zealously on the appeal. The arduous process moved at a snail's pace. No one seemed to be in a rush to stay a capital offense.

In the early fall of 1985, his lawyer made his appeal to the Eighth Judicial District Court of Clark, Nevada, Judge Addeliar D. Guy presiding. Thomas Rigsby, along with public defender Morgan Harris, offered thirteen objections to the trial which they had hoped would sway the judge into a stay, perhaps an exoneration of the crime altogether. With legal posturing, they deftly laid out the case for reexamination of facts in the hopes this judge would overturn the original verdict. Commencing with the arrest whereby Roberto gave initial inadmissible testimony to the police that he had not gone to the victim's home, and knew nothing about the crime. The district court erred by refusing to admit into evidence an out of court statement made by Emmett Anderson, the person who Fernando Cabrera claimed accompanied Miranda and Fernando to the victim's home the day after the murder. Anderson was not available to testify at the trial on his behalf. Miranda attempted to introduce into evidence a statement made by Anderson to the police prior to the trial indicating that he had not gone to the victim's home with Miranda and Cabrera and that he knew nothing of the murder. The district court refused to allow this evidence, or to locate anyone who might concur with the statement. The defense lawyers argued that statute NRS 51.315, permitted a district court to admit out of court statements of a non-testifying party when the declarant was not available to testify at the trial and when the nature of the statement was made with strong assurances of accuracy. It seemed as though the courts cherry-picked testimony, allowing in only that which would vilify the defendant. The appeal contended that the district court further erred in excluding from evidence certain transcribed statements Fernando Cabrera made to the police prior to the trial, evidence which might have exonerated their client of the crime.

On his own behalf, Miranda presented several witnesses who testified that Cabrera had told them that Fernando had actually been the one who had committed the murder. Several of those witnesses testified that they had seen Fernando in blood stained clothing shortly after the murder occurred. But this was not enough to sway the jury at the time of trial, not even enough to kindle an inkling of doubt. Both Judge, and defending lawyers allowed this piece of evidence to shape or alter the outcome of the trial. One could only wonder what the jury was thinking when those witnesses exposed those salient bits of information. Wouldn't simple human curiosity have served up an explanation? Beyond all rational doubt, became suspect when blatant evidence was presented, but never questioned or investigated. A man was on trial for his life, mandating nothing less than extreme prudence when any doubt could be sustained. And where was the judge's wisdom? Why did he allow this damning piece of evidence to skate by the jury as if never presented? Was the lack of interest, the routine of the case so meaningless as to cast a predisposition? Did the Judge's body language, the lack of interpretation provide an unconscious message to the jury that the defendant was guilty, and that they just let bothersome and time-consuming evidence ride by as if it never existed?

During the course of the trial the prosecutor referred to the defendant as, "A Cuban who arrived in this country on a flotilla, another immigrant who did not speak English, and that fact alone should be cause for doubting his testimony." How utterly prejudicial was this statement? Where was the Judge's outcry when such absurd words were allowed to be uttered in a fair unbiased courtroom? What was in the heart of a prosecutor who would say or do anything to get a conviction, even from an innocent man? Another notch on his belt, another inch up the ladder? Was all this commentary necessary to win the case? The answer was yes. Without setting a tone of disqualification of the defendant's words, Roberto could have walked out of the case a free man. Using scare tactics, including the infiltration of runaway Communists, the jury would feel secure in knowing they put away a potentially dangerous man.

It was common knowledge that Castro opened the gates of the jails and psychiatric wards and allowed the populace to escape in waiting fishing boats. The man who had sat at the defendant's table could surely have been one of those escaped convicts or mentally deranged patients. It took little convincing to alter the objectiveness in the minds of the jury. The prosecutor kept reiterating the lack of information of the accused background. Where was he born? What schools did he attend? How were his grades? His friends? His family? Who were they? Casting doubts about his "secret " life further exaggerated the possibility that he was one of those unwanted citizens unleashed by Castro's regime, and if Castro didn't want him then neither did America. The jury couldn't send the defendant back to Cuba, but they had the power to make sure he was isolated from society, and then executed.

The other damning inflammatory evidence alluded to the pardon of President Nixon. "Everybody knew that people could be pardoned — look at President Nixon — but not just by the governor, it also included actions by the State Board of Pardons in commuting or reducing the defendant's punishment of life without the possibility of parole....So I caution you not to shy away from something that you feel you should do simply because you feel the defendant could be taken off the streets for the rest of his natural life. That may or may not be the case," touted the District Attorney.

The comparison was inappropriate, inaccurate (as in comparing oranges to donkeys), and further exemplified the innate badness hidden underneath a foreigner's skin. Those derogatory remarks were also allowed by the judge, who did nothing to taint the absurdity of the comparison; as a juror, receiving instructions from the judge, the statements became part and parcel to the evidence of the case, and would be warranted in the decision making process.

Prejudicial evidence was argued by the public defenders, but this was not a strong enough response to alter reversal of the death penalty. On October 7,1985, Judge Guy struck down the first appeal. The State of Nevada, case number 14553, summation was as follows:

Defendant was convicted in the district court of first degree murder with the use a deadly weapon, robbery with use of deadly weapon, and grand larceny, and he appealed. The Supreme Court held that the witness' statements were not of a trustworthy nature and were inadmissible. Defendant was not prejudiced by error in failure to admit transcribed statements of witness, sufficient evidence existed for state's use of aggravating circumstance. Defendant was not prejudiced by prosecutor's reference to his nationality and mode of entry into the country, or by reference to executive pardon, and imposition of death sentence was not disproportionate.

Summed up: the first appeal was a complete and utter failure. The public defender's case would not stand the rigors at the district level. Brian McKay, Attorney General for the State of Nevada put on such a strong response, the judge maintained status quo, retaining the decision on the initial verdict.

The State answered the appeal as follows:

"In reviewing the record before us, we cannot perceive a fundamental lack of fairness or a miscarriage of justice emanating from the forgoing prosecutorial improprieties. Viewed from the vantage point of the entire proceeding, Miranda was fairly tried. The facts elicited at trial reveal that Miranda violently stabbed his victim and thereafter, wearing gloves, went about taking the victim's property. Considering the circumstances of Miranda's crime and the lack of any mitigating factor upon which a determination of disproportionately might be based, we conclude that the sentence of death was fairly imposed." And thus the chance to free Miranda of the death penalty had been swept away. The judgment affirmed on behalf of the state.

The two public defenders had the unseemly job of reporting the outcome to their client, a job no lawyer wished to do. True, they lost that round, but there would be other chances to appeal in the future. So backlogged with clients and pending cases, so lacking in funds, and astute seasoned lawyers, promises made would be hard to keep. A man's life hung in suspension by their ability to challenge and re-challenge the decisions handed down by a jury who had received biased facts. The public defender's office, lacking necessary resources to overturn the verdict, would have to reroute whatever manpower they had in order to prevail. Not unlike an emergency medical room where the triage nurse assigns the most critical cases to the immediate care of a doctor, so too, did the office of the public defender. Inundated with needy clients, who was to decide which ones would receive life and death saving aid? Would it be more expeditious to take on the easier cases, saving more people, or spend uncountable hours fighting a case that seemed doomed to failure? These were questions that would be answered by an "angel" in the future.

Bad news traveled fast as the Death Row inmates offered condolences to the newest member of the convicted. Inconsolable, Roberto became deeply depressed. All his newly found faith disintegrated instantly. Painstakingly, he had studied the Bible, had learned to communicate in English, had tried to better himself in preparation to rejoin the outside world. Now there was no reason. He had lost the appeal, and death would surely come. Again, his cellmates explained that the possibility of appeals in the future were readily available; to continue studying and reading, he would find a reason, a way out of this hellhole.

That day the inmates set aside their usual nocturnal activities, using the sun-light to shed illumination on Roberto's verdict. There were books, cases, alternative arguments, and perhaps, alternative lawyers. Although this thought had crossed his mind, the judge had over ruled his request. The state had provided him with free legal council. How could he look a gift horse in the mouth? Who was he to complain that his defense was less than ideal, that mistakes had been made, that evidence wasn't presented, that the prosecutor's statements were prejudicial, that his case was fought with an inferior professional, to the point of complete ineptness?

Roberto was considered a nobody, just another Mulatto who had escaped the loss of freedom in Cuba to have it taken away in America; freedom twice lost.

At this juncture Roberto calculated he had three choices: suicide, the easy way out, accept the verdict and live with impending death; or God help him, fight the system until the very last breath had left his body. Fight, fight with all your heart and soul, ranted the cellmates. "Gentlemen," addressed a lifer, "What we have here is an innocent man. Lets do for him what we can't do for ourselves, lets fight, and lets win." Backed with an honest to goodness cheering squad, his hopes blossomed into faith that one day he might prevail. For once, he didn't feel alone. He had friends who were willing to truly help him, who truly believed in him. Giving him strength and friendship, he forged ahead with the third option, swearing to fight his case until the Lord himself set him free.

Unable to sleep, he stared up at the ceiling of his tiny cell. So quiet and calm, he could hear his heart beating, feel his chest moving up and down with each measured breath. He was poignantly aware that he was still alive, and as long as it was God's will to keep him that way, he should try to survive. He had read the story of David and Goliath, that fighting the giants and winning was a possibility, but it was the brilliant mind of David that allowed him to prevail. He acknowledged if he kept studying, he too might find a way to slay the dragon. The Bible would show the way. Turning to thoughts of his family, he longed to see their faces, hear their soft words of compassion, taste the joy in being within their presence. He prayed the day would come when he would be reunited with his siblings and mother. The sky darkened, hall lights dimmed, the siren blasted the end of another day, while Roberto had fallen asleep to the thoughts of a man who would one day be free.

# A WITNESS
# COMES FORWARD

Letters were slow in coming, but Valentin, in jail for a petty crime, one of the few Las Vegas friends, maintained a steady course of correspondence that would prove to be one of the keys to Roberto's innocence. On July 13,1984, Valentin delivered the first of many confessions to his incarcerated comrade." I felt sad because I couldn't get you out of that mess but, look, all you were told about Fernando is true. Being honest with you, I couldn't say any of that because, before I testified in your case, I talked to my attorney and told him everything and he told me that if I said that about Fernando's bloodied clothes were at my house the prosecutor would accuse me of receiving stolen property and I could be sentenced to more than ten years. Damn it, Roberto, you know I did all I could. I did what I had never done, snitch on a man. And you know that I snitched on Fernando but it doesn't matter. Some day the truth will be known. The only thing I say is that you trust me till death, because it doesn't matter what happens or what is said. I will always help you. If I didn't say anything that happened before, I, at your next court appearance, I, Valentin Franco Rodriguez , will let the court know that you are innocent and Fernando is the guilty one."

A week later another letter arrived, more revealing than the first. "I am answering your letter to let you know that I am here crying. Not out of being a coward or a sissy, but out of feeling. Look, it is very much true that I know that whole story. I will tell you here why I never said any of this in court. Before I answered, I called the late Wilfredo and I read the letter to him over the phone to ask what he thought of it and he said these words to me. 'Valentin you are a kid and have a lot of courage and I know very well you don't care what anyone says but you should realize that if you say all of that (testimony) you are getting into the fire since the prosecutor can come hard on you and give you another charge for accomplice of a murder. Besides, if you rat on those people everything you say is going to be in the newspapers and you are in a place where people don't like that kind of snitching and they aren't going to believe that you did it to defend a man but rather you did it because you are a snitch and you are going to bring many problems to yourself.'

"Roberto," continued Valentin's correspondence, "No matter what people say my concept of a man doesn't allow me to rat on anyone. Now if in the future you are called to court you send your attorney to me and this kid who speaks to you today with his hand over his heart will testify in front of any jury that you are innocent and that you never killed no one. You must understand that if I talked about the clothing full of blood, and I'm given more time than what I have to serve, I'll really be lost inside these prison walls."

Several weeks later, Valentin again wrote his friend and offered the most profound statement on his behalf, a promise to testify. "I am willing to help but before I do anything I have to receive a letter signed by the judge and the prosecutor that they can't do anything to me for testifying all of the truth. So if you want to write to your attorney, and tell him that I have decided to testify. I will tell all the truth but with that condition that I will not get additional time in jail. If your lawyer gets that letter, I swear to you on my brother's grave that I will save your life, otherwise I can't gamble with my life that way. Because I do indeed know how and why everything was done and I know who drove the truck of the dead man, and I know why that man was killed And I know what happened with the loot, and I know what happened with the keys of the truck and I know what happened with the guitar, the record player and many other things. That is why I tell you that if the judge and prosecutor sign a letter saying that nothing can be done to me for testifying I testify the whole truth. Damn it, Roberto, understand me. I know that your whole life is in my hands, but you must realize that if they give me any more years than what I already got, then I loose my youth. I hope you understand what I explain to you and don't worry, I will never abandon you, nor will I let those people kill you."

The correspondence brought Roberto into a true level of hope; that someone would come through for him just as the warden would be administering the toxic gas. Although Valentin's letters were illuminating, he had never explained in detail exactly what he knew. That was to come in the next correspondence:

"Roberto, after having read your letter, I'm answering it, to tell you that the day I sold the loot Fernando was with me and my brother Ramon. I took the loot out of my house the night before the police found the truck parked in front of my house. The person we sold the loot to, they call him Matraca, and I don't know if you knew him but I do know his name and where he works and I also know what he did with a portion of the loot. If I tell you that this is so, that you know that I indeed knew everything regarding the murder and the robbery. Regarding the print on the glass, I'll tell you that Fernando took advantage of the day we were drinking at my house. When my brother Luis was outside making the barbecue. I don't know what glass you were drinking from, but I witnessed Fernando slipping it into his jacket. Then he and I went to buy a few beers at Food Kim that is next to the Chusmita. He borrowed five dollars from me to get gas for the truck so he could go downtown close to the casino where they put pennies in the slots. I believe the street where he parked was number ten and he got out of the truck and told me to wait for him that he'd come right back. I did see him carrying something in his hand but I couldn't figure out what he was carrying. When he returned, I asked him who lived there and he answered that it was from where he had stolen the things. Right away, I realized that inside the apartment was the dead guy. He told me that after what he had placed inside there nothing could happen to him. If I tell you this, it is so that you know in advance that this is the surprise I had for the day we are called to court. Roberto, if the prosecutor does not accept, I swear to you on my brother who is in heaven that you will not be killed, because pretty soon I'll make the whole statement and I'm going to write it on paper, and after I finish I'm going to send it to the Federals to see who tells the truth. Don't think I'll abandon you, I am not that way because first of all I am a man and second it doesn't matter what those Cubans say about me, but I act and do things my way and he who doesn't like it can stay away from me."

Like a revelation from heaven, those letters would serve to save his life, standing as proof for the world to see that he was an innocent man. He understood Valentin's fears of elongating a jail sentence; prison life was sheer hell. He wondered if the tables had been turned would he have spoken up for his friend. Would he be willing to risk extra jail time to save a life? He couldn't answer his own questions except to rejoice in the fact that finally the truth would come out and he would once again be a free man.

As the months passed, the convict heard little from his lawyer, but he maintained rigorous correspondence and hoped to have the case retried. On October 7,1983, Rigsby kept his word. He entered the second appeal. Although the death sentence had been rescheduled for November 7,1983, Judge Guy granted a ninety-day extension. Appeals were forthcoming as Rigsby kept the state at bay. With each extension, Roberto received letters of further extensions. The advice the doctor and his inmates had given him was correct. Appeals could continue for many, but not endless years.

In spite of the fact Rigsby had continued to challenge the death sentence, he did nothing to supplement the errors of the trial, so Roberto thrust ahead on the battle to have his name exonerated based upon inadequate legal representation. On March 7,1986, Roberto won the right to a hearing of his petition, the District Attorney Robert Miller acquiescing to the petition. The judge notified the warden to release the inmate for the court hearing. And on one sunny hopeful morning, dressed in street clothes, he was transported back to Las Vegas to appear before the court. Armed with improved English skills, and legal jargon, he passionately stated his case, listing citations, and giving specific examples. But his rhetoric fell on deaf ears. Judge Guy was not impressed enough to grant a retrial or relinquish the death sentence. Back to death row he returned, heart broken and desperate.

His years on death row were slowly mounting up. He had seen inmates executed, and as days ticked away, it became clearer his time would soon be arriving. Helpless, pitiful, he slumped into a deep depression, sensing all options had been exhausted. He had no money, few friends, and far away family. He could see no way out of his dilemma. Every avenue for another trial or extension of appeal seemed to have evaporated. Alone and miserable, he laid down on his cot, sulking for days at a time.

The small surroundings were interspersed with visits out to

the exercise yard where socialization took place on many levels. It was not Roberto's good fortune to be allowed out on this particular sun-drenched morning, but inmates had no say in routines. Standing erectly in line, the members of the cellblock were herded out to the glare of the sunny desert sky, which was so strong many shielded their eyes until their pupils could adjust. Circumventing the perimeter, Roberto kept his head down and his mouth shut. He feared the violence and demeanor of most of the inmates, and avoided as much contact with them as possible. From the corner of his eye he detected a cache of men who were behaving improperly. Measuring his gait, he strolled nonchalantly to investigate the purpose of the assembly. Shocked, he observed three black men in the process of raping a white male. "You guys are sissies," Roberto vehemently yelled, "Cause only sissies would attack a man. You are men. You don't do this to other men, unless of course you are sissies." Even in the hellish state of incarceration, Roberto's values would never bend or lapse. Unable to stand by and see another person violated was incomprehensible.

"But we have no women," retorted one of the aggressors.

"Well, then you all must be sissies," he rebutted. And something remarkable happened. All three men walked away from the white male. Relieved, the terrified young man thanked Roberto profoundly.

Back in confinement Roberto felt safe, but feared reprisals from the three men he had humiliated in the open yard. Before the week was out they took out their revenge on the inmate, Roberto, whom they nicknamed Castro. Standing in line for breakfast he didn't see it coming, although there were at least twenty inmates who did. A man, suddenly springing from the back of a cement post, attacked Roberto. The inmate was one of the men who Roberto had poked fun of in the exercise yard. Using a make shift knife, he brutally stabbed Roberto several times; once above the heart, on his lower left side, and on his back, until he weakly dropped to his knees, blood spurting in every direction. No one would help, and no one would notify the guards. They all just stood by silently watching. Reaching deep into his soul for strength, Roberto grabbed the knife and threw it down on the floor, thwarting the last vicious attempt at murder. As he was lying in a pool of blood, the guards alerted the medics who rushed in with a stretcher, steadfastly carrying him to the infirmary "It was not my turn to die today," he weakly stated as he shook his finger at the gawking crowd. "God has better plans for me than to die worthlessly in this jail." And God did, because Roberto survived the stabbing that would have put most men into a quick and ultimate grave. For several weeks his wounds were nursed as he slowly regained strength, but he would never forget the force and brutality of this attack. Those wounds would serve as constant reminders of the hell of prison life, a life he never deserved.

Banging the thick cell bars the guard notified Roberto that a visitor had arrived and was waiting in the glassed-off section near the entrance. Unlatching the door, the guard escorted him to the visitor's window where Mark Bailus introduced himself as Roberto's new counsel. "I represent the law firm of Manos and Cherry, and I am here to try and help you."

For the first time in months, a sly smile crossed Roberto's face, "I don't know how I can pay you," the inmate explained, "I have no money."

"We know. But my firm believes in your case, and we want to help you. Sometimes lawyers take on cases they feel were incorrectly tried and try to change the outcome. The judge has asked my firm to take over your case, he wishes to honor your petition for new legal counsel," he stated clearly. "Can I represent you? If so please sign these papers that allow a change of representation and gives us the right to handle your case."

Happily, Roberto signed each document, promising to pay back what he could if he should ever get out of jail. "I appreciate all you can do for me. I am an innocent man. I did not commit that murder. You must believe I did not do it," he spoke.

"After looking at the evidence, our law firm took the case because we truly believe you did not commit the murder, otherwise I would not be standing here now, asking you to sign these papers," he empathetically spoke. "So I guess we understand each other?" Because of the glass window, they could not shake hands. Both merely nodded. "I will be in touch soon, you have our address, anything you need to know call or write and we will get back to you," Mark warmly spoke, as he departed abruptly.

On this mild May afternoon, Roberto's spirits had finally lifted as the meeting played back in his mind a thousand times. "Somebody finally believed me and is willing to help me get out." He worried how he would be able to pay the law fees, and he worried that the same judge who appointed Rigsby also appointed this lawyer. Back in his cell, he had lots of time to think. He had two choices — he could either dwell on his pending execution, or he could dwell on hope. For the moment, he chose to think of the positive outcome. He might again taste freedom, feel the warmth of another human being, love again, and live again. Mark would be able to grant him his rightful day in court. The cell-block was quiet. It was naptime for the death row inmates. Excited, he had no one to share the good news with. He would have to wait until supper.

A week or so passed until he received a reply from Mark's firm. Opening up the large yellow envelope, which had been inspected by the guards, he began reading an extensive brief filed with the court. Over forty pages long, it eloquently stated numerous arguments on the nature of trial, refuting all of the evidence, and asked the court to lay aside the verdicts. Reading the weighty documents, Roberto came to realize what it meant to have excellent representation, and how his life would have been different if this quality of lawyer had been present at his trial. It further emphasized the fact he should never have been found guilty in the first place. The brief fought each charge with a vengeance, stating that there was insufficient evidence on the charges of robbery, grand larceny, and murder. The most compelling portion of the brief was the defendant's pleas for better representation. Honing in on those points, the appeal centered on the right for everyone to have competent lawyers, and clearly in this case the defendant was left wanting. Using the defendant's poignant testimony, Mark believed, would establish the basis not only for an appeal, but retrial or complete dismissal of all charges.

In a letter written by Roberto to the judge he protests, describing a conversation he had with his lawyer "I would like to tell you, your Honor, from the beginning, I have told my attorney (Rigsby) I am innocent. They have tried to accuse me, and they have tried to tell me if I don't plead guilty they are going to give me the gas chamber. By me pleading guilty, this man would give me the gas chamber or life in prison. And the attorney tells me no matter what happens I will be convicted just because of the fact I am black and I am a Cuban and then if I ask him if this was right Rigsby says 'Yes, because all of the jury here is racist.' So what am I going to trial for? I am not guilty of this. I have six witnesses."

Using this outrageous conversation, Balius prayed the judge would see the absurd nature of the defense lawyer. Not only was this neophyte lacking in common sense, but, his advice was so illogical that it bordered on insanity. It mocked the justice system, dooming his client to execution even before the trial started. In Rigsby's own words he stated the jury was prejudiced, yet he had a heavy hand in selecting the participants. The inescapable conclusion was that the judge himself should have been held accountable for the negligence of his appointee. It should have raised an eyebrow of both the judge and jury, when Mark revealed emphatically that no fieldwork was ever presented in the case. No attempt was made to interview witnesses, no additional forensic evidence was amassed, no subpoenas were issued, and no research into backgrounds was completed. The measly, bare defense lead an undercurrent that the defendant was guilty and that it would be futile and useless to prove otherwise. Because the judge allowed this inferior quality of defense it fed the undercurrent — why bother with a lengthy trial when this man was guilty?

The petitioning process began again, this time with a more learned and thorough professional. Judge Guy would not be stirred by the appeal on April 88, nor the appeal on May 88, but he did allow two additional witnesses to be called to testify on the following September: Rene Carbonell and Ramon Macuran, who both stated that Fernando had been seen driving the deceased man's truck and both had observed blood-stained clothing on that man. Again, Judge Guy turned a deaf ear as a motion for retrial on March 1989 was petitioned. Rather than cast doubt on the case, Rex Bell District Attorney for Clark County, entered and was granted a supplemental order of execution. Frustrated, angry, overwrought with defeatism, Mark Balius withdrew as attorney of record. In all, he had committed 3000 pages to research, filed fifty-six separate legal documents and rebuttals, spending hundreds of hours on a case that appeared to be futile. His competency proved to be insufficient for the prowess of the judge, who was looking for a lot more evidence to overturn the verdict.

In spite of the attorney's utter frustration, he was able to touch a nerve of Justice Steffen, the first judge to ever respond positively to the petitions. Reading the brief, the newest member of the bench felt a tugging in his mind and sensed that the case was much more complex than he had been led to believe. After prudent reading of the appeal he wrote the prosecutor,

"Well counsel, I, (Justice Steffen) have an uneasy feeling about this case I have no hesitancy to impose death penalty if we have the right man. But when you start reading, at least based upon what our staff has presented to us as evidence that could have been produced, that the Anderson testimony wasn't allowed. And the fact that Cabrera apparently had a fight with the decedent, the victim, the fact that apparently there was another witness who at least would have stated that Cabrera had indicated to him about the time of the murder, and in this case that he had killed someone. Now if all these facts are true, the thing that bothers me, and I would think it would bother you, if there's any truth to them, because I'm sure that no one on the part of the state would want to participate in executing someone who's innocent of the murder."

This powerful admission would serve as fodder to light the fire for the defendant's freedom.


Mail call arrived as usual in the early morning hours of the Ely Penitentiary, as the guards carefully handed out envelopes of varying sizes and small care packages. Most arrived in the hands of the inmates already opened and inspected. Privacy was an element of life none of the men would be allowed, as each moment, every movement was perpetually observed from a battalion of cameras poised in every nook and cranny of the institution. Many of the inmates hated this part of the day as it exaggerated their loneliness, and emphasized being shunned from society. It was rare that Roberto would receive correspondence, but today a correspondence arrived auspiciously addressed in a thick cream colored envelope with gold inscription. Handing the letter to Roberto, the guard smirked, "Must be from one of your lawyer friends. No one else could send such fancy writing." Extracting the pages his face bristled with a pathetic grimace as he read Mark Balius' notice that he was bowing out as his attorney. He provided no explanation except to say he had exhausted every avenue. Listing all the appeals, legal petitions, time spent, he limply excused himself as the counsel of record.

The devastation of this insidious news grabbed him by the throat, generating an anxiety attack of monstrous proportions. He envisioned his body incinerating. He felt his nerves gyrate as electrical impulses flashed through his arteries, instantly killing him. "I'm doomed," he screamed. " My lawyer has given up on me, I know now that I will die. There is nobody left to save me." The tide of hope he had been carrying had swiftly washed out to sea. He was overcome with grief and the realization of the finality of his life. In days, weeks, perhaps months, he would be executed, and the simplest of life's pleasures would be replaced by an eternity in death. He wasn't ready to die. He did not choose to die. He was still young — mid-forties. He had a lot of living to do. The preverbal writing was on the wall: his last chance for an appeal had dried up. Penniless, poor, Cuban, black, single and without family his fate was sealed. Nobody wanted to save him. Acceptance of death was inevitable, but his acceptance had to come decades before God's will.

Tumbling into melancholy, he slept an inordinate amount each day because  dreaming protected him from the constant reminder of death. His only pleasure was gambling, which he carried on more fervently, using the excuse that with death imminently arriving, he would hardly have to repay debts. Trading cigarettes, television privileges, and toiletries, he quickly racked up a substantial amount owed to his fellow inmates. Days, and weeks continued as the mundane routine kept him alive.

# AN ANGEL
# ARRIVES

Late one morning, he heard the unexpected footsteps of the guard announcing he had a visitor. Ely was so remote, he never had visitors. Surprised he asked, "Are you sure the visitor is for me? No one wrote to tell me they were coming."

"A young lady is in the visitor's room and she is asking for you," he responded.

Hoisting himself up from the cot, he fastened his buttons and followed the guard to the waiting visitor. A thin, attractive, woman in her mid-thirties, with long soft brown hair, soft eyes, and a slight smile on her face greeted him warmly.

"My name is Laura Fitzsimmons. I am a lawyer in the state of Nevada and I would like to take your case. I will take you out of prison," she promised.

"Lady, I don't care. If they want to kill me then they will kill me. It's that simple."

"Please," she reiterated, "Let me take your case, I know I can get you out of this prison. I have read and studied your case. I know you are innocent. The district attorney knows a mistake was made. Please let me get you out."

"I don't have any faith in anybody," the prisoner spoke. "I have been stuck on Death Row for so many years, and each day I wake up and think. 'Is today the day they will kill me?'

Other lawyers have given up on my case. I am innocent and I will say this until the last moment before they kill me, but I did not kill anyone."

"I know you didn't," she sympathized. "I will do what the other lawyers failed to do. I will find all the missing evidence and all the missing witnesses and then you will be out of this prison. You just have to agree to allow me to be your lawyer."

His emotions exhibited signs of despair, yet the pleading in her eyes, and her genuine nature rekindled his hope. Peering through the thick glass window, he could see a satchel stuffed with papers. "What do you have there?" he questioned.

"These are documents from the trial, and investigations I have done on my own," she responded. Well before she had made the long trip up to Ely, the shrewd attorney had begun intensely studying the case, sending investigators out to the field to validate her theory; Roberto had been framed. Pointing to the bulging case, she began explaining, detailing the court records, documents, and the investigations she had been tirelessly working on. As reticent as the inmate was, he couldn't help but be impressed with the amount of work this unsolicited professional had accumulated. "I have enough evidence to set you free." she repeated, "And I will set you free."

"You know," he said, "Everything I told Rigsby in confidence, he told to the district attorney. I have a very hard time trusting lawyers, that is why I am here now."

"I promise you, every move I make, you will be informed and it will be discussed, I am here to save your life, not destroy it."

Signing an assortment of documents stating that Ms. Fitzsimmons would be retained, she thanked her newest client, promising he would hear from her very soon. Gathering the mélange of papers, and neatly stuffing them back into the brief-case, she slowly stood up, smoothed back her hair, then looked deeply into Roberto's somber eyes again and reminded him of her promise. For the first time in days, he felt his cheekbones rise as the essence of a smile crossed his face. "You are an angel, " he murmured. "If you can get me out of this place, then you must an angel."

Walking back to his cell, he had much to muse and much to be hopeful for. He would once again retrace all the steps leading up to the trail to help the field investigators gather all the evidence. He would have plenty to do in the next few weeks, summoning up the depths of his memory so all names, evidence and conversations could be implemented as proof of his innocence.

But he did worry. After two disasters, he was reluctant to give away his heart and his soul, yielding to yet another failure. Two lawyers had offered their professional services, yet execution loomed over his head every waking moment. He was terrified to allow himself the joy, the hope, that this woman could do what the other two had not done; set him free. As at each level of court, judges turned down his appeal, he knew his chances were running out. Having lost all appeals, Laura would be working directly with the Supreme Court of Nevada. She couldn't fail. This would be his last chance. "Hey," he thought ."Is this lady crazy or what? Can't believe anyone can set me free, after Rigsby betrayed me, sold me to the prosecutor, breached my trust and confidence I can't believe anyone could be able to set me free of this place. I am going to die and nobody can stop it. But maybe, just maybe she might be able to help me. It's my last chance and I have to take it," he contemplated.

In February 1993, a formal petition was filed with the Supreme Court asking for a prayer for relief and a continued stay of execution pending final disposition. The stay was granted while the lawyer began an intensive field investigation. Laura sent out investigators to take testimonies. She gathered additional forensic information, retrieved statements from the police. She left no stone unturned. The truth would be documented, and Miranda would get his day in court.

The judge was more benevolent this time around, allowing the stay, and accepting a court hearing for a retrial. Reading the introduction to the case would make anyone who had owned a sense of fairness rethink the rationale of those originally trying the case.

"The petition challenged convictions, and sentences, including the sentence of death that were imposed against the Petitioner. In the course of those proceedings Miranda was represented by counsel who conducted no meaningful investigation in the state's allegation, and who failed to locate, and interview known witnesses whose testimony would have materially altered the outcome of the proceedings. The prosecution failed to disclose material evidence and engaged in other forms of misconduct. Those defects were enhanced by many erroneous rulings and instructions of the Court. The material omissions that occurred prior to and during trial resulted in a proceeding in which the truth concerning the victim and the innocence of Mr. Miranda were both obscured. As a result there was no meaningful testing of the state's allegations. There was no meaningful determination as to whether he should live or die. Had the allegations against him been subjected to a fair adversarial process, he would have been acquitted."

This was the bodacious attempt to solicit the court for retrial. Not only did Ms. Fitzsimmons blast the ineptness of the defense lawyer, but that of the District Attorney and the Judge himself. Laura had amassed enough evidence to more than prove the outlandish unfairness of the proceedings. Although Rigsby was incredibly inept, both the judge and the District Attorney were painfully aware of his inadequacy, taking untold advantage of the situation. Each had their own agenda for the trial: the District Attorney wanted to win, no matter what the cost, even if laws were compromised, and the Judge wanted the case to be expeditious, out with the old and in with the new. But no matter what motivations spurned the trial, Ms. Fitzsimmons was determined to undo the wrongs, petitioning the court until someone somewhere would view this case in a fair and unfettered light. Tenacity was her middle name; her determination to make things right for her latest client was unstoppable. Exhausting all legal options, implementing every investigator, she would unbury the truth. She would free a man who was pitifully tried by a court system that had been touted as free, unprejudiced and impartial.

There were numerous petitions presented to court, many demanding the convicted be present. The difficulty for Roberto was the remoteness of the location. Ely was far north of Las Vegas. Leaving the confines of death row was not a simple task. This was no party place, with twenty-three out of twenty-four hours in lock down. In a petition filed March 1995, Roberto requested to waive his rights to appear at the hearing because it was standard policy for the jail to confiscate any vacated cell and give it to another inmate. When this happened, he would not be allowed access to his old cell, thus forfeiting all few personal possessions. But the worst part of this situation was a return to solitary confinement. "I do not wish it to appear that I don't care about my case, I care about my case more than anything, but I feel it is out of my hands and in the hands of God. It's just that I can't stand living in solitary, and it could be months before any cells are available," Roberto explained to the court.

Appreciating this fact of jail life, the judge acquiesced to his wishes allowing Ms. Fitzsimmons into the court, freely representing her client's wishes. Roberto had been living on death row for so many years, nearly a dozen, adding any additional hardship to his life would be irreprehensible. He trusted Laura, he knew she would do her best, but he would not give up one tiny morsel of human comfort to return to a living hell, just for a brief court appearance.

Working diligently, she assembled a brief over one hundred forty pages long, detailing every error, omission, fault, and all prejudicial evidence. She then asked for a new trial. On February 13,1996, Roberto received some of the most hopeful words he would ever hear: Senior Judge Norman Robison granted him the right to a new trial. For the first time in over a decade he had real hope. He wasn't free yet, but a new trial, with all the evidence exposed, and he knew he would be exonerated. There was a God, and He gave him an angel.

As the inmates began their nocturnal conversations, they congratulated Roberto's chance at a real life. They continued to tutor him in reading and writing English, he learned everything from these guys. He learned how to communicate, and how to sound intelligent so no one would think he was stupid. He owed those guys a lot. They talked about freedom, how great it would be just to take a walk, see the sky, smell the trees, feel the touch of another human, and have the chance to love again. All those years living without the warmth of another human, without the love of another, had taken its toll. Hardened, and bitter, Roberto would have to rediscover himself. Reaching into his past, he would have to remember how to behave. For the last twelve years, living with asocial men, he would have to relearn how to interact with average good quality people. Losing all trust, he would have to force himself to believe and love again, otherwise he would end up lonely and miserable. All the therapy in the world would never bring back years served, nor redeem his mental distress, but with help, he knew he could lead a happy life.

Rejuvenated, the next morning, he remained up after break-fast was served, and began to change his life. After all those years in jail, it would take months, perhaps years to alter his internal time clock, perception, depleted physical condition and destroyed emotional state. He had spent years contemplating death and now he had to address the reality that he might actually live a natural life. This meant dealing with the simplest of tasks such as shopping for groceries, doing laundry, buying clothes, and paying bills. A job, he would have to find a real job! He was hopeful and anxious, and was smart enough to realize that he needed reprogramming in order to survive in the changing American culture. The only bad habit imparted by his fellow inmates was gambling. He would learn to cope with this bad habit once he was released. He knew money would be hard to come by. Before he landed in this hellhole, making a liveli-hood had been arduous. Lacking skills, saddled now with almost fourteen years on death row, he wasn't prime employ-able material.

Along with rethinking his new life, he wanted complete exoneration from his past life. Extracting pen and paper from a worn shoebox, he wrote a letter to the parents of Manuel Torres. Describing his sorrow, he bestowed sympathy, elaborating that he was not the person who had murdered their son, that soon they would be told who had committed the crime. It was as if Roberto was washing away those eternal endless years of his life. Exoneration was the first step; he wanted the Torres family to know he was not the murderer, but mostly he wanted their apol-ogy for an error that cost two men their lives. As he eloquently wrote, the words would serve to commence a lengthy healing process for both the grieving and the incarcerated. Carefully fold-ing the three-page note, he addressed the envelope, licked the stamp, and handed it remorsefully to the guard.

Ms. Fitzsimmons continued the relentless quest to retry the case. The district attorney, uneasy by her claims of inappropriate behavior and illegal mishandling of the case, proposed a deal. As promised, Laura brought this quickly to Roberto. "The only deal I can make with you, " he responded," is for you to let me go and put Fernando Cabrera here in my place."

"Sorry," answered the district attorney. We can't do that as we had given him immunity before the trial began."

"So you gave immunity to the real killer and you put me in jail to die? To die for somebody else's crimes?"

Taken aback, both attorney and client were outraged.

Returning back to her brief, Fitzsimmons, augmented it by an additional fifty pages, resolutely shattering the state's case. But this time, she would not ask for a retrial. She would beg the court to dismiss the entire case. Incensed at the abominations incurred before, during and even after the case, she would put things right She would do as  promised and get her client out of jail. In September 1996, she re-filed the petition and asked for an order dismissing the case. When she was certain this case would be upheld, the judge ordered Roberto to appear in court. Understanding the hell he would return to in jail if the judge were to knock down the appeal, she had to be very, very right.

# AN ANGEL DELIVERS
# A PROMISE

Early that September morning the guards once again rattled the keys, and unlatched the cell door. Panning the tiny musty overheated cell, Roberto stood proud as he passed the other twelve death row inmates who were yelling out "Good luck, don't return."

Chiding him, the guard said, "You'll be back, they all come back. Haven't had one of you guys ever get off of death row. Everyone ends up coming back."

Undeterred, the cuffed convict walked through endless sets of security gates, to an awaiting van, then to a tiny prop plane. Once again he was absurdly ill on the short flight, but having faith, he believed he would land in one piece. And he did.

The date set for the hearing was September 3,1996, but there was a postponement. Rather than sending him back to death row, the judge allowed him to cool his heels at the local county jail. Gravely disappointed, Roberto accepted the situation, abiding by all the rules and constraints; he would do nothing to alter the path his lawyer had established.

For the past fourteen years, the wrongly accused had been isolated from society. Roberto lived a lonely existence with little interaction from outsiders. The appeal brought to the Supreme Court of Nevada would catapult him from an isolated life into the public limelight. Smoldering publicity was slowly beginning to erupt, putting this man smack into the middle of a news frenzy. Ms. Fitzsimmons' work was beginning to pay off as reporters were following the appeals and reading the case, and gathering public sympathy. An outrage, the initial trial was like a festering wound that would not heal. It was an embarrassment not only to the legal profession, but elected officials. It was time to put it right. On this everyone agreed.

Sitting in his new surroundings, he would be ill prepared for the attention that would be showered his way. Jail had not prepared him for public speaking, crowds of people, microphones shoved into his face or loyal followers against the death penalty. Cast away for so long, he had no idea how much publicity this case had aroused.

Two months had passed since his arrival at the county jail, and although life was easier, he was not free. Visitors arrived more frequently — his attorney, friends, and chaplains, making the transition back into American society easier. Each day he would seek another way to improve himself so he would be successful when the day would arrive that he would be set free. The outside world had provided little support for the possibility of transitioning into society, but there was a special group of volunteers who helped the inmate, the First Church of the Nazarene. Volunteers would come directly to the jails and counsel the inmates. "It wasn't a formal church service," explained Jan Hoffman, a chaplain. "We would just talk to them, listen to their feelings and try to guide them into a better path of thinking."

A newsletter "The Rising Sun" was mailed directly to the inmates, serving as another form of communication. Because Roberto had not believed in God, had never been taught the comforts religion could offer, these visitations and publications enriched his life by helping him get through many stormy days.

Mostly, religion gave him faith in another being, much higher than any he would know on earth. Seated in the jail cell, he gazed through a glass window, and picked up the phone listening intently to Jan's bible reading and thoughtful religious guidance. Drinking in the words like a thirsty child, his heart began to stir with feelings of love, compassion, and trust. Jan was laying down the emotional groundwork for him to rediscover and reclaim his life. The years on death row had annihilated his faith in mankind. He trusted no one. He believed in no one, but this lovely, smiling woman would begin to reverse his anger, putting trust and faith in a higher form of life. Her letters and discussion of Jesus added a broader dimension of humanity. So much of his soul had been lost in the unseemly years in prison, humanity vanishing under the auspices of penitentiary life He had finally found a way to rekindle his soul. Believing in his innocence, Jan diligently corresponded often, writing letters filled with hope, and love. Although she discussed the bible, she allowed Roberto to be privy to insignificant details of her life, making him feel that his life had value and meaning. No other outsider had generated those feelings, besides Laura Fitzsimmons in the past decade. The endless hours spent tucked away in the county jail were beginning to be filled with thoughts of a higher nature. Through Jan, Laura, and a scattering of friends, he would take back civilization, becoming a valued member of society.

Roberto had absolute faith that the final petition would turn even the coldest, most cynical heart into a believer of his innocence. So beautifully written, every detail was in place, every piece of evidence was articulately described, every incriminating letter included, every piece of forensic evidence, all the lost interviews and witnesses' statements fully documented. What Judge Robison held in his hands was the complete truth. Every footstep retraced, there was no room for interpretation; all the facts had been meticulously laid out from beginning to end. The final brief was brilliant by any standards. No honest judge could have had any doubts as to the outcome.

"In 1982, Petitioner was convicted of one count of murder with use of a deadly weapon, one count grand larceny, and one count robbery with use of a deadly weapon. On September 3,1996, this matter came before the Court for a status check regarding a new trial date. Petitioner was present and was represented by Laura Fitzsimmons. The State was present and through Deputy District Attorney Eric Jorgenson. At that time, the State informed the court that it did not intend to retry the case. Petitioner's counsel then moved to dismiss all charges and there was NO opposition."

Dressed in a pinstripe suit, shined shoes, and a sparkling crisp white shirt, Roberto stood nervously before the Supreme Court Judge.

"Mr. Miranda," the judge solemnly addressed, "You have suffered enough. You have paid for a crime you did not commit. It is hereby ordered that case known as State of Nevada Versus Miranda is dismissed in its entirety. You are free to go."

Ecstasy replaced all thoughts in his mind. He was going to live. It took the Supreme Court of Nevada, and a fair judge to rectify all the wrongs the state had heaped upon him. Finally free, he could march proudly out of the crowded courtroom, becoming part of society. As tears spewed forth, Laura grabbed her client and joyously kissed and hugged him. Overwhelmed by the press, friends, and lawyers, he felt weak, his trembling limbs had waited over fourteen years for this moment. Now that it had arrived it was almost surreal.

Ms. Fitzsimmons had many legal successes, but this one tugged at her heartstrings more than most. Perhaps it was the outlandish ineptness of the legal system, or the blatant fact he was innocent, or the reality that she had come to truly care for this good man. But true to her word, she had kept her promise. Today, her client walked out a free man. She was ecstatic Although she had an ego, she was scared. The legal system could be fickle at times, and she agonized that the judge may have had a change of heart. Nothing was certain until she heard the words ceremoniously uttered from the judge's lips that her client was truly free. Her flowing tears represented months of arduous work coming to a successful climax.  Slinking an arm around her client's waist, she ushered him to the top step of the courthouse where they were greeted by a large contingent of news reporters, both local and national papers.

Roberto had no idea how closely his case was being monitored, nor the extent to which the public was aware of his ordeal. An endless list of political, religious and civil rights groups had used this case to exemplify their goals — elimination of the death penalty, equal legal representation for the poor, civil rights for immigrants, and fairer treatment for inmates. The crowd was holding placards and screaming out words of support. Roberto was overcome by the support of strangers. Secluded in jail, he had no idea how important this case was, nor the affect it had and would have on the future of the legal system.

This story was not over.

# A SLIGHT SNAFU

Departing the courtroom, Roberto was carrying his sole possession — the suit of clothes on his back. In his early fifties he would begin life anew, with literally nothing. Anticipating this moment, his lawyer had been searching out financial aid to facilitate the transition from cell life to public life. Locating a small apartment in the south side of town, she felt relieved that he would at least have a roof over his head for six months. "Come with me, " she demanded. "I want to show you something."

Like a newborn puppy, he would have followed her to the ends of the earth. Gleefully, he plopped down in the front seat of her comfortable, air-conditioned car, remaining silent as Laura babbled continuously of her joy and faith in his future.

Driving through the congested streets of Las Vegas, his silence quickly evaporated, he was shocked by the numerous changes, "Oh my goodness, " he exclaimed. "The city got so big, so many new casinos, and apartments, and the park where I gathered with my friends is gone. Just look at that huge thing."

Laughing, she explained the "thing" was part of a new casino called the Stratosphere, with a roller coaster at the top. Pointing southward, she listed all the new buildings, including a brand new federal courthouse. Arriving at a quiet side street, gliding the car to a stop, she rummaged through her satchel, extracting a set of keys and an envelope containing cash.

"These are for you, at least temporarily until you can get your feet on the ground. I have rented this small apartment. It's not a palace, but you will have a place to call home until you can afford something better."

So moved by her generosity, he could hardly speak. Thoughtfully taking the keys, he thanked her profusely, vowing to make his new life successful. Putting out her hand, she shook Roberto's hand goodbye, wishing him happiness and health. "Anything you need," she added, "Do not hesitate to call."

Walking up the steps to his new home anxiety set in. Free, but truly alone, he would have a lot to do to make life successful. Unlocking the door to the one bedroom apartment, he smiled. Privacy, liberation, finally. Scanning the room he was surprised by the thoughtfulness his lawyer had showered upon him; there was a bed with sheets and a blanket, toiletries placed fastidiously in the bathroom, and food in the refrigerator. She had thought of everything. Exhausted, he took a lingering warm shower, and dropped on the bed, sleeping until dusk.

Wednesday morning, Laura met her client at a local sandwich shop where they discussed another nagging problem: immigration. The U. S Immigration and Naturalization Service planned a hearing for deportation. There was no choice. He would not evade the law. He would do whatever it took to set things straight. After a delicious lunch of ice-cream and sweet rolls, they returned to the jail where he surrendered to authorities. "Don't worry," the confident attorney decried. "I will have you out soon." Again, she would be true to her word, and he would be released on his own recognizance within twenty-four hours.

Back in jail, his heart pounded. His life was in a tail spin. Not one day out of death row and there he was back in jail. This time it was not a capital crime, but the evaluation of his status. With unwavering faith, he knew Laura would again rescue him, and again true to her word she did. Thursday morning he was set free. The local press had a field day publicizing the arrest. Headlines, such as, "Still Chasing Freedom, and "Miranda Set Free," euphemisms for "Let the Guy Alone," splattered the front pages of the week day papers. Roberto, already a humiliation to the legal system, the arrest added salt to an already gaping wound. There was no doubt where the press stood. They liberally backed this wronged man, unabashedly supporting him through editorials and photographs. "A former death row inmate spends another restless night in jail before being released Thursday," portrayed the seemingly unending saga of Roberto's troubled life.

A much relieved Fitzsimmons deftly completed the paperwork extricating her client out of the confines of the county jail and back into public life. Admitting that this sordid situation was depressing, it was a legal step that had to be taken in order to once and for all secure his lawful status in America. Traversing this hurdle meant he would carry the proper papers which would allow him to work and travel freely.

The guard, showing respect and deference for the famous inmate, quickly led him out of the jail. Signing papers, and pocketing his personal affects Roberto lumbered into the sunshine and was jubilantly greeted by Janalee, President of the Rising Sun Ministries. Perceptive, this church had taken on the responsibility of administrating to inmates, teaching them faith and Christian values, continuing the guidance after release from custody. Years of ministry work gave the church credibility in dealing with the reality of freedom once inmates were released. All too many inmates returned back to jail, but this case was special. Roberto wouldn't be returning. Taking him under her wing, she ushered him back to the apartment, promising to return early Sunday morning for church services.

"I don't know how to thank you," he uttered. "You have been so kind to me, I am so happy for all your help."

"Just be ready around eight and I will show you what real love and caring can be about," she dutifully promised.

Closing the door of the scantily furnished apartment, he felt safe inside. He was terrified of leaving a secure place, fearful the police would be scrutinizing every move he made. Although free, a sensation that someone was always looking over his shoulder, watching and waiting for him to make a slip up, stalked his psyche. He shut the dusty Venetian blinds. Sequestered in the cozy home, he didn't venture out until Sunday morning.

He dressed for his first outing — religious services at a small Lutheran Church in the southeast section of Las Vegas. As Janelee, the representative of the Rising Sons Ministry, chauffeured him through the quiet streets, he marveled at the continued changes of the landscape. Gone were the endless acres of desert foliage and wisping sagebrush. They had been replaced by towering casinos and resort hotels. With each venture into various parts of the city, he was astonished by the transformation; he had left a small town returning to a lively sprawling metropolis. The developing city left room for economic opportunity. He shrewdly realized that perhaps there were many possibilities for employment. Noticing the plethora of construction trucks dotting Las Vegas Boulevard, it seemed logical that numerous jobs existed. Hopeful, he discussed the prospects of finding a job with Janelee.

"I will do as much for you as I possibly can," she promised, turning the wheel of the van into a black-topped parking lot.

Restrained, he slowly opened the van door, and gathered emotional strength to meet the religious community. Guarded, each word would be thoughtfully executed, each gesture understated, so as not to alarm or frighten potential friends. Seated at the end of a bench, it was easy to notice he was the only black face in the entire Christian congregation. Odd, he just waved it off as another quirk. Grasping a prayer book, listening intently to the service, the newest member voraciously drank in the beauty of the psalms, savoring the sounds emanating from the small choir. At the end of the sermon, the minister spoke of charity, love, and understanding that in the midst of their congregation was a very special attendee. "Mr. Miranda, " he boasted pointing a finger at the congregant, "Is our very special friend, and we would like to introduce you to him." A slight applause filled the room as Janelee grabbed his hand, and forced him to stand and acknowledge the support.

Continuing, the pastor explained how the work of the Rising Sons Ministry, had helped hundreds of inmates find a richer, more meaningful life, but once in a while a special person emerged who needed additional help and sacrifice from others. Briefly explaining the death row experience and the fourteen-year incarceration, an appeal was sent out from the pulpit and pleaded for assistance in any way possible. With just the shirt on his back, he could use any of the help and support this church could offer. A tearful Janalee added commentary about Roberto's unique situation and she thanked anyone who could assist this needy gentleman.

And they did. Many parishioners came forward and filled up his refrigerator with food, his closet with slightly worn clothing, his parking spot with a used car, and the empty hours with rich personal attention.

# FRIENDS EMERGE

Kerry, a successful woman with an outreaching heart became a proponent to his cause. Her intellect and education was matched by her sharp wit. With two college degrees, a Masters in Business, and a PhD in Education, she could converse with anyone about anything. At forty, she rid herself of her first bohemian husband, exchanging him for Jim, a man who shared her goals — making lots of money. In good health, Kerry knew her nest egg would not take her comfortably into retirement, so she changed professions, turning towards investing. Her ability to network allowed the business to grow geometrically. By her mid-forties, the nest egg had grown large enough so that she would never have to worry about creature comforts, even if she lived to be ninety-nine. Using every single opportunity to meet clients, Kerry became active in the community Lutheran Church. Every Sunday, she and Jim, would dress up and spend two hours holding hands while the pastor conducted services. But Kerry spent those hours mentally surveying the congregation, listing potential clients. Although she believed in Jesus, the almighty dollar caught her attention, at least at this stage in her life. Her soft spots centered around her love for her brilliant son, and new husband.

Life as an investment consultant freed up the late afternoons, as her clock was set to Wall Street time. Rising early, she turned on the computer, traded with the finesse of a sooth-sayer, completing the workday by two in the afternoon. As her business became successful, she devoted more time and money to benevolent projects. Charity functions were her pet projects. Raising money for the homeless, or children, or some exotic disease, allowed her the opportunity to mingle with potential clients, and give back to the community. Analyzing each proposal, she cunningly selected only those projects that would reap her the greatest benefits. That was until she was introduced to Roberto. Tentative at first, the two became close friends. Her sparkly eyes and warm voice offered Roberto compassion and honest friendship, without which he might not have survived successfully.

Terrified of leaving the confines of the tiny apartment, she cajoled him into going out for ice-cream, his favorite source of calories, then to the movies, to church, and the grocery store. All those simple acts taken for granted by others were difficult for a man who had not interacted in the public world in fourteen years. Not only had so much changed, but his terror of being placed back in jail resembled paranoia. Feeling safe in the company of friends like Kerry, he began a slow process of socialization into Las Vegas society.

He was miffed, the only car he had owned was confiscated by the police in California. He was thankful an overly generous gentleman had signed over a used car in his name. The only problem was getting a driver's license, as that too had been taken away from him. Offering to solve this problem, Kerry volunteered enthusiastically to escort him to the motor vehicle department where he began the process of obtaining a license. Stubborn, he refused to take the written test in Spanish, as his grasp of English was stellar, but unfortunately he had forgotten to study and promptly failed the exam. On the sullen drive back to his apartment, Kerry explained that the rulebook had to be memorized to pass the state test. Like a little kid, she took him out for ice-cream, reminding him to study hard. She would be back in one week for the next try.

True to her word, Kerry, dressed in a pastel summer cotton suit, and with her meticulously manicured nails and artistically applied make-up, appeared at his doorstep with a broad smile, touting a large plastic garbage bag filled with gently used clothes collected from friends and neighbors. This beautiful caller made Roberto feel important, stirring lost passions for female companionship. Love and women were an important part of his life until he was slammed away from society. There was much to make up for in his new public free life. Finding love would be a top priority. Thanking her profusely, the two set out to conquer the written test. But it was not to be: again he failed miserably. It took two more tries before he finally achieved a passing mark. Elated, they celebrated at the local Dairy Queen, with oversized chocolate sundaes. "Well you did it," exclaimed Kerry. "I knew you would pass the test. You put your mind to the task and you succeeded."

Thanking his friend, he asked her if she would help him take the driving test, although she was more than happy to do so, she offered the services of her husband, Jim. That Sunday, Roberto would have his first behind the wheel experience in his new used car. After church services, Kerry dropped Jim off at Roberto's apartment where the practice session would commence. Keys jangling from his pocket, Roberto glided into the driver's seat, turning on the car, listening to the lovely sound of the engine purring. Reading the fuel gauge, Jim quickly realized the lesson wouldn't be longer than ten minutes if they didn't fill up the tank. Pointing to the nearest gas station, Roberto timidly eased the car perfectly parallel to the pump. The problem occurred when it dawned on the new driver that he was not in possession of a credit card. Coming to his rescue, Jim opened up his wallet and inserted the card while Roberto pulled out the nozzle, filling the empty tank. "Lesson number one," laughed his instructor. "Always make sure there is gas in the car. And lesson number two, we will see about getting you a credit card."

Thanking his friend, the two began the first driving lesson, and a lifelong lesson of sharing, learning, companionship, and love. Opening up his heart as well as his pocketbook, Jim would experience a deep friendship with a man he would never have considered his peer. Through endless dinners, movies, and church services, the three of them became intertwined in a deepening friendship that would span decades.

Prior to their meeting, Kerry had contacted an old friend in the construction business, and inquired if there were any openings. After elaborating Roberto's dilemma, her friend explained there would be an opening at a new site on the southern end of the strip. "Not a fancy job," the contractor explained, "but it would be a start. If he works out, I could use him for the more difficult jobs that none of the others wanted".

Thanking him sincerely, she wrote down the address, and handed it to Jim. "Please explain to Roberto that this was a starting point, and that if he worked hard he could make a decent living."

Grabbing the note, Jim tucked it into his shirt pocket, saving it as a surprise. He would reward Roberto with the potential for the job after he had passed his driver's test. The reality of the situation was without a license he would have no way to get to a job, and then he would be endlessly frustrated. One step at a time, Jim told himself. This man has gone through sheer hell. He only wanted to make his life easier. By taunting him with a job without a driver's license would be cruel. Holding the note in abeyance, he would wait for the proper time to reward Roberto.

The written test was arduous to pass, but the driving test was easy. One try and the State of Nevada bestowed Miranda with the official identification card of an authorized legal driver. This additional liberty added another dimension to his life. Now free to come and go as he wished, to be able to flash an identification as necessary, he felt important. The elements needed for self-esteem slowly proceeded to enter his psychological make-up. "Now," reminded Jim. "All you need is a job." Shaking his head in agreement, they both knew this task was daunting. Extracting the note tucked in the shirt pocket, Jim handed it ceremoniously to his friend. "This is an excellent lead. Kerry called an old friend, and its possible you could have a job soon. It's a construction job, nothing glamorous, but it should help pay your bills for a while."

"Every job application asked you if you have ever been arrested, or spent time in jail," explained Roberto. "If I checked that I had never been in jail or arrested and they look up my record they would say I was lying, but if I put down that I had been arrested and spent time in jail, they don't hire me. Its so aggravating, it seems I can't win." Jim and Ms. Laura Fitzsimmons both knew this would be a huge problem upon release. After fourteen years of unfairly being incarcerated for a capital murder case, he wasn't exactly a prime candidate for most jobs. Even though the town of Las Vegas was bursting with expansion it would prove to be an obstinate fact to overcome in landing a job of any kind.

As his self esteem precipitously evolved with each job application, he began the realization of how unfairly he had been treated. Yes, he had some friends, but so much had been stolen from his life, his heart and his soul. He bitterly wanted the lost years back. How to accomplish this he wasn't sure, but he would find a way. All this suffering, starting over, lost loves, life, money, and family — it just wasn't remotely fair, and it was high time that somebody, something, pay for the gross errors thrust upon him.

When the judge dismissed the case, he neither pardoned nor exonerated Roberto. He couldn't be pardoned for a crime never committed, and exoneration could be bestowed only after another trial. Left in limbo, forced to carry a red card boldly reading "Convicted Felon," jobs and relationships would be hard to come by. Standing naked in front of the long mirror, he didn't look so bad. Handsome, his face didn't exhibit the scars left from prison life, but psychologically, that was an entirely different matter. His heart had been broken, his spirits trodden on by years of the threat of execution hanging over his head. Resentful for the hardships life handed him, he sought fairness. Needing advice, he phoned Kerry, and ranted about his difficult life.

"I will pick you up later this afternoon, " she spoke encouragingly. "Let me think over your options." Believing that all of her friend's problems could be solved at the bottom of a deep ice-cream bowl, they chatted at the nearby coffee shop.

Confessing his tendency to continuously complain, he sought refuge in her advice. "I need help I am at a loss as to what to do and where to go," he said gulping down the last bit of chocolate ice-cream.

Extracting a five-dollar bill from her Chanel pocketbook, Kerry earnestly grabbed Roberto's arm and announced they were going to solve this problem, right then.

# SEEKING RESTITUTION

Driving to the local mammoth booksellers, the saleswoman guided them to the help section, plucking a book written by Gerry Spence, a nationally known lawyer for taking on special landmark cases. "I think you qualify for his services, " she confidently announced. "Now all we have to do is to get him to represent you."

Dismayed, he never in a million years believed the most famous lawyer in America would take his case, but on the other hand, he had absolutely nothing to lose. "I can't believe how strong you can be, " he reiterated to Kerry. "Do you really truly think this lawyer would even look at me? I am a poor black Cuban. Those lawyers, they ask for a lot of money. You know I don't have any money. I couldn't even pay for the ice-cream today."

"Have a little faith. You might be surprised what direction your life can turn. Hope is a good thing. Let's hope he might take your case. He is the most fair lawyer in the country, and if we can show him the grave injustices done to you maybe, he will take your case," she said.

Standing in line, she quickly pulled out her credit card, purchasing the book before her companion changed his mind. With a slow, pensive gait back to the parked car, the two began plotting how they might approach the famous Mr. Spence. Simplicity, they both agreed. They would try to explain the outlandish injustices as simply as possible. With that in mind, Kerry hastily dropped off Roberto, rushing home to compose a letter.

*"Dear Mr. Spence,*

*I'm writing today to tell you about a man who was released in early September 1996, from prison here in the State of Nevada. He spent fourteen years on death row for a murder he didn't commit. I have enclosed two newspaper articles that outline his release. Mr. Miranda has asked for my assistance in helping him find an attorney to represent him in his actions against the state of Nevada and Clark County for his wrongful imprisonment. The case would have to be taken on contingency as he is living in Las Vegas with no family and little means of support. Ms. Fitzsimmons, the attorney who represented him in the US District Court could not represent him as her husband works for the public defender's office resulting in a conflict of interest.*

*If you have time, please review the paperwork. If you wish to pursue the case further, I will be happy to furnish you with a complete copy of the petitions. I keep informing Mr. Miranda to be patient with the legal system and he keeps reminding me that he is patient but he doesn't want to wait fourteen years to get satisfaction against his wrongful imprisonment,"*

*Sincerely, Kerry.*

Back in his apartment, he began to realize that to get ahead, to make his way in the world, he would have to be aggressive. No one was going to come to him, he had to venture out into civilization to make an active meaningful life. Ms. Fitzsimmons had done all that was possible. She had obtained enough money to sustain Roberto's needs for six months. After that time period, her client had to make it on his own. And her telephone was ringing all day long with clients, like Roberto, desperate for legal advice.

Seated at the desk overlooking the street, he composed a list of goals, promising to work each day to make these goals; a new car, a house, a good woman, a good job, a lot of money, a better place to live, and a small group of close friends. At the bottom of the page he annotated, "Very easy? No way Jose."

A sudden loud knock at the door surprised him. Two people introduced themselves as reporters from People Magazine, explaining they had been reading about his case and wanted to do a story about the trial. They published a full page on December 2, 2002, describing his near brushes with death. "I have all my anger in a black box, and I don't touch it, " Roberto said in the article. The article briefly explained the trial, and sported a large photograph of him standing in front of the Lutheran Church. "Currently unemployed, Miranda, who has no family in this country, combs help-wanted ads and attends church twice a week. I can't blame America: America didn't do this to me, a judge and a lousy lawyer did. The judge is dead now, and I am alive. There is a God.' "

Although many articles had been written about the grave injustices he had survived, this article won him the fifteen minutes of fame he well deserved. His luck would change. Millions of people read this magazine and would begin to understand the hardships endured since landing in Florida.

Waking up early, dressing in hand-me-down-shirt, pants, and loafers, he headed out the door. He was resolute in procuring a job, it truly didn't matter what the job entailed, but money was important. Parking the car at the local coffee shop, he purchased the morning paper, borrowed a pencil and a piece of paper from the haggard looking waitress and began earnestly searching the help wanted section for work. Seated in the corner booth his privacy was uninterrupted as he diligently searched through the want ads and jotted down every possibility. Constantly warming the oversized coffee mug, the attentive waitress intuitively understood her customer's needs, and placed the plate of eggs and toast silently on the table.

"Thank you, " he responded. "I am trying so hard to find a job. It's not easy, but I believe if I keep trying something will come up."

"You know," the waitress replied, turning her view to the windows. "Over there, just down the street about a half mile, some trucks came in rearranging the dirt on the ground. It looks like something big is going to be built. Why don't you take a hike down there and check it out."

Gulping the last drop of rich black coffee, he placed several single dollars on the table, grabbed his notes, and thanked the kind waitress who had energized his day. Looking down at the bills, he noticed a piece of paper. It was the job site that Kerry had helped arrange. Referring to the address, and the insight from the waitress, he realized that this was the same place. What luck. Pledging to return, he jumped into his car, and headed up the street. Slowing the car, carefully parking on the gravel, he walked toward a cluster of men, all wearing hardhats. Shyly, Roberto asked if there was work to be had. Nodding, a heavy set man with thick, curly, black hair, and biceps larger than his neck, pointed to a tall, thin, blonde man. "Be strong," he coached himself. "Believe in yourself and someone will hire you."

Shouting above the sounds of the huge yellow John Deere forklifts, he introduced himself and asked if there was any work. Shocked, the blonde man obliged him, offering him a position.

Stating that they needed a few extra hands for the next months until the building was back on schedule. Agreeing on a wage, Roger Jamison, the head foreman shook his new employee's hand telling him to be there bright and early the next morning. Afraid to smile, he walked back to the pack of men introduced himself, stating he would be there early the next morning.

Elated, he drove back to the coffee shop, boldly walked through the door, and kissed the pretty waitress. Taken aback, her droopy eyes popped up, as Roberto thanked her for the tip. He explained every detail, as she smiled widely. "Tomorrow," he promised, "You get a bigger tip from me, this is my favorite place to eat, and you are my favorite waitress."

Mentally referring to his wish list, he knew he had definitely made some strides, with a job, and maybe even a new friend, life was looking up. He also was aware of his lack of organization. Had the paper that Jim had given him not dropped on the table at the coffee shop, the foreman may not have been so quick to hire him. Roberto had to learn to listen and pay attention. The foreman had been honest with him about the length of the job, but at least he would have money in his pocket while continuing searching for a more permanent job. He would do well so he could have a good reference for the next job. Spending the balance of the day alone, he took a walk in his neighborhood, enjoying the simplicity of freedom.

When Friday arrived, ending the first workweek, he took his check and cashed it seeking out fun in the lively city of Las Vegas. Settling on a local casino, he entered the noisy bingo parlor, bought two boards, located a table filled with smokers, and grabbed the seat at the end of the row. For the first time in over fourteen years, he could feel the jingle of change in his pockets. It was the first paycheck in over fourteen years. The most basic things in life had escaped him. Listening to the coins jangling around the insides of his pant's pocket, he was drawn back to his old habit of gambling. Intensely studying the cards, anxiously waiting for the numbers to be called, a woman seated directly across the table caught his eye. Returning the smile, they began sporadically conversing, pointing to the called numbers, and discussing each other's chances for a bingo. Drawing a pack of cigarettes tucked in his breast pocket, Roberto shook the pack, offering one to his new acquaintance. Shaking her head, he was surprised she refused the offer.

"I don't smoke," she confessed "And by the way my name is Alice."

"My name is Roberto, and it's nice to meet you. Why did you turn down my offer for a smoke, this is the smoking section? I see you carry cigarettes too."

The chubby brunette, with a mass of thick curls, replied that she met the nicest people sitting in the smoking section. Explaining her passion for bingo, and all the wins, she discovered the patrons were genuinely kinder, more interesting, and more fun, than the nonsmokers.

"Since my husband left me, I feel the need to get out and meet people. This is the best place in the city. The locals are kind, and fun loving; we all enjoy socializing. Stick with me and I will show you how to play the game, and make lots of friends along the way."

They played for a couple hours, and as Roberto's money was waning, he said good night, promising to see her the following Friday. Waving her sun-tanned arm, she made him promise to keep his word. She would be counting on his appearance the next weekend. He did keep his word, meeting her the following Friday evening and the dozens of Fridays after that. They had become fast friends. It wasn't a sexual relationship, just a repartee between two lonely people.

Alice's ruddy complexion reflected the hard work required as an appliance contractor. Her rough fingernails and poorly arranged hair, portrayed a woman who spent her energy on her business rather than herself. Selling and hooking up appliances in new homes was a tough job. Riding the rising tide of tremendous growth in the Las Vegas area kept the business lucrative and active. Because she needed space for three large trucks, she lived on the outskirts of the city, close to the air-force base. She kept a small ranch house and her ex-husband kept a larger mobile home.

When the weekends arrived, Alice, now single, found bingo parlors a satisfying social outlet. Carting a pack of cigarettes and a twenty-dollar bill, she loved playing the game. Talkative, she met many locals, a few who had used the services of her business. Her kind words and endearing smile compensated for her lack of natural beauty. But, Alice kept in great shape, often catching men glimpsing at her more formidable features, a great butt, and full breasts. After two disastrous marriages, she was looking for a good time and a good companion.

Often the two would share a soda or ice-cream after a couple hours of play, talking about their lives, their problems, their families, and work. This was the first true friend he had made on his own. Each had no ulterior motive; it was purely friendship they sought in each other. Alice was married almost two decades when her husband decided a younger, thinner version of her would satisfy his needs. One spring morning he packed his bags, leaving her the house, the mobile home, and a bag filled with overdue bills. Listening intently, Roberto began to have empathy for someone other than himself. This was a symbiotic meeting of the minds, each giving the other what was lacking in their lives. And although times were tough, and money nonexistent, he never gave up his bingo evenings with his friend.

Times did get tough. Unable to keep up, or understand what was expected of him, he lost his job at the construction site. Kerry was annoyed, but after fourteen years locked in a jail cell, he had to retrain his mind and body, not an easy task. After years in lock-up, he resented anyone telling him what or how to do something. Plainly, he begrudged authority at any level. It was time for him to be the boss of his life. Although this didn't make him the ideal employee, it was easy to understand the intense loathing for authoritative figures. He would have to learn how to accept direction without blowing each incident out of proportion.

Hanging his head low, he cashed the last paycheck, determined to find a better job. As usual he met Alice on that Friday night. He cried bitterly about the job loss, but after a couple of hours at bingo, some hot coffee and cigarettes, his spirits were lifted. Alice's warm personality, and softly smiling cheeks, offered encouragement and sympathy to her glum friend. Grabbing a small cozy table in the casino lounge, they lingered for an hour or two and chatted endlessly, sharing their problems and aspirations. The smoke filled air, vibrating with sensual sounds of a jazz band, provided a relaxed atmosphere, allowing the couple to converse freely concerning their problems, if only for a fleeting time. Although Roberto did not deem it as such, this was a therapeutic relationship, each helping the other to cope with life's challenges.

Glancing at her watch, Alice announced her departure. Kissing each other good evening, they went their separate ways. For Roberto it was the beginning of a long weekend. With little money, and little time left in the apartment, he would have to scrounge for a new place to live, and find a new job. Ms. Fitzsimmons had found the apartment but the rent was paid for only six months. After that, he was on his own. The state felt that in six months his life would be turned around, that he would have landed a great paying position, that he would know how to take care of all his needs, that he would want for nothing. But such was not the case. He needed help, therapy, financial support, training, education, health benefits, and socialization. It was as if he were Rip Van Winkle who had slept for decades waking up and finding the world around him had changed. Although Ms. Fitzsimmons was his savior, she had limited resources to offer her client.

Leaving the excitement of the casino, he drove home moaning over the prospects of beginning again. He wasn't prepared for the vicissitudes thrown his way, and coping was becoming more difficult with each failure. He saw every morsel of his life disproportionately, the onset of failure brought waves of depression and insecurity. Fear had become an enormous factor that played out in every aspect of his life. Fear of getting arrested, of being homeless, going without food, friends, and money, of becoming ill, too ill to work, all these thoughts stalked him obsessively, to the point of paranoia.

Entering the dark apartment, he took a long, warm shower, turned on the television falling asleep to the boisterous sounds of a Spanish sit-com. His sleep was fraught with nightmares of prison life He often woke up completely drenched with sweat, and disorientated. He would literally shake himself up out the stupor, look around the apartment, feel his heart beat, before assuring himself of his current reality; that he was free, and alive. Tossing in the rumpled bed, the problems kept sleep at bay while he wrestled with probable solutions. Within a short period of time he would be homeless, and jobless, both time and options appeared to be running out as disillusioned thoughts permeated his psyche.

# REALITY
# SINKS IN

The summer heat was beating down mercilessly on the crowded pavement of the strip. Lying on a discarded quilt, Roberto, now homeless, woke in the corner of a quiet alley to the sounds of a street entertainer playing a saxophone. Living with the heat of Cuba was nothing like the intensity of the mid-summer desert temperatures. Miserable, dehydrated, and hungry, he forced himself up, checked the contents of his emptied pockets for change, and headed northwest to the cooler mountains. His worst fears had come to fruition. He was now homeless. The streets of Las Vegas became his home. In the fleeting six months living in the apartment, he had not learned how to use his money wisely. He had not saved a dime. Upon receipt of each paycheck, he spent nearly all of it before the beginning of the next workweek. He had completely forgotten how to handle money. Dismayed, he looked at his surroundings and decided he needed a change of scenery.

Mt. Charleston loomed over the city as the one place guaranteed to be cool and green, an oasis in the midst of endless sagebrush and cactus. Checking the fuel gauge, assured there was enough gas to reach the peak, he turned on the ignition and slowly pulled the choking car out of the deserted alley. Although he had not yet to stoop to rummaging through trash cans for food, he feared that would soon become his next source of food.

Although he had lived on the streets of Cuba, he had been younger, and there was always his family to go home to. But in Las Vegas, he was without a safety net. Unable to apply for welfare, because of his immigrant status, or accept services offered by parole, his situation had slipped through all the bureaucratic cracks, there was no social agency that could or would help him. Because the judge dismissed the case, by the state statutes, he was no longer under the auspicious of the penal system, and therefore the parole system. The usual support offered by the state for inmates was not available to him. Although the patrons at the Lutheran Church had opened up their pockets, they too had run out of patience. Everyone thought he had more than enough time to get his life in order, but this was far from the reality of the situation. Seven and a half months out of prison, and his options were quickly drying up.

Climbing up the curved road, cool air slowly began replacing the stuffiness of the interior of the car. Taking a deep breath, he began to feel invigorated, his mind clearing from the fog of the past two weeks. Creeping up further toward the peak, the desert foliage was replaced by tall evergreens, the sagebrush by green grasses, and small desert rodents by deer and coyotes. The azure blue cloudless sky was peaceful, reminding him of lazy days spent on the beaches of Cuba. This, he thought, would be a private retreat, a chance to regroup, and rethink the future. As if his life had become a scale, he mentally balanced the good with the bad; his assets and his liabilities. As long as he had hope, then life would be worth living. He did not merely want to exist, that he had done for fourteen years, but to seek joy and true happiness for the years God saw fit.

Remembering Kerry's earnest try to seek justice, there was hope that he would have his day in court, receiving fair retribution for the atrocities endured from the legal system. This thought alone sent vibrations of optimism reverberating through his soul; concentrating on those positive thoughts lifted his spirits, creating the desire to push on with life. Spending three days in the comfort of crisp, cool mountain air revived and replenished his core, allowing confidence and anticipation to replace all dismal thoughts. Hiking the luscious paths, sleeping under the star lit skies, observing the brilliant colors of the forest birds, chatting with fellow campers, gazing at the colors of dusk, drinking from the ice-cold streams, and resting on fallen tree trunks, changed his entire outlook. The wide expanse of the skies allowed him a chance to regain a sense freedom. Smelling the freshness of the higher altitude invigorated his senses, causing reflection to the moments in his life that had meaning. There were people who had cared about him, who had gathered strength to help him win the ultimate battle with the legal system. Janelle, who grabbed Valentin's letters, forcing the prosecutor to read the glaring truth. Written on yellowed sheets of lined paper, this petite spiritual leader ambushed the prosecutor, "If you don't free Roberto," she demanded, "Then I shall go straight to every single news media in this country."

Roberto knew he was fortunate to have bodacious people on his side, that he truly was not alone. The battle cry was heard by several new acquaintances, from Janelle, to his slowly building procession of lawyers, who came to his aid. It was an assembly of true believers rallying around him that propelled the courts to set his release. A silent cloud passed overhead, he bowed in prayer thanking God for the efforts of all those altruistic people. Lifting up his deep brown eyes, grabbing a branch of a huge evergreen. he was ready, he would return to town fortified with emotional strength to face and conquer all the problems life would throw his way.

Returning to the city, he remained homeless for many nights to come, yet in this squalor, he would find the deepest love he would ever know. Not in what she said, but in the deeds themselves do we come to truly know and understand a person.

Locating a public shower, he cleaned himself up, shaved, brushed his yellowed teeth, dressed in simple khakis, a buttoned down striped shirt, and dark tennis shoes and he began the strenuous task of finding another job. The want ads were filled with menial summer jobs. The Las Vegas heat was so demanding that many outdoor workers were forced to quit, thus work could be found if an applicant was willing and able to withstand the elements. Strolling into a rental car company, Roberto timidly asked to make an application. When he got down to the pivotal question concerning jail or convictions, he conveniently forgot to check the appropriate boxes. Shaking hands with the office manager, they chatted about the job, and the business of car rentals. Impressed with Roberto's stature, strength, and appearance, he was hired to detail cars. The outdoor covered lot held the intense summer heat, making the job even more physically taxing. But Roberto desperately needed the money and was willing to do whatever it took to put his life back on the upward path. Sweating profusely, he grabbed a plastic water bottle, and headed off to the lunchroom for another refill. A beautiful young Spanish woman, seated on a metal chair in the corner of the lunchroom, caught his eye. "Good afternoon," Roberto gently called out. Lifting her dark brown eyes off the book, she smiled, introducing herself as Juanita.

"Do you work here?" he inquired.

"Yes, I have been here for over a year, its hard work, but the office manager keeps promising me a promotion to the back office, I just have to learn to speak and write English a bit better," she relayed.

"I would be happy to help you. I have been studying for years," he replied.

This conversation would be the beginning of the strongest love he would ever know. They began dating, both falling helplessly in love with the other. In spite of his sordid background, Juanita quickly came to believe in his spirit. Although they saw each other often, she found it very odd that he never took her back to his home. Most of their dates were in public places, or at the apartment she shared with her younger sister. Roberto was too embarrassed to admit he was homeless. Until he could put together a couple of paychecks, he would live under the stars.

Seeing each other at the car rental business brightened her spirits, balancing the drudgery of the intense physical labor, but the situation did not last. As the early fall approached, Roberto got into a squabble with another detailer, hearing the yelling the office manager ran out of his air-conditioned comfortable office, and promptly fired both men. Roberto was left with no job and no money. The job lasted less than four months.

Juanita's call from her lover sounded odd, and she quickly agreed to meet him at some obscure corner off the busy strip. Worried, she held her concern in abeyance until he could explain the pressing problem. Easing her car into a tiny space, she saw his familiar smile. Returning the wave, she jumped out of the car and she wrapped her willowy arms around his torso. "You see this spot," he announced. "This is my home, and this is where I will have to stay until a job or money comes my way. How can I see you, when I am dirty because there is no place to shower. I want to be with you, but not like this. I don't want pity either." Shaking his head in despair, he could think of no other words to utter.

Taking his face in her hands, Juanita lovingly offered up her home, exclaiming that what was hers was his. But in his stubborn chauvinistic frame of mind, he would have no part of her charity, stating that a man had to make his own way and if he couldn't then he had to suffer. "If you have to suffer," she pleaded. "Then you shall not suffer alone." Without further confrontation, she pulled a blanket from his bag, and saddled up beside him, lying underneath the starlit sky. Closing her eyes she whispered, "I will stay with you wherever you may be, so tonight it's under the blanket of God's glorious stars."

For two days she stayed with him wandering the streets, watching the people and traffic, eating junk from whatever left-over sources they could find. Hot, sticky and dirty, they drove to Lake Mead, found a secluded spot, stripped naked and jumped into the tepid water. Frolicking in the midst of the lake made them feel like two dolphins who had discovered nirvana. Both good swimmers, they tired after extended long lap races into the deeper sections of the calm lake. Dressing, he grabbed her tightly. "I will love you forever, he promised. You are my true angel."

Kissing him intensely, she held him close, nestling her brunette wet hair underneath his arm. Not a word was returned. She had no words to articulate the love she felt for this man. All she wanted was to cling to this moment, and pray it would last until eternity.

Without a place to stay or the guarantee of a restful night sleep and a hot shower, job prospects would prove more dismal than they already were. Any kind of permanent place would be better than living homeless on the streets of Las Vegas. Mustering up the courage, he would phone Kerry, pleading for money as soon as his feet hit the pavement of the city. The short drive back in the searing sunlight reinforced the fact he needed the comfort of air conditioning, at least until late fall arrived. It was likely any job available would be outdoors. After a full day laboring in the summer heat, coming home to a cool apartment would be the

only way he could survive. Pulling the dented used car up to the
7-11, he plucked the last quarter form his pocket and called his
friend. As the rings grew longer and longer, it never occurred to
him she wouldn't be home. How he would suffer until he knew
she would be able to lend him some money!

"Hello," Kerry answered. "Where have you been? We have
worried about you, tried calling, and then Jim and I went to your
apartment and were told you had packed up and left. I am so
sorry. Laura did all she could to pay for additional months, but
the money just wasn't there, and she is busy trying to get other
people out of prison like yourself."

Hesitating, his parched lips could hardly utter the words.
"Look, I am kind of broke, I know I screwed up at the job, but I
promise it will not happen again. It was my second job and I
guess I made a lot of mistakes."

"I will meet you at the local coffee shop tonight around
seven. Until then try to find a place to stay and Jim and I will
write you out a check," she earnestly spoke.

"I can't thank you enough," he stuttered. "I swear I will pay
you back, you can bring me a paper and I will sign an IOU, I
don't want charity, just a chance."

"Say no more," she chirped. "I'll see you tonight."

Hanging up the phone, he realized God had sent him a third
angel. He would spend the rest of the day finding a room, and
then survey the paper for any kind of job that would put food in
his grumbling belly. Too many times he had gone hungry. He
would set out to rectify this problem immediately. Hunger had
stalked his entire life. Here in America, he should not have to
worry about food; it was abundant everywhere one looked,
everywhere one went. Eating out of garbage cans was no civil
way to solve this problem. Animals ate garbage, but he was a
human being deserving of some semblance of dignity. Growing

up in Cuba he had begged for pennies to help put food on the table, and in prison the inmates went to bed every night with empty stomachs. Hunger was painful, and he was just plain tired of going without.

Driving toward the northern section of the strip, vigilantly looking for cheap rooms, he spotted older motels one block east. Turning onto Freemont, he meandered down the side streets until a vivid sign announcing cheap monthly rates caught his attention. Pulling into the empty parking lot, it signaled lots of empty rooms, perhaps even a chance to negotiate a better price. Entering the dimly lit lobby, it was plainly clear the décor had not changed in the forty odd years in business. Peeling wallpaper, cracked linoleum floors, and outdated electrical outlets assured the guests this was not on AAA's list of preferred lodgings. The parrot rattling his feathers in the brass cage appeared the same age as the hotel, and the manager behind the high wooden desk.

"How much for a room?" Roberto shyly asked.

"Usually its four hundred dollars a month, but let me see what I can do for you," the portly, mustached man replied. In a thick Spanish accent, he began bartering, until both had come to terms. "Alright. Two hundred fifty for the month, but when winter arrives, the prices will go up."

"I will return at eight tonight with a check for you. Please hold the room until then," Roberto said. Shaking hands he walked two long paces to the door, stopping suddenly to grab the local paper.

"Go on take it," yelled the lobby clerk. "See you later"

Mentally counting down one hurdle, locating a place to live, he forged ahead to cross the next hurdle, locating a job. His empty pockets wouldn't allow him a seat in a coffee shop, so he strolled to the outside mall on Freemont Street, taking a seat on an empty bench. Scrutinizing every single job, circling potential positions, he organized a list based on location. Starting at the southern tip of Las Vegas Boulevard, he would work his way north until someone offered him a job. He did not care what the job was, as long as it put food in his stomach and paid for his modest, yet unseen room. Two jobs were listed within a block of each other, two blocks north of the airport. Jotting down all the addresses and phone numbers, he neatly folded the borrowed paper in half, and strutted to his decrepit used car. Driving slowly down the side streets, he located the first job on his list. Sauntering into the rubbish removal company, he inquired about the open position.

"Sorry, Mister," piped the young, scruffy receptionist. "we filled the position yesterday, but we are still taking applications, you know, in case it doesn't work out."

Why bother, he thought, as he quickly exited the smelly office. Scanning the next address, he found himself at a rental car place. Again inquiring about the position, he was given a short application to fill out. For some reason, it did not ask if there were any convictions on his record. For once he would not have to explain the last fifteen years of his sad life. Carefully filling out all the information, he silently handed it back to the middle-aged, heavy-set woman. She motioned for him to take a seat until the manager had completed his phone call. Patiently, he sat for almost a half hour when a scrawny, elderly man appeared in the waiting room. Shaking the applicant's hand, he ushered him into his tiny, cluttered office. After a short perusal of the application, he looked up and asked if he minded hard work.

"No, he responded vigorously. "I do not mind hard work as long as I get paid."

Explaining the job, the manager elaborated the importance of cleaning and preparing rented cars. The business was competitive and he wanted the customers to have the cleanest, best driving rentals in town. After further explanations of the job, he again asked Roberto if he would mind the hard work, and again he responded he would love the hard work. A wage was agreed upon; he would begin working that Sunday morning. Giving up early morning church services was the sacrifice he would have to make until a better, easier paying job would come his way. At least when he met with Kerry, he could give her the good news, with a stern committed promise to repay her shortly after he began the job. Using his wit, Roberto did not avail his new boss of his prior job, as he feared the office manager would not offer a good reference. It was much easier not introducing past work experience. Let the new boss think he was a quick study, and an earnest worker.

The restaurant was unusually crowded with summer tourists, as Kerry waved to Roberto from the corner booth of their favorite coffee shop. A new waitress brought over the greasy menus, frowning from exhaustion and chaos of the overcrowded restaurant. Ordering for the both of them, Kerry brought out the glimmer of a concealed smile as she relayed the reply from the law firm they had corresponded with concerning the case.

"Remember the lawyer I wrote to about your case? The famous one on the cover of the book? Well, Spence is extremely interested in taking your case," she brightly explained, "There was a ton of paperwork to complete, but I just know it will be well worth your while. You will have to sign a letter stating their share of fees, and how the case will be handled. I will be happy to help you, but this is truly exciting news." Extracting a letter from her brief case, she allowed her friend several quiet minutes to methodically read the response. Watching his face perk up with a smile as he continued reading, they both understood the impact and the potential the case would have if it went all the way to district court. Happily he grabbed the pen and signed his name to the proposal with the understanding that the case could take a long time crawling through the court system.

"He truly seems to want to help me. This is the best news. This could mean a chance to free myself from the past, and let those awful people pay up for their horrible treatment. I bet the public defender, district attorney, and those cops won't like it when they have to face a judge, a fair judge, and this time they will be the ones paying for their crimes. Maybe they won't have to go to jail, but they will have to pay up, and that will hurt them. All the money in the world can't make up for the fourteen years I spent in a jail cell the size of a tiny closet. Nothing, absolutely nothing. But if this is my revenge then so be it, but let them all pay for what they did to me," he ranted.

Touching his arm, Kerry tried to calm Roberto down. He was so excited, he had hardly touched the large bowl of chocolate ice-cream the waitress had flung on the table. "I have some good news too, I got a job, not great money but it's a start," Roberto said. Explaining the interview at the auto rental company, he promised to repay her back as quickly as possible. Almost forgetting the purpose of the meeting, Kerry handed Roberto an envelope brimming with twenty-dollar bills, then pulled out a note, handing him a pen to sign the IOU. Never would she allow him to believe he was a charity case. So many times her heart ached for his sorrow, for all the losses he had suffered, yet another part of her realized that showing signs of weakness was probably the worst thing she could offer. She would never cry, or spout words of pity. She would never allow him to see into her aching heart. He needed strength, he needed someone to believe in him, guide him, pushing him to succeed. She was keenly aware of his fragile shattered ego, but placating it would not help him gain the resolve needed to cope and endure in a tough world. In prison there was no need to ever make a decision; all decisions were made by the warden.

Grabbing his hands, she assured him the future was looking up, that God had a soft spot in his heart. Roberto's life would be better, "Just keep the faith," she persuaded, "You will reap your rewards, even though it may take a very long time. Almost every Sunday in church we say a prayer for you asking the Lord to be kind and grant you peace. Many people come up to me after services asking if there is anything they can do to help you. Everyone wants your life to be successful. If there is good news we share it and if there is bad, we share that too." Kissing each other on the cheek, they hugged good night and she assured him a visit at his new place soon. Wadding the money up inside the shirt pocket, he hopped sprightly into the sorry excuse for a car, steering uptown to his new home.

With a lazy stretch, he rolled out of the lumpy bed, and he padded to the bathroom taking a lengthy shower. The water dripped down his large frame, first warm and then cool. Wanting to be fully prepared for the long work day ahead, knowing the work would be grueling in the midst of the summer heat. A clean tee shirt, khaki shorts, and worn sneakers were all he needed for the arduous task of detailing rented cars. Reaching up for the car keys lying on the only piece of furniture in the room other than the television, he grabbed what was left of the money Kerry had given him, closed the blinds, turned off the lights and departed. "Even though it was a dingy place," he ruminated, "I can only hope to do better." Anxious about the job, he replaced sulking with anticipation. "Maybe they will like me, and give me a fat raise soon" A sudden ring of the phone startled him, "Yes, " he replied sharply.

"Roberto, my name is Ron Smythe. I belong to the same church as your friend Kerry. She told me all about your life and I would love to meet you. We could sit down and have a little chat," he proposed.

"I guess that would be fine, when would you like to meet, I can't go far as my car is not running so well," he responded.

"How about I just meet you at your place? Say tomorrow around six, maybe we could go out for dinner," Smythe suggested.

"Sounds like it would be fine," responded Roberto. "I will see you tomorrow night." Giving Ron the address to his apartment, they hung up. Roberto was curious, perhaps God would send him a fourth angel, this time, it would be a man.

Unable to fill the tank with gas, he opted to take the bus down Las Vegas Boulevard. It was a sleepy, warm morning as he quietly rode down the most electrifying street in the world. Too early for the tourists, he enjoyed the elegance of the grand architecture lining the street mixed with the beauty of towering, lean palm trees. This was a city to enjoy, if one had money, but even without a lot of money there was endless free music, street entertainers, and sights such as the Bellagio's dancing musical water show. He felt happy to be alive, to imbibe in the gifts God had given man, and the richness of talent and art filling up the town. Making up his mind, he decided to make the best of it, live as much as he could for as long as he could, in the best way he could.

Walking up to the front desk of the rental car company, he introduced himself to the elder man, who appeared annoyed at the intrusion. Picking up a shirt, he told the new employee to wear it while on the job, then pointed to the garage where the manager would show him what to do. Nodding, Roberto grabbed the fresh cotton shirt, and removed his worn one; now he felt like an official employee of the international rental car company. The manager put him immediately to work on what seemed to be an endless parade of returning cars; first cleaning out the interiors, then scrubbing down the exteriors. "Sunday mornings," the manager explained. "Is the busiest day, everyone returns the cars to fly home, Monday a flock of people come in for midweek excursions, then Friday, well that is truly the busiest day of the week. I call the Monday renters mid-weekers, because they all get these great rates from the casinos, and they don't tip that good either. Stick with me and I will show you the ropes."

Lunch could hardly come fast enough as his rumbling stomach talked loudly. In the corner of the main office a small, clean employee lunchroom allowed a respite from the heat and the toil of the detailing. Dropping some coins in a vending machine, Roberto took his Coke, bag of chips, and candy bar to a vacant seat. Memories of Juanita flooded his thoughts. How he missed not working in the same location! But circumstances arose that he could not justify. He would have to settle for seeing her after work and days off.

Living with her unmarried sister, who was burdened by a young infant, frightened Juanita. The thought of having to raise a child alone terrified her. Juanita would never ever give birth. Watching her sister struggle to feed and clothe the baby was more responsibility than she was ready and willing to take on. Roberto would do just fine, she thought, handsome, strong, smart, kind, but most of all, he was romantic and loving. She knew he had fathered children in Cuba. Having another hungry mouth to feed was the farthest thing on his mind. A truer love she would never find. Although they did not live together, many nights were shared at his simple apartment. They would meet each day after work for dinner, talking endlessly, confiding, and exchanging parts of their lives. Her broad smile, doting eyes, and tender kisses showered Roberto with the kind of love his heart had ached for. Truly God had answered his prayers by bringing this lovely woman to love him. He loved her back, caressing her shoulders, holding her tightly, so tightly that he feared to let go. "I love you," he professed. Her passion was just as profound as his; they would be a couple forever.

Often he would simply stare into Juanita's dark eyes, so round, and deep. Her lips were bow shaped, not too thin not too full. Although short, her shapely, thin body was exactly what he had in mind when dreaming up his perfect mate. Finding no faults in this ideal woman, he would never cheat on her. Sexually starved for endless years, he would confide to her she was well worth waiting for, a love so profound came only once in a lifetime. It came late for both of them, but it did arrive. Her entrance into his life brought meaning and an urgency to the value of his life. For once he felt as if he were living with a purpose. He had yet to mention the lawsuit, but in time, she would come to know every detail of his life. Her love would sustain him, and he would make sure she would always be taken care of financially, if the money should ever come to fruition. He was keenly aware of their age difference — the two decades over her age would justify his intent to give her a substantial portion of whatever monies he would receive. Even though they were not married, and may never marry, he promised himself he would take care of her well after he had departed the earth. Her love was the power that would ensure his substance on earth, and from heaven, he could assure her sustenance with enough funds to see her comfortably through her life.

Opening the door to the motel room he heard the crying sounds of the phone. It was Ron Smythe reminding him of their dinner together. So intoxicated by the thoughts of Juanita, was all that he had time for he had totally forgotten the meeting. Thinking that a good meal was just what his empty stomach required, he readily agreed. Ron would pick him in a few minutes. Although Roberto knew nothing about this man, he was a parishioner at Kerry's church so he figured he must be a good guy. Never for a moment did it cross his mind that anyone would have ulterior motives in developing a friendship, yet this naïve attitude would abruptly change. Although trust was a trait Roberto had long forsaken, it never occurred to him that anyone would intentionally hurt him After the hellish life already endured, and with Ron's knowledge of his situation, Roberto naively assumed their meeting was based upon empathy and compassion. Ron's unknown background could lead Roberto in harm's way.

Sharply dressed in a simple khaki cotton suit and open tattersol shirt, Ron extended his hand and firmly shook his newest friend. Gesturing to the car, Roberto took a seat in the roomy Cadillac, enjoying the ice-cold air-conditioned interior. The discussion centered around a quiet restaurant to eat, with the companion assuring his driver the simpler the better. After a short drive, Ron pulled into a Texas style steak house, just the right place for a man who spent so many years in jail. A nice juicy steak with delicious baked potato was not the typical fare on death row, unless of course, it was the last meal. Chuckling to himself, Ron figured this man was an easy target for his conniving, he would be easily sucked into his prepared underhanded financial scheme. Just one decent meal, and Roberto would be eating out of his hand. Ron Smythe had plenty of practice in cheating people out of their money, so much so that he had served a year in prison for defrauding several people out of millions of dollars in phony investments. This man seated across from him chewing on the biggest piece of steak he had probably seen in twenty years, would play right into his hands. Although

Roberto never drank, Ron was chugging down his fourth beer when he finally had enough alcohol in his brain to broach the reason for this meeting. Pulling out a document from his lizard skin briefcase, he explained that he was an investment agent, and he took care of peoples' finances. Detailing his vast accomplishments, avoiding the part where he was found guilty of fraud, he coyly convinced Roberto of his professionalism.

Before the ice-cream had been consumed, Roberto signed on the dotted line, giving Ron the right to handle his finances. Ron was a member of the Lutheran Church, he too used the Sunday morning services to gather clients. It was his good fortune to eavesdrop on a conversation Kerry had with another worshiper. Ron had listened to the awesome fact that a famous lawyer would be suing on behalf of Roberto and the suit could settle in the millions of dollars. This was a slam-dunk for Mr. Smythe, another fool sold a bill of goods. But this scheme would be worth waiting for as the settlement would be huge, and he would have complete control over all the funds. Smiling, he imagined the fat check he would be writing himself each month as sole manipulator of the funds. Quickly grabbing the document, he asked Roberto if he would like anything else. Hugging his swollen stomach, Roberto declined, but thanked Ron for the wonderful meal. Although naïve, Roberto was not dumb. Driving back to his motel room, he turned to his new friend asking him if he could get a copy of what he had just signed. Taken aback, Ron nervously twitched his nose, but promised to mail him a copy of the agreement the very next day. Shaking hands the two departed in utter silence.

For a while, Roberto's life became routine as he worked, slept, dated, and shopped. He was moody, agitated, often morose over the loss of so much of his life, but his mind would wander to thoughts of Juanita, Alice, and Kerry, and then his spirits would brighten. He felt like he had his own private harem; he had more women friends than male friends; simply, he trusted women more than men. Although he could no longer attend church services, Janelle kept in touch, often reminding the parishioners to give what they could to help him out of his poverty. Unable to budget money, he lived from paycheck to paycheck, never putting any money in the bank. He didn't trust banks, in fact he didn't trust any institution that would use power over him. His shirt pockets held all the money he owned. Often he daydreamed what he would do if the law-suit was ever settled, and he would have several million dollars. Laughing, he knew he could not stuff it all into his shirt pockets. Perhaps he would stuff it under the mattress.

One quiet, cloudless evening he composed two letters, one assigning Kerry sole executor of his will, placing her in charge of all substantial fiduciary responsibilities, and the other to the Spence law firm. Kerry had advised him to formalize the relationship with the law firm by writing a letter of representation. "I want you to represent me against those who may be liable for all damages as a result of my fourteen-year imprisonment in the Nevada State Penitentiary. It is my desire to engage you as my attorney to investigate this matter fully and to take whatever action may be necessary, including a suit, to recover for me the loss and damages which have been sustained by me as a result of this incident. In this respect, you are authorized to negotiate, compromise, or settle any claims I may have which in your judgment you think best." Rereading this significant letter, he would give it to Kerry to proofread thoroughly before mailing. Knowing the importance of stating the proper facts, he didn't trust his command of the language to cover all the bases.

The letter for Kerry was based upon his complete trust and

faith in her. It was obvious that she cared a great deal, and if something should happen, he knew in his heart she would do the right thing; she would take care of his family in Cuba. Many an ice-cream bowl had lead to discussions of sending money to his mother and to his sisters, how this could be accomplished. Mail was tampered with, thus it was unsafe to enclose cash in a letter or package, especially if it had come from America. Still waiting for proper legal papers, he could not travel to Cuba. This left Kerry as the courier for the funds. Making a solemn oath, she promised if upon his demise the lawsuit hadn't been settled, she would take control of the funds and make the pilgrimage to Cuba, personally handing the money to his family. At this point, he had totally forgotten the document signed with Smythe, but Roberto was a man of the moment. The relationship forged with Kerry and Attorney Spence would be all he would consider as relevant and legal.

As the lawsuit proceeded and the possibility became real that he might actually see substantial sums of money, he was smart enough to know what he didn't know; how to invest and manage money. Kerry, with her MBA and PHD degrees, was well-suited to take care of whatever should fall his way. He knew he had to put his trust in someone, and she was his best friend. She would never, ever cheat him. Sitting on his bed, he wrote out a two-page letter explaining his trust and faith in her judgments; he would abide by her decisions when it came to large sums of money. Allowing her to make decisions as to how the money should be allocated eased his mind. After all the struggles and horrific hardships he had endured, he did not want any large sums of money to slip through his fingertips, nor did he want outsiders to cheat or steal from him. He wanted to make provisions for Juanita, and also he wanted Kerry to continue advising and investing. Poverty stricken, like himself, Juanita had no idea how to handle potentially large sums of money. Sometimes love wasn't enough. It didn't make you smart.

Rereading the letter, he annotated it as best he could, signed and dated it, then slipped it into an envelope located in the motel desk drawer. Turning on the television, he stripped off his filthy work clothes, taking a lengthy cool shower. His mind would often jump from the present to the past, daydreaming of the hell endured on death row. The simple smell of soap, adjusting the faucet to a comfortable temperature, reaching for a clean soft towel, shaving with a new triple edged razor, brushing his teeth with spearmint flavored toothpaste, was lost to him for fourteen years. These basic necessities had been stolen from his life, never to be replaced. Relishing and rejoicing in freedom, he bitterly reflected the unfairness he had endured. Playing with the water temperature, he shouted out, "I will have a long shower. I will make it any temperature I want. I will stay in here all day"

Juanita was not a jealous person, and quickly came to terms with her boyfriend's numerous girlfriends. (Kerry, and Alice). Every Friday night still belonged to Alice and the bingo games. Gambling was a huge part of jail life, a habit hard to break even in the free world. Carrying nothing more than a twenty-dollar bill, Roberto controlled the losses, as detailing cars was not a lucrative paying job, and he absolutely could not afford to lose any more than this small amount. Kerry had set up a budget, helping him control and stretch his modest weekly wages. Every Friday night, Juanita would search his pockets, pulling out all the cash and leave him with only the predetermined measly sum. Often Alice's sympathy got the best of her, spotting her friend with a five or ten-dollar bill until his luck would turn around.

Nor was Alice jealous of Juanita as she listened to Roberto's

rendition of their love for each other. Companionship and cama-
raderie was the basis of their deepening friendship. For hours
each Friday, they talked endlessly about their problems, revealing
personal details he dared not ever tell Juanita. Alice was an
ardent listener as well as a candid, liberated thinker who could
absorb, cogitate, and analyze rhetoric, then reply in a logical,
philosophical answer that would appear valid to the most erudite. Those prolonged bingo evenings, proved beneficial for both
their emotional health. Juanita understood their relationship,
which was why she never balked nor nagged at the intrusion of
time. Some weeks he would return with more than the twenty
dollars, but most weeks his pockets were empty. Regardless, he
always returned with a smile on his face, and an overly zealous
hug. Coming home to Juanita was like coming home to a minia-
ture paradise. He would never ever take her for granted. He
would cherish her, and love her forever.

The routine of work continued uneventfully until one
warm fall afternoon. Another worker challenged Roberto, dis-
placing the manager's authority. Demanding to take the easier
cars to clean, he left Roberto in dire straits struggling with the
larger vehicles. "You can't tell me what to do," yelled Roberto.
"You are not the boss." And with that, a screaming match
ensued where upon both men were abruptly asked to join the
ranks of the unemployed. That night Roberto was terrified to
meet Juanita, but he had to face up to the fact that yet another
job had been lost. Taking him aside, calming him down, she
extracted the story, then told him to cool off, and calm down.
She was upset. She knew how difficult it would be for him to
obtain another job. Perhaps, she contemplated, she could talk
the manager into keeping him. Just one obstacle stood in the
way — her lack of the English language. She was useless to his
cause. It was at this moment that she decided to attend night

school, Roberto had a strong grasp of the language. It was time for her to learn it as well. Kissing her good night, he ambled home shadowed in self-pity.

Back in his tiny motel room, he struggled with his temper. The vestiges of prison life had left deep crevices in his deflated ego. There were some incidences that instilled core values couldn't override, and at times those incidences got the best of him. So tainted from the adversities suffered in jail, all the power he could summon would not be enough to carry him through tough confrontational situations. Try as he may, he never again could accept authority thrust at him without valid rationale. Suffering under the thumb of prison guards, authority figures usurping more than their due, was unacceptable. He was unable to deal with bullies. He would rather walk away than suffer any deflation of self worth. Asking himself if these thoughts were justified, the answer would haunt him to his grave — yes. He had to fight, he had to preserve what little dignity and self-value was left in his heart and soul.

Although he was able to pay off Kerry for the loan, if another job didn't come along soon, he would be forced to ask for another, or take the route of homelessness. Too depressed and tired to open up the want ads of the local paper, he tossed the blankets back, and plunked down into the sagging mattress for a long afternoon siesta. Dreams had always been the escape hatch to reality of consciousness; life there was serene, flawless, and freedom prevailed. Oftentimes, he dreamed of being a bird, or a wild stallion on the desert prairies, or a whale swimming in the ocean, but always he was free to roam the planet uninhibited by any constraints. A jarring ring of the phone interrupted the pleasures of sleep. Grabbing the receiver, the familiar voice of Kerry echoed into his ears. Listening intently, she explained she wanted to meet him that evening to go over some exciting correspondence received from the law firm in Wyoming.

Because Roberto roamed from place to place, all vital correspondence was sent to her home bearing his name, but she never opened it without his presence.

Groggy from sleep, he conjured up a positive answer, promising to meet her at the usual coffee shop. With lackluster energy, he forced himself out of bed, plunging to a cold refreshing shower. The usual t-shirt would not be ample clothing to combat the strong fall winds. Grabbing a worn sweatshirt he dressed for the elements. So used to warm weather, the slightest cool breeze sent shivers down his spine. The extra layer would provide warmth for the evening ahead. Grabbing the car keys, he carefully closed the motel room door, and turned on the reluctant engine of his car and slowly cruised to the restaurant. Relentlessly checking the gas gauge, he was overly cautious about running out of gas. Rolling down the window, the cool evening breezes caressed his head, reminiscent of the tropical nights in Cuba. Often the smallest stimuli would trigger vivid memories of childhood memories of a life long gone, never to be revisited. He remembered his last conversation with Kerry, when he explained why he could not travel back to his home land. "I never would give up my Cuban citizenship." If Cuba ever became a free country, I would have no problem coming and going. I live for the day when it will be easy to visit my family."

Rattling the thoughts out of his brain, the smiling face of Kerry easily drifted his thoughts to more pressing problems. Facing her with the prospect that again he had lost another job, would more than anger her usually congenial nature. She on the other hand kept the conversation light, as she was aglow with good news. Reaching into her briefcase, she pulled out a thick letter from the Spence legal firm in Wyoming. "You know," she said. "I receive all your correspondence because you move around a lot, and we can't afford to miss any important letters."

Shaking his head, he understood the purpose of her statement. "Kerry, I appreciate all you do for me you know I trust you with my life, all your help, encouragement, I could never repay you for all your kindness."

Holding up the letter, she ceremoniously handed it over, relishing the gusto of observing her friend reading the reply from the famous law firm. Both smiling, the letter informed them the firm would be taking the case, and they were requesting Roberto's presence in Jackson. An airline ticket was enclosed; now all he had to do was pack. The timing could not have been better. With no job to worry about, time was something he had a lot of. Kerry congratulated her friend and hoped that this would be his chance for exoneration.

"I know money is the main thing. All those people should pay for what they did to me, but I want to be fully exonerated. I don't want to carry this red card that states I am a convicted felon. Now way Jose, " he stated.

"I am just happy you will get your day in court. Just remember that this entire ordeal may take a very long time, and it's hard, but please try and be patient. This firm never takes a case they don't think they can win, so this is a very good sign. I just knew when Gerry Spence read your case his heart would melt. It does not surprise me that the law firm wishes to support your cause. This will be the first case of its kind tried in the district courts and there will be a lot of legal precedents set. All this takes a lot of time, research and manpower. Just promise me you will not lose faith, even though it may take years. In the end you will prevail, and then you will look back and say it was worth it."

Roberto was so involved in thought, he hardly realized he had consumed three scoops of chocolate ice-cream. As they stood up to leave, he held his stomach, not realizing how much food he had eaten. "My goodness, I am stuffed, " he laughed. "Kerry, I know this isn't such good news, but I lost my job, again. This guy, he was so obstinate. Ordering me around, treating me badly — well, to tell the truth, the manager fired us both."

Handing him three twenty dollar bills, she told him she would update the IOU, but he couldn't very well go all the way to Jackson without a cent in his pocket. Kissing her lightly on the cheek, he thanked her again, then in gentlemanly fashion walked her to the car, opened the door, and made sure she safely departed the parking lot before he retreated back to the motel room. Holding the letter and the ticket in his hand, he felt empowered, energized to face the lawsuit with the most brilliant assemblage of lawyers in the country. Faith had played into his destiny. The prayers of Janelle, his family and friends were about to be answered. No, there would never ever be a replacement for the years on death row, but thanks to Kerry, he would have the opportunity for justice to be done.

Lying in bed, the mantra played over and over in his head: "I am the only person ever released from death row in the state of Nevada, the only one, the only one...." He closed his eyes and fell into a deep relaxed sleep.

The crashing noises of the garbage truck brusquely shook him awake. Juanita was already at work, so he would have to impatiently wait until the shift had ended to surprise her with the good news. Removing a pen from the desk, he scrounged around the room for pieces of paper, and began composing a letter to his family. He couldn't wait to tell all his friends and family about the impending case, how finally he would be exonerated for the crimes he didn't commit, how his family could restore their honor and faith. The humiliation endured for having a son convicted of murder in the first degree destroyed his mother, taking years off her life. Now she could hold her head high when talking about her eldest son. Sending Teresa all the news and magazine clippings meant she would finally finish the scrapbook with photos of Roberto standing amongst the finest of American attorneys, as they all smiled victoriously.

The timing was auspicious for a short trip. Without a job he had complete freedom to come and go as he chose. Collecting a few articles of clothing, he packed a worn suitcase given to him by a generous parishioner, and swiftly exited the dank motel room. Dropping by the old job site, he waved at Juanita, as he sat patiently in the car while she crossed the busy intersection. "I just wanted to say goodbye. I should be back in a couple of days. I will miss you and think about you every day." He kissed her gently on the lips. She hugged his shoulders and waved as he continued driving south toward the airport. He knew he couldn't afford to park at the main airport lot, it was too expensive for his depleted funds, so he veered off at the signs pointing to remote parking. This, he realized, was what he could afford. Perhaps if all went well, he would never have to be troubled with trivial sums of money.

He rolled up the windows and locked the doors. He grabbed the suitcase, the ticket and the large envelope containing documents assembled by Kerry and began a half-mile hike in the crisp fall air. The walk would help relax his jittery nerves as he contemplated the lengthy plane ride. Loathing flying, he promised to control his fear by concentrating on the impending meeting with the Spence law firm. Anxious, excited, hopeful, and curious, his mind had ample thoughts for distraction. Kerry had packed extra paper and pens in case he wanted to ask questions or jot notes of the meeting. In prison, he had learned rudimentary legal lingo and procedures. He knew this information would come in handy when the attorneys began working their magic. Completely ignorant during the initial case, he never again wanted to put his life in someone's hands without a base of basic knowledge. Armed with an elementary understanding of the law and inherited intuition, he would be able to properly judge the meaning, value and purpose the lawyers would offer.

Climbing the outer steps to the moving ramp, he patted his shirt pocket, and assured himself that the ticket and wallet were in place, and ready for inspection. Jumping off the people mover, and walking through the automatic sliding doors, he noticed the crowded airport was jammed with tourists seeking transportation into and out of the city. So busy, he observed, so much tumult and noise. Scanning the electronic boards, and locating the gate, he walked purposefully to the security checkpoint, and removed the ticket and picture ID. Laying the small case on the x-ray machine, he slowly walked through the screening. For once, he was scrutinized the same as everyone else. He was the same as any other passenger taking any flight. Grabbing the ragged case, he strolled to the boarding gate gazing into the boutiques. Prolonging the eventual realization that boarding time had commenced, he stood diligently in line, grasping his belongings, as he was gasping for air. Remembering Juanita chastising his poor behavior, he began silently muttering; "Soon the plane will land. Soon the plane will land."

The loud roar of the engines signaled the beginning of the flight. Tugging at the seat pocket, he searched for the ubiquitous white bag, and was sorely disappointed when none existed. Turning to the elderly woman seated in the center, he asked if she had a bag. It seemed as though the airlines stopped equipping each seat, as so few passengers ever became airsick. Tickled, the woman turned to Roberto and assured him he would be just fine, to think about other things, and to just relax. She began a lengthy banter about her endless airplane trips. "This woman won't shut up," he mused. "Next time I will keep my fear to myself, or feign sleep." It was too late. She had a captive audience, and without missing a beat, chatted on until the plane had safely landed.

Stepping off the plane, his wobbly legs barely made it to the baggage claim area. Scanning the small crowd, he spied his name written on a large tablet. Smiling proudly, he walked over to the young couple, announced his name. They fervently shook his hand, and lead him into the biting cold winds of Jackson, Wyoming. Introducing themselves as representatives of the firm of Spence, Moriarity and Schuster, they prodigiously escorted their newest client through the congested streets, motioning the driver to bring the car around to the sidewalk. Roberto grasped the thin coat tightly around his torso, as they quickly stepped into an oversized Jeep wagon. It had been over 17 years since he had felt this cold. The air woke up his senses, evaporating the trepidations of travel. Inquiring about his flight, the lawyers appeared honest and concerned. Before he had time to respond, they began pointing to the landscape — the mountains, lakes, and various tourist sites. It was a magnificent place, the deep blue cloudless sky meeting the giant heights of the towering mountains, flowing into the lush green meadows laced with snow and crystal clear streams. "Beautiful," he exclaimed. "But way too cold for my Cuban bones."

"You get used to it," the young woman piped up. "It is so restful, so calm Your mind has a chance to think, to allow the senses a rest from the tumult of city life. Speaking for my colleagues, we all love this place. You might be surprised how many of our clients are from other states, and fly in just like you did today to visit us. We can do almost all of our work here. But don't worry, when the time comes, we fly wherever we need to. This environment really allows us the space to explore, to think freely. Maybe that is why we win all of our cases."

"I think you win all of your cases because you are all very, very, smart," Roberto chuckled.

As they drove up to the law offices, Roberto was surprised by the simple beauty of the buildings; the natural woods reflected surrounding forests. It was as if the architect grabbed the bounty of the woods and captured it as a building for man to learn and prosper. The splendor was not intimidating. One sensed a warm glow from the clean lines of the uncomplicated buildings. The Spence name had become a legend in the field of law in its own time, so much so that a school had been erected to teach the methodology. Although money was plentiful, there was no great ostentatious display of wealth. Simplicity was the basis of the design and instruction. Famous for reigning in the old Christian values founding the American legal system, the Spence name implied purity of thought, honesty, and purposeful litigation. Frivolous cases never made entré to his pulpit. Only cases warranting the highest human values caught his attention. This was the sole reason Mr. Miranda was summoned to the great law offices of the revered Spence firm.

Kent Spence, the protégé of the legal legacy, confidently strutted into the conference room, and greeted his new client with a sturdy frontier handshake. Smiling, he picked up an assortment of documents, and looked purposefully into Roberto's face announcing they had better get started, as much ground work had to be laid prior to winning this case. Careful not to seem condescending or to speak in useless legal vocabulary, he treated his client with utmost respect and dignity. Elaborating results from initial investigations, there appeared to be a lengthy arduous fight ahead; this case would not only set a legal precedent but would forever change the disposition of law in the

United States. These were powerful statements from a young energetic man, yet this young man had the backing of the greatest legal minds in the country. Roberto knew Kent would not compromise on a promise: his skills and intellect spoke potently for themselves. This was the time when Roberto would see a man who was thoroughly convinced of the rights of his client and the wrongs committed by entrusted public officials of the state. Neither God nor complacent judges would stand in Kent's way as he sought vindication for the sacred rights of his client. Caged in a tiny cell, awaiting the knock upon hell's gate for a crime not committed, raised the dander of every lawyer housed in the Spence's firm. There was no doubt in anyone's mind they would prevail; all it would take was tenacity, money, and time. Roberto would learn to be patient. He was free, truly. Freedom was all he cared about. Sure he wanted money. Payback time was in the distant future. He would be patient, and when his turn in court would come to fruition, he knew the law firm would prevail.

As the meeting came to a close, all stood shaking hands, offering smiles of future meetings. Carrying a small package of documents, Roberto was cautioned to carefully read and absorb the material. Reminding himself he was currently unemployed, there was ample time in his empty schedule to follow orders. Gathering his few possessions, the youngest attorney guided him back to the van and sped back to the small Jackson airport. Chatting endlessly, the driver delivered an ongoing pep talk filled with empathy and hope — the perfect ending to the perfect meeting. Listening intently, Roberto gleaned additional information which added to the brightness in his future. Remembering the checklist he had made when released from prison, each day he was inching toward accomplishing the goals. He had made friends, found love, was now on his way to vindication and monetary security. Still left was that tugging thought of finding the right job. The money would be years away. He still had to survive until the money rolled in.

The beauty of the countryside was astounding. He observed tiny crystals of snow brushing the soaring evergreens. If it weren't for his loathing of snow and cold, he would deem this place heaven on earth. In the distance, he could spot a small herd of deer drinking in the half-frozen streams, and one dark brown antelope. "You have a lot of animals here," he noted, "Not like in Las Vegas, where we don't even see any jack rabbits I think the rattlesnakes lost too much money at the tables, and they seemed to have vanished too."

Driving up to the passenger drop-off, the lawyer handed Roberto extra business cards, thanked him for coming, and promised to be in contact shortly. Shaking hands, they parted, each heading back to continue working on the case. The airport was quiet as it was midweek and few flights were leaving. Locating the gate, he swiftly passed through security, taking a seat near the window for a front row seat of the scenery. The airport had yet to be converted like its busier counterparts. Passengers were led to their planes directly from the tarmac and walked up a metal ladder to enter the plane. A loud announcement by the warmly dressed agent signaled the small jet was ready for boarding. Instructing the passengers to form a line, they would be led out to the tarmac, climbing up the movable steps. Noticing the wind had picked up, Roberto lifted up the collar of his jacket, buttoned his coat, clutched his case and yellow envelope and began to board the plane. Following the footsteps of the passengers in front of him he cautiously stepped on the ground as fresh snow had fallen. The brief walk against the harsh arctic winds shortened his breath as he tentatively trudged toward the waiting jet. Without warning, he unexpectedly slipped on unforeseen black ice. He screamed loudly. A crack, crunch rang in his ears as he lay on the ground. A passenger yelled out to the flight attendants that someone had fallen and needed immediate attention. Staving off the winds, several passengers surrounded Roberto until help arrived. The pain was excruciating. He couldn't move. The brutal cold winds overcame his ability to breath. Strength faded away as he went into shock. Although the passengers spoke kindly and tried to aid the victim, no one dared move him until the medics arrived with a stretcher. It seemed as if an eternity passed until he was lifted into the ambulance, and speedily taken to the local hospital. The attending paramedics roused the patient into consciousness as the warmth of the emergency vehicle enveloped his lungs and heart. Again screaming out in pain, he pointed to his leg. "I heard it snap," he uttered weakly. "Oh my God am I in pain. My leg."

Assuring him he would be fine, the rapidly moving ambulance arrived a few minutes later at the emergency room, with its attendants in preparation to receive the latest victim of the cruel winter weather. Wrapped up in blankets, the nurses began an IV, then whisked him off to the x-ray lab, where he was given the sad news he had broken his ankle in two different places. "Guess you will have to extend your stay in Jackson," they joked as the various doctors and nurses diligently cared for this middle-aged visitor. The nurses administered pain medication and his mind began to function. Without money, friends, or health insurance he was overcome with fear. Remembering the card the lawyer had given him, he asked the nurse to help him find his pants, as he needed to make a call. Manipulating the bed, the benevolent aid helped him make the call to the law office, and in the groggiest of voices, he weakly explained what had happened and where he was. Shocked, Kent Spence assured him he would be taken care of, and not to worry about the medical bills. Getting better would be all that was important. Promising to see him sooner than anticipated, he sent the same young attorney to back to the hospital to check up on their newest client. Handing the phone back to the doting aid Roberto announced his lawyers would be visiting soon, then promptly fell asleep.

The glaring light reflecting off the freshly fallen snow permeated the astringently sparse hospital room. Because most skiers were presently on the slopes and intact, he had the space to himself. Still groggy from the various medications, he slowly opened his eyes, remembering where and why he was lying in the hospital bed. Sitting up, dizziness overcame his ability to balance and he swiftly realized he wouldn't make it to the bathroom without help. He buzzed the nurse's station, and an aid quickly arrived with a bedpan. "You will not be leaving this bed for a while, " she admonished. "That was a nasty fall you took, shattering your bones, and creating two different breaks. Get used to us helping you for a while."

"Oh my goodness," the patient squawked. "When can I get out of this place and go home?" Remembering his last kiss on Juanita's lips, he had promised to return within a day or two. This stop was not in the plans.

Elaborating the doctor would be in to fully explain the nature and extent of the injuries, the nurse handed him the remote to the television, and suggested he expend whatever energy he had changing the channels. Taking the remote, she reiterated that even though they seemed far from civilization, there were numerous cable channels. Breakfast arrived shortly; lifting the plastic lid, he smelled the sweetness of pancakes and bacon, and realized he was hungry. After opening the plastic utensils, he gobbled the food, washing it down with a hot cup of weak coffee. Surfing the channels for a movie that would captivate his interest, although it would not camouflage the pain. That was an impossibility. The swollen ankle throbbed deeply. Sweat poured down his dry unshaven cheeks as he once again summoned the nurse begging for relief from the relentless pain. Prudently referring to the chart, she nodded her head agreeably, adding pain medicine to the IV drip. In a caring manner, she assured the patient he would feel relief momentarily, then darted out of the room.

As the morning sun crossed to the western horizon, Roberto awakened to the sounds of visitors. The lawyers had not forgotten him. They had come to console his sorry state of affairs. Making light jokes, they cajoled him into a happier consciousness. "We don't work on these types of legal suits," they admitted. But another law firm had already been contacted and they would be handling yet another law suit on his behalf. Bringing flowers and various and sundry snacks, and magazines, they departed, quickly explaining he was in dire need of rest. Limply shaking their hands, and thanking them for the gifts, Roberto fell back into a fitful sleep. He hated being in the hospital, as he loathed any and every type of institution. For him it stirred memories of jail life. He desperately wanted to leave, but the pain and the extent of the injuries were too overpowering. Having no choice but to surrender to the situation, he would do what the doctors and nurses commanded, and therefore expedite a speedy recovery.

Several days into his unplanned stay, two strangers appeared, introducing themselves as representing the law firm Spence had contacted to handle the injury case. Kind, patient, reflecting down home simplicity, they explored, questioned and investigated the nature of the circumstances. "Witnesses needed to be contacted, photos taken, and statements recorded. Time was of the essence," they elaborated. Although the lawyers were by no way famous, their professionalism was reflected in the extensive list of affirmed court cases. The locals didn't want to meet with this tiny well-appointed army of lawyers in the courtroom, as past wins tilted the scoreboard well on their side. "Hopefully," the shorter attorney added, "This can be settled out of court." The smartly dressed secretary took copious notes as the client replied to abundant questions, detailing as much as he could remember. Leaving two business cards, a legal pad, and several pens, the lawyer asked him to write down any additional points that might be helpful to the case. Shaking their heads in despair pointing to his broken ankle, they promised to be in touch soon.

Laying back his weary head, the patient laughed at himself, thinking out loud, that he had come to Jackson for one suit, but was leaving with two, each represented by a different firm. Life was unpredictable. That was the only thing he could count on.

The nurses had easily grown fond of the Cuban patient, who sneaked phone calls to his girlfriend back home. Empathetic, they knew the cure for his state of mind was hearing the voice of his lover. If nothing else, it made their jobs easier. A short chat with Juanita would assuage his pain for long periods of time, leaving the call bell untouched for hours. Because of the extent of the break, progress was slow. Discovering he was a diabetic would prolong the healing process. It was days before he could stand, and days after that before he could take a step. Annoying the nurses, he insisted on as many outings as they would allow. Leaving the hospital as quickly as possible was paramount on his mind.

After a nineteen-day stay, the doctors handed the patient a crutch, pronouncing he was well enough to leave. Immediately calling his lawyers, they told him to wait, and that a car would be sent right away to take him to the airport. Happily, he hopped into the wheelchair, wrapping the worn coat tightly around his torso, as the nurse rolled him down to the front entrance of the county hospital. The muddy van whisked him to the airport. Bombarded by questions, the two familiar faces from the Spence firm fettered over the health of their client. "I will be alright," he answered. "As soon as I land in my hometown."

This time, they promised, he would safely make it to the plane. They had taken the liberty of ordering a wheel chair. Taken aback by their thoughtfulness, saying thank you, seemed far from adequate for the care showered upon him.

"I can't thank you enough. I don't know any other words to express how I feel. Your help has been so great, and all I can say is thank you again," he professed. Waving goodbye to the lawyers, the airport attendant took his bag as he settled into the shiny steel wheelchair. Traversing the windy tarmac, the black ice had been replaced by scatterings of salt and de-icer. He slowly crawled up the ladder. The smiling stewardesses gave him a first class seat nearest the door, pampering the indigent passenger with drinks, food, and magazines. Leaning the crutch against the floor, he wrapped the thin blue blankets around his legs and stomach, and lay his head into the small spongy pillow. The aisle seat was occupied by a local rancher contemplating a few days of rest and relaxation in the lively town of Las Vegas. This time the trip was filled with continuous banter from Roberto, whose story easily filled the two-hour flight. Listening incredulously, the rancher was highly entertained with the saga Glancing out of the window, Roberto began to appreciate the beauty and the sense of freedom flying provided. The vast expanse of the continent could be taken in with an amazing perspective. How beautiful and bountiful America could be. Searching his soul, he knew this metaphor also included opportunity; that he had truly not taken advantage of all that America could be. Reverting his gaze back to his ankle, it was painfully clear he was in no shape to go in search of a job. In fact, he was in dire need of physical therapy. With no health insurance this was an impossibility; he would make do, simply learning to live with whatever pain or scars the break would leave. Intently listening to the captain announce it was time to buckle the seat belts in preparation for landing, he was anxiously ready to set foot on solid ground. He had missed Juanita, other friends, and even the crumby old motel room. Picking up his life, he would make the best of whatever was to come. The hopefulness, and prosperity promised by the Jackson law firm, perked up his future. Yes, he thought, I do have a future, and I should live as if I owned a piece of the future. Promising to improve himself, he hobbled off the plane to an awaiting wheelchair. Thoughtfulness had continually prevailed as Kerry was contacted by one of the dozens of Jackson lawyers, and stood prepared to take her crippled friend home.

"My goodness," she exclaimed. "Just look at you! Could you believe all this would happen? Sometimes I just wonder about your luck, but I think you are more like a cat with at least nine lives. You seem to survive anything."

Thanking his friend incessantly, he retold the ironic story of woe, crisscrossing from one lawsuit to the next. "I think I am the only person in this country who has two law suits going at one time, one with the Spence firm and another with a firm specializing in injuries," he chuckled. Although still in dire pain, the sight of his friend, and the warmth of the city cheered up his spirits.

"I called Juanita, and she will be over as soon as she finishes her shift," explained Kerry, "She really missed you, as we all did. We even said special prayers for your health in church on Sunday. We all think of you, and want you to get better."

"There so much I have to tell you. The law suits, how to handle my future. I will need your help and support. This is all too much for me," he admitted. "With my leg like this, I can't get a job. I don't know what the hell I am going to do. But on the other hand, the future looks bright with the impending cases going to court. Yet I still have to eat and live today."

"We will think of something, I promise you will not go without," she said as she parked the car in the empty motel lot. The front desk clerk had cleaned the room, removing all Roberto's personal articles to a locked closet, explaining that without money the room was rented out. Hanging his head deeply into his chin, the disappointment on his face could easily be detected. Kerry reached inside her heart and pocketbook and extracted the credit card that would magically perform the trick of reopening the closet and the room. Brushing away a slight mist of tears, he profusely thanked his friend, solemnly reminding her he would payback all the loans, with interest. Handing over several bags, the clerk walked them to the room, opened the doors, and offered to help rearrange the confiscated personal affects. Nodding, he again apologized, and wished him a good stay.

Kerry gave a quick glance at her Rolex, and kissed her companion goodbye, shaking a finger in the air, as if scolding a young child. "You do what the doctors ordered you to do, " she warned. "Keep your leg elevated, take your medicine, and try not to worry too much. You are not alone. You have lots of friends and we will all help you get through this ordeal. Maybe a nice quiet desk job," she joked, closing the creaky door behind her.

Alone, in his home, he had plenty of time to reflect on Kerry's words, and his future. With the injured leg, he couldn't think of any job he was suited for. Hard labor was the only type of job he had ever been able to get, and now, that would be an impossibility for several months. Although he had a strong command of the English language, his thick Spanish accent made conversation difficult, and the fact that he was an immigrant, not a citizen, made other positions unattainable.

What a mess life seemed to be. If ever he needed friends now was the time. No one was ever bored in the company of Roberto as conversation was filled with fascinating experiences and interspersed with a deep sense of values creating a character that both intrigued and mesmerized listeners. He spoke from strength not from weakness. His persona glowed with an inner light, capturing the most jaded men and women. It was as if he had a magnet that attached itself to the listener's heart; anyone meeting Roberto would walk away a better person; chastising themselves for ever complaining about life's tribulations. But all of these traits would not put bread on his table.

Looking at the local paper spread on top of the desk, he realized it was Friday; remembering the routine date with Alice at the bingo parlor, he truly intended to keep it. With no paycheck on this Friday, going to the casino was out of the question. It would be embarrassing to have her spot him a twenty for the evening Moping, he decided to meet Juanita at the car dealership. It would surprise her, and cheer him up. Still cool, he pulled on white athletic socks, and a hand me down Ralph Lauren windbreaker He grabbed some loose change and hopped the bus downtown. Roberto entered the rental company and sat patiently with the new walking cane. Juanita's wide smile signaled surprised as she walked out of the office and hugged her lover There was no hiding his dismay over the loss of income. A perfect lover and friend, she read the sobering signs his face was unable to conceal. Reaching into her wallet, she pealed off two ten-dollar bills, folding them in his right hand. "Now go," she demanded. "Meet your friend Alice, I will be busy tonight anyway. My sister needs help," she demurely lied. "Watching my sister's kid. You go and have fun. You can pay me back next week."

Shaking his head incredulously, he kissed those bountiful lips, thanked her again and again, and promised to win back every cent. Opening up the front door of the aging Chevy, she opted to take the main boulevard uptown. Friday night on the strip was the most exciting as the town filled up with raucous tourists. Neither uttered a word as they slowly crept up the congested noisy street. Juanita dropped him off at the corner of a busy intersection. He promised to call the moment reaching home. A short peck on the cheek was all the time heavy traffic would permit as he extricated himself quickly from the front seat. Adjusting the cane, he shuffled into the lively casino, and headed for the bingo parlor. Spying Alice in the smoking section, he flayed his arms in the air, and purchased two cards, taking an empty seat across from his companion. "I need luck tonight," he complained pointing to his injured leg. "Alice, you have to bring me luck tonight, here, blow on my cards."

Laughing, they spent the next two hours concentrating on their cards. So close, so many times, but no bingo. The smoky casino was filled with small time gamblers, all hoping to win the thousand dollar prize. A hush grew over the crowd as the numbers were pulled from the rotating bin. "And its number eight," declared the caller. Shocked, Roberto screamed out. "Bingo" There were times when Lady Luck was on his side, and tonight was that night. Verifying that the correct numbers were all covered, he was handed a chit, then limped over to the cashier. Counting out ten one hundred dollar bills he felt flush for the first time in months. Returning to the table, he handed Alice one of the bills explaining that so many times she had been generous to him, and now it was his turn. Insisting she take the bill, he dropped it down the front of her black V-neck sweater. Secure the money was in a safe place, he kissed her good night, and threatened to win again the following week.

# UNANSWERED QUESTIONS

It was during restless dreams that the nagging unanswered question resurfaced time and time again. "Where was the killer? Where had Franco gone? He couldn't have just vanished into thin air. And if he had died, I would have known." Over and over these thoughts turned in his mind. No one, not the police, nor any of his lawyers, had suggested searching for the true perpetrator of the crime. Exoneration would come if he could locate Franco, bringing him into the authorities, forcing them to hear the truth, forcing the guilty man to confess to the murder.

It was early Saturday morning as the desert sun crept into the darkness of the rented room. Unable to sleep, he looked down at his left ankle, now unencumbered with a cast, and realized the one thing he could do was drive. Looking at the pile of hundred dollar bills lying on top of the dresser, he realized there was ample money to take a short journey back to California. Calling Juanita, he suggested a surprise trip. She should be ready. He would pick her up in a few minutes. Still sleepy, she acquiesced to his mysterious proposal. Dressing slowly, as to not lose his balance, he took an extra sweater, his thin wallet, and a pair of sunglasses. Backing out the car, checking the gas gauge, he was set for the four hour drive to Los Angeles, and the Cuban community, where he would initiate a private investigation into the whereabouts of Franco. Although many thousands of Cubans encompassed the ghetto, it was a tight knit community. Everyone knew everyone else, or knew of someone who knew that person. Eventually, anticipated Roberto, he would locate the murderer. If he could do this, a chapter of his life could be officially closed forever. He would never be haunted by doubt. To him, this was more valuable than any money the lawsuits would reap.

Roberto honked the car horn. Juanita opened the small bedroom window, waving, then put her finger to her lips, signaling him to be quiet as her sister's baby was sleeping. Carrying a sweater, a thermos filled with coffee and a bag of jelly donuts, they drove southward through the desert toward Los Angeles. After an hour had passed, Roberto relayed the purpose of the trip. He feared Juanita would not wish to be a part of this investigation. "Be careful," she warned. "You might get yourself killed too. That's if you are lucky enough to find him. Besides, he might be dead for all you know. So much time. Fifteen, sixteen years have passed. Who knows if he is still around. A guy like that lives dangerously. Someone might have already taken his life."

"You might be right," he agreed, "But this has been driving me crazy. If the police don't look for him, then I will. I can't work. About the only thing I can do is drive a car. I figure if I put out the word that this guy is a killer, that he is a very dangerous person, maybe someone will turn him in. I want to at least try; you can appreciate that. If this guy surfaces and is brought to the police, his confession will finally exonerate me, and you know how much that means. Just believe in me. Lets just make an effort to find him, then I can sleep at night."

Unable to argue with the logic, she agreed to his plan, cautioning him not to do anything crazy, that he was in no shape to act like one of those private eyes on television. He was barely able to walk, let alone jump over walls and fly effortlessly through the air while accurately shooting off a pistol. Laughing, he reassured her it would just be simple talk. He would interview as many acquaintances as time allowed, putting out the word in the neighborhood that he was looking for a killer, that Franco was an evil man not to be reckoned with and the best place he could be was locked up tightly inside a jail cell. Murder for the sake of stealing a few items was intolerable; if he had done it once, for so little, he could have done it again, or might do it again. Convincing as many people as possible of. the evil nature of this killer might help to bring him to the surface. Someone would snitch. With no money as a reward, the fact that Franco might kill again might prove enough of an incentive to move someone to call the police. There was little time, and lots of work, anxiously he sped directly to the city of Angels, hoping one would land on his shoulder. Roberto did not care that close to two decades had passed, he was on a mission and logic was replaced by obsession.

Following the street signs, Juanita pointed out directions based upon the map hastily grabbed at the local grocery store. Overcast, the early afternoon stank of auto emissions and garbage cans overflowing with leftover food from weekend shoppers. Selecting a restaurant whose lot was sparsely filled with cars, they parked, and headed inside to use the facilities and eat an authentic Cuban meal. There was no doubt this was a rough neighborhood: the graffiti, drug paraphernalia, dilapidated store-fronts, and wandering homeless were blatant signs of an impoverished ghetto. Staring out the window, Juanita was shocked at the dilapidated neighborhood. Yes, she thought, Las Vegas had its bad areas, but nothing like Los Angeles — the poverty was astounding, so much, spread over so blocks, it seemed to go on forever. Grasping Roberto's thick hands, she prayed he knew what he was doing.

The steaming plates of food smelled like his grandparent's home. The marinated roasted chicken, the Spanish rice, and a rich bowl of beans tasted just like the Cuban recipes his grandmother cooked. Food this good was never prepared at his mom's home. They didn't have the money to buy the chicken, let alone have both soup and a main course. Picking up the last chicken leg, he gobbled down the meal in record time while Juanita played with her portion. Patting his stomach he told the waitress the food was delicious, and asked for two scoops of ice-cream. Shaking her head from side to side, Juanita turned down any additional food. She was too nervous to eat. Just sitting in the restaurant, occasionally glimpsing out the cracked window, reminded her where they were. She was anxious to leave the neighborhood as quickly as possible.

Opening up his usually thin wallet, Roberto looked at the expression on Juanita's face, she was surprised at the cash. Handing her a hundred dollar bill, he thanked her for her loan, and gave her a little extra. Vividly explaining his good luck, he assured her the two ten dollar bills had brought him all the good fortune. He reminded her that she was his good luck charm. "Lady Luck," he laughed gently squeezing her hand.

He paid the bill, and they walked directly to the car, and headed deeper into the Cuban ghetto. Driving through the crowded streets, it conjured memories of the places he had lived, and people he had met. A street sign, a store would help jar his memory. Pulling onto a side street, squinting at the faded signs precariously hung on the apartments, he hoped something would be familiar. Cruising slowly through street after street, he vigilantly scrutinized every building, anything that would remind him of his short stay. Patiently, Juanita sat in the car, pointing out anything that appeared to be of interest. Disappointed, Roberto suggested they spend the balance of the day at the beach. Referring to the map, they turned the car west, driving to the lively Santa Monica pier.

Both smiling at the sight of the ocean, Roberto remarked how beautiful Juanita looked when she was happy. The cool breezes of the Pacific Ocean smelled fresh. A taste of salt covered her lips as they kissed and cuddled on the clean beach. Sitting with his arm wrapped tightly around his lover, he realized how wonderful life could be; there were many moments worth living for. Looking at the scars on the left arm from three attempts to commit suicide, he was thankful to be alive, to love and to be free. If he were dead he wouldn't be able to enjoy the company of this beautiful woman, smell the sea breezes, eat delicious food, or feel loved. It was impossible to shove the past out of his memory even for a fleeting moment as the signs of jail life could be visibly detected from the physical scars along with the unseen signs of emotional scars. But he had slowly learned to enjoy life. This moment held a blissful place as a memory worth savoring.

The brilliant shades of orange and red lighting up the early evening sky reminded them the sun was setting and they should look for a place to stay. Arm in arm, the couple walked unsteadily to the car, Roberto's gait was uneven from months of pain and lack of physical therapy. As they were opening the car doors, Juanita spotted a motel directly across the street. Rather than bothering to drive further, they joined a huge crowd of pedestrians crossing the wide boulevard. Luckily, the desk clerk had two cancellations and happily gave them a room with no minimum stay. Placing the key in his hand, they walked back across the street, moving the worn car into the safety of the motel lot. Still stuffed from their Cuban meal, she suggested they have a drink on the wharf, then maybe he could take advantage of her, she suggested winking demurely.

The weekend brought masses of tourists and locals to the wharf; it was an ongoing carnival of rides, music and entertainment. The waitress brought over two glasses of draft beer, as they took a seat near the window of the bar watching the dusk turn into night, illuminating the glittery lights of the Ferris wheel. Conversations could be detected in numerous languages, and the noise level seemed to escalate with the appearance of a local jazz ensemble. Listening intently, they overheard several conversations in Spanish. One caught his ear as the dialect was reminiscent of Cuban speech. Turning his head, he introduced himself and inquired if the man had lived in Cuba, or if he was just visiting. Responding in Spanish, the middle-age gentleman explained he had lived in Los Angeles his entire life, and loved escaping to the beaches on the warm weekends.

Roberto told the stranger that he was looking for an old friend who would be living in the Cuban neighborhoods, and asked the stranger where one might begin searching. Pensively scratching his brown curly short beard, he began rattling off a list of streets. He paused to think, then continued listing several possible locations. Grabbing a cocktail napkin, Juanita copied down the information neatly, asking the proper spelling of some of the more difficult names. When the gentleman was finished, they had compiled a list of over twenty different locations. Asking the Cuban to join them in another beer, they exchanged names. "Jose Garcia," he said, shaking their hands. "It's a pleasure to meet you, especially such a beautiful young woman." The three of them lingered at the bar until Juanita coaxed Roberto into leaving. Hungry, she suggested they walk out to the boardwalk and grab a few hotdogs or freshly prepared burritos. Not one to argue, he excused himself, shaking hands, thanking Jose for all his help.

Munching on the bean burritos they agreed to call it a night. They would pick up the investigation in the morning. The rare treat of sleeping outside their humble apartments, put them in a romantic state. The smell of the salt-moistened air, the gentle slap of the waves hitting the beach, and the effects of one too many beers, added to their passions. One night of love-making with someone he loved, had been a constant dream on death row. Blinking, he wasn't sure if this was real or if he was back in the jail cell. To be confined in the tiniest of spaces for such an enormous amount of time, many lose sanity, or a part of their sanity. Housed like an animal, treated worse than any animal, that way of life, so ingrained in his conscious, often distorted perception. Not wanting the loving to end, he held Juanita tightly as if clinging for dear life. He needed her, needed her love, her compassion, her touch, her kisses. Gazing into those deep round eyes, she met his look with a wide smile and a deep kiss. "I love you," she whispered. "You are my hero."

Lying back he uttered a silent prayer that this deep passion would never end.

Sunday morning they arose to an overcast sky. The light gray clouds stubbornly wouldn't give up the sunlight until noon, so they packed up and headed back to the ghetto in search of Franco. Realistically, Roberto knew he might not find him, at least on the first try, but he wouldn't give up easily. Making simple inquiries and letting a few people know he was looking for Fernando might prove to shed light on his whereabouts. Roberto disregarded the idea that by now the killer might be dead. Until there was absolute proof of this, he would continue pursuit.

By midmorning, the sun had broken up the clouds in the downtown area, warming up the air and the streets. Pointing out an older Spanish shopping plaza, Juanita suggested stopping to browse, explaining this might be a good place to investigate.

Shop owners knew a lot of people. Hearing much local gossip they might be in a position to help find clues that would lead to finding Franco. Roberto busied himself chatting with the locals, while Juanita happily searched for gifts to bring back to her sister and baby. The booths were laden with brightly colored blankets, leather goods, hand painted clay pots, and endless pottery fashioned into various animals and fruits. Locating a lace shawl, she began bargaining with the young Mexican girl until they finally agreed upon a price. Proudly, she carried the bundle and went in search of her lover. Because it was early Sunday morning and most customers were attending mass, they had the street to themselves. In a moment, she spied Robert deeply involved in conversation with a rotund elderly Mexican man inside a small store crammed with art from the floor to the ceiling. She had never seen so much merchandise in such a tiny space. Feeling claustrophobic she waved, then stood at the doorstep waiting for Roberto to finish his conversation.

The reality of finding Franco was like looking for a needle in a haystack. Although she had to indulge her lover in his need to find the murderer, too much time had passed. She didn't want to discourage him, but he needed to be nudged into acknowledging the likelihood that finding this man after more than sixteen years might be unfeasible. Weighing the needs with the wants, she treaded on a delicate balance of encouragement with reality. Never one to nag or disparage, she would follow his lead until obsession or danger was imminent.

Meeting Juanita in the sunlight, Roberto appeared disturbed and agitated as the possibility of locating Fernando seemed an impossibility. The shop owner explained the neighborhood had changed over the last two decades. The Cubans had moved toward the center of the city leaving their homes for other ghetto inhabitants. Finding someone from so long ago would be difficult at best. Immediately after the trial, Roberto was told that Fernando had left Las Vegas for Los Angeles. It only made sense that Fernando would choose to live among Cubans. But, this was so long ago. Visualizing the murderer, Fernando's well chiseled torso, sharp jaw line, the dark curly hair worn shortly cropped, and his eyes, so deeply set into his skull, Roberto understood this description would hardly be accurate of the same man today. Wondering if he would be able to recognize Fernando when so much time had elapsed, put a thorn in his goal. With the possibility of a name change the potential to unearth him became more remote. He kicked himself for spending all those years in jail, without ever pushing the lawyers to find the true murderer.

With deep disappointment, he suggested they pack it in and drive back to town before the Sunday evening rush began. Taking his hand, Juanita asked for one more moment as she purchased a puppet clothed in Mexican velvet for her nephew. Both of Juanita's hands were overloaded with packages. Roberto joked it was time to leave anyway since she couldn't carry another item. Hugging her, he grabbed the bulky parcels so she could barter for the last purchase. Seated in the car, she was bursting with excitement from all her purchases, boastfully relaying the story of how she had bargained for each and every one. Laughing to himself, he knew the four-hour ride home would pass quickly.

As Roberto was lying on the bed in the rented motel room, he realized money was running out, and with his bum leg getting a job would be difficult if not utterly impossible. He wasn't scared, but living on the streets became the only viable alternative he might have. Tossing off his clothes, he took a long lazy shower anticipating there might be days when he wouldn't have this luxury. The warm water cascading down his limbs relaxed his mood causing his mind to drift to the romantic moments with Juanita. He realized how lucky he was to have a woman willing to put up with his poverty and financial insecurity. Clearly she loved him for who he was. The simple unaffected, pure love they shared would take them into the future for many decades to come. Juanita did not want children. Living with the daily reminder of her sister's trepidations of feeding and caring for an infant was more than she could contend with. Between her and Roberto, just taking care of their basic needs was more than they could financially muster. Besides, he had his share with three children. Smiling, he sometimes whimsically imagined what his lover would look like pregnant with child; large breasts, and a huge rotund stomach. Not a pretty sight, he chuckled. For now, their relationship was perfect, each willing to give and take as necessary. They saw each other often, but not everyday, keeping their dates together fresh and filled with anticipation. Always sporting a radiant smile, Juanita was his ideal mate. He would love her until the day he died.

Flipping on the television, he fell deeply asleep to the sounds of a Spanish movie. The answers to all his worries always seemed less pressing in the crispness of the warm desert morning.

Meanwhile back at the ranch, and in this case it truly was, the Spence law team was assembling their case in meticulous fashion. Knowing this precedent would snake through the legal system at a snail's pace, they diligently gathered all necessary materials in preparation for hearings. The constant reminder of, "fourteen years on death row" added momentum to the case serving as fuel for future appeals. One million per year was a paltry amount to sue for, yet the firm did not want to be greedy, nor ask for such an exhorbant amount of money that no judge would grant the claim. Although money would be the main issue and Roberto's consolation for wrongful imprisonment, the grant for complete exoneration was the ultimate goal.

The lengthy list of defendants accumulated each day as more facts were gathered. Starting with the arresting police officers, to the district attorney's office, to the public defender's office, the string of improprieties committed along each step of the nightmare constituted the basis for the case. Knowing the panel of federal judges might disqualify or excuse some defendants, the lawyers prepared a hefty, imposing list. In 1998, the firm filed a formal lawsuit against the State of Nevada citing the Clark County public defender's office and two former detectives as the defendants. The fifty-two page complaint named Morgan Harris, head of the public defender's office, along with Thomas Rigsby and two former detectives, Robert Leonard and Michael Maddock. Although the focus of the lawsuit was the inept performance of Rigsby, public defender, the other parties had a hand in the wrongful imprisonment. The suit elaborated the hardships and mental destruction suffered. "Extreme emotional physical and economic damage as a result of the violation of constitutional rights," and asked for damages of lost wages, loss of future earning capacity, medical expenses, past and future emotional and physical pain and suffering, and loss of enjoyment of life. In addition there were punitive damages demanded, none of which could fairly add up to the destruction of a life by an unfair legal system.

This initial suit shook up the legal system of Clark County, rattling the core and the validity of those in power. Las Vegas is a town based on tourism, and negative publicity was the worst thing that could happen in a city that purports family values and pleasure seekers. From the mayor down to the street cop, everyone wanted this lawsuit to roll up and go away, but the relentless team of lawyers would never let this happen. They assured their client he would have his day in court no matter how long it took. The presentation of the initial lawsuit met with a partial denial and some names being revoked from the list. Although this did not surprise the team, they went back to the drawing board, resubmitting the case given the thirty day limit by federal Judge. Holding all public officials accountable for their actions was at the heart of the suit. When entrusted with power given by the people, it is to be used for the people. In this situation there was abuse of power from the beginning to the end of the case; it was time to make all those accountable. From afar, it would seem as if a conspiracy had taken place. Each level of the legal system acted in total disregard for the rights of the accused. If nothing else, the suit served as a wake-up call to all levels of legal enforcement. The message clearly stated that being poor or an immigrant does not make one guilty.

Unafraid of negative publicity, the Las Vegas Journal reported the case in a balanced manner, stating both sides of the lawsuit. The article pictured Roberto being hugged by Janalee of the Rising Sun Ministries. He was treated with dignity and respect in the press. The saga did not bode well for the city, and perhaps Carri Geer, the writer of the news releases, sensed this, yet the presentation of facts led any follower of the story to have a sympathetic position for Roberto. The city, county, and the state would have to pay for the mess some of the employees had been privy to, but this was a small price to pay had the death row inmate been wrongfully executed. The publicity for the possibility of that error might have cost the state untold millions in revenue, and bad public relations. The top officials of Nevada are keenly aware of how their bread gets buttered — tourism, and allowing anti-death penalty marchers down the city streets would reap havoc on the image and goals that make the State of Nevada financially sound.

This lawsuit would not go away. With the press observing every twist and turn, the reporters wanted the public to be aware of the salience and the ramifications. A year later the same journalist headlined a story: "Much of Miranda Lawsuit Rejected," again picturing a flattering photo of the subject standing outside the meager apartment. The story reported that much of the suit had been rejected by a federal judge, but the Spence firm would be appealing to the 9th U.S. Circuit Court of Appeals in San Francisco. Quoting directly from Spence, the story unveiled the humanistic base of the suit; "We pray that court will see it differently. If ever there was a case that cried out for justice, this is it. And it's not just for Roberto. It's for all those people who end up in that situation. He is a man who, if anybody in this country has ever been treated unjustly, has been treated unjustly." Ironically, the story had nothing new to report. Nothing had changed in the case in over a year, yet this journalist kept the story fresh and ongoing in the public eye.

Roberto obtained a job at another car rental company. As time had trudged on he eked out a substandard living returning to detailing and cleaning cars. It was important that a paycheck was made each week, he wanted to take care of himself and Juanita, but the weekly wages barely covered the rent. Not forgotten by Kerry, Alice and Janelee, who continued to support him through gifts of food, second-hand clothing, and furniture, Roberto was able to survive. Kerry continually reminded the pastor of the church to make a plea for donations, while she and her husband persisted with their weekly support.

It was late on Monday evening when Kerry phoned Roberto

and asked to meet for ice-cream at their usual coffee shop. Cognizant that he was hard pressed for funds, she did not want him to end up out on the street again, so she cashed a check, enough that would cover the rent for the coming months, wrapped it in an envelope, and prepared to hand it over. Pride was a portion of his ego she did not wish to offend, yet no one wanted him sleeping on the streets. It was simple. She cared a great deal. He was an easy person to love, and she wanted him safe and comfortable. Greeting her with a broad smile, he slid into the bright red booth. Disregarding the menu, he ordered coffee and double scoops of chocolate ice-cream. It had been a couple of weeks since they met, and they both became quickly lost in conversation. Sharing the latest correspondence from the law firm, she again reminded him to have patience. This suit would take a long time to resolve, but when that time arrived, it will have been well worth the wait.

"Kerry," he solemnly initiated. "At the rate this case is going, I might be dead. I need to make a will, to establish who would receive the money from the suit in case I am not around when it finally is settled."

Taken aback, Kerry's cocked head and disparaged look reflected her shock at his suggestion, yet he did have a point. If there were no person named, who would reap the financial rewards of the case but the state. "You know, " she acknowledged. "You have a very good point, and I agree with you." Pulling out a rumpled sheet torn from a legal pad, she copied down his updated requests: money to his family in Cuba, money to Juanita, money to Kerry, and contributions to Janelee's church. Paying close attention, Kerry promised to type the document, have it notarized, sending a copy to both sets of lawyers in Wyoming. Although they had previously discussed the allocation of funds, neither had formalized it.Looking into his eyes, she sensed a sadness that had not been present in their last meetings together. Without saying the words, it was clear to both of them that time was running out. His ability to enjoy life, to relish in the enjoyment of carefree living was slipping away from his reach as each day passed. So much of his life had wasted away; he had lost patience, and at times hope that the case would be solved in a timely manner.

Opening up her beige pocketbook, she extracted the cash, whispering that it might help him pay the rent. Taking his hand, she placed the small envelope in the middle of his palm and offered her usual wide smile. She would never understand how difficult his life had been. He could sit for hours explaining what life was like living on death row, and she would listen intently, and empathetically, yet she would not truly comprehend how he felt. She once bought a cage for her dog, but was unable to place her in it, deeming it too cruel. As the words rolled off his tongue detailing the size of the cell, the daily hunger, the middle of the night screams from other inmates, Kerry wondered how Roberto summoned the resolve to stay alive. Searching her soul, she knew she would never survive such an ordeal. It was easy to understand why her friend had tried suicide so many times. It was not easy to understand how he mustered the strength to stay alive. Perhaps this was the attraction — Roberto represented an inner strength so profound that he could never be shaken. Listening to him elaborate jail life, she tried to compare him to all the hundreds of people who had crossed her path, and no one even came close to having the qualities he encompassed.

Emotionally exhausted from the meeting, she dropped two dollars on the table, picked up the check, and pecked a kiss on her friend's cheek, as she extricated herself from the plastic covered booth. Parting in the parking lot, she turned on the engine, while the tears trickled down her glistening skin. Overwrought, she pledged to continue fighting for his cause, making sure none of the lawyers nor the legal system would sweep this case under the carpet. She would make noise, stir the press, appeal to the anti-death penalty groups, anything to maintain the interest and keep it in the limelight. Circling the car around the parking lot, she waved as Roberto pulled his dilapidated used car from the parking lot, slowly creeping onto the boulevard.

Waiting for the glow of the late afternoon sun to cast a shadow over the dining room, Kerry lit a match to dimly illuminate the Thanksgiving table. Surveying her handiwork, she was thoroughly satisfied with the décor; the cream colored fluted dinner plates from England, the ornate sterling silver from Germany, the finely beveled French crystal glasses, and the delicate Swedish crocheted table linens, sumptuously set the scene for her favorite holiday. She celebrated this occasion with more rituals and decorum than any other holiday, even more than the traditionally religious Lutheran Christmas. The purpose of the holiday was based upon sharing, kinship, hope, faith, and the adventure of a new country, all values any American could celebrate with understanding and commitment. She had warned her husband she would not be taking the usual chair at the other end of the table. That would be reserved for the guest of honor, Roberto. He had rarely come to their home, and she wanted to make him feel welcome, loved, but mostly important, that his life mattered and that he was appreciated. Preparing the turkey, she glanced at her watch and vividly remembered her guest should arrive at four, but her watch read almost five. Worried, she phoned his apartment; no answer, she continued for another half hour and still there was no answer. Something was very wrong.

During the last month, Roberto had again found himself unemployed as the rental business had slowed down to a standstill. He was one of the first let go. November was the slowest month of the year for this type of business as the usual throng of visitors to the city stayed at home for the Thanksgiving Holiday. Having used his last cent to pay the rent, he was now homeless, again. Unable to budget, as soon as Roberto cashed his paycheck it was gone. He simply did not anticipate that he would lose his job, and had not put back any money. Carting the last package into his car, Roberto left the motel, now officially homeless. The rent money was due and without a job, or a decent prospect in sight, he simply could not stay. Begging the desk clerk to allow a few extra days, by noting the severity of the weather, and the fact it was a holiday, the clerk obstinately refused to oblige, stating that he wasn't running a charity organization. It was a business, and if his boss knew he had allowed a customer to stay without paying, his butt would in a sling. With no options, Roberto left the motel and cruised the streets hoping to come up with a quick solution. The warmth of the late afternoon was quickly replaced by the severe cold of the cloudless evening sky. Living out of the car, Roberto rifled through his belongings, pulling out a ripped quilt and an old dirty blanket, these would provide the only shelter from the autumn cold. Opening the car door, he carried the blankets to the nearest park bench, and pulled them tightly around his neck and feet, then twisted around so he could fall asleep under the twinkling stars. The autumn evenings in the desert were chilly. He would not be able to live in these elements for long as winter was beckoning, promising bitter cold temperatures. Either the cold or pure exhaustion set in, and allowed him to become immersed in a deep sleep.

Roberto was too proud to stay with Juanita, and too ashamed to ask Kerry for another handout. He would make do for the moment.

A sharp jarring jab hit deeply into his ribs. "Get up you vagrant," shouted a police officer. "Got any identification? Let me have it," he kept shouting. Completely disorientated, Roberto was terrified, unsure if he was still sleeping or awake. Groggy, he reached for his wallet, but the officer screamed for him to put his hands in the air.

"My wallet is in my pocket. If you want to see my ID, that's were it is," he stuttered.

"Please get up, and drop your wallet on the ground so I can examine it." Without further intercourse, Roberto pushed back the frayed blankets, unsteadily stood, then extracted the wallet from the back pocket of his trousers. Examining the sleepy man's credentials, the cop barked again, and ordered him to get inside the police wagon. He would be taken to the county lock up.

"But why?" the vagrant screamed. "I have done nothing wrong. I have not hurt anyone. Please just leave me alone."

"We have our orders," was the cop's only response.

Locked up in an old-fashioned paddy wagon, Roberto, along with three other vagrants, were taken to the all too familiar county jail. The conversation inside the van was fraught with anger and resentment, as the men shouted to the driver to cut them some slack. After all, it was a holiday, and they just wanted to be left alone. Roberto was mute during the short ride to the county lock-up. Fearing reprisal, he kept his feelings to himself. Unlatching the door, the cop escorted the motley group as they descended into the bowels of the jail. Nervously turning his head looking in every direction, Roberto's memories of the place resurfaced. The building had changed little, if at all, from his initial stay: the floors, still gray, the walls still were wearing the same washed out color, the radiating overhead lights still lighting the hallway, and the bellows of incarcerated men begging to be released. Collecting his nerves, he ordered himself to be calm, that this was just overnight He would be released in the morning, pending the cops finding a valid reason for him to stay. But he was not charged with any crime, merely lifted off the streets away form the view of the public. He was not alone. This time he had a small army of friends and lawyers watching over his rights: Spence, Alice, Kerry and Janelee.

Following the uniformed guard the men relinquished all personal property at the front desk, then were somberly walked to a holding cell. Again loudly protesting, the clerk explained he could be held overnight without cause. "Without cause," Roberto rebutted. "This is America, they can't just arrest you for no reason."

"That's right without cause. I suggest you contact your lawyer," he cynically remarked. "But since its Thanksgiving, I doubt anyone will come to get you out."

"Oh my goodness. It's Thanksgiving," he cried, because he suddenly remembered where he was supposed to be. "Please, can I make one phone call?" With tears in his eyes, he dialed Kerry's number and elaborated his unending tail of woe with the legal system. There was nothing which could be done until the next morning, and he was extremely apologetic he could not make it to her house for the holiday. They had not spoken in a couple of weeks, and Kerry was unaware that her dear friend was homeless.

Angry beyond reproach, Kerry swore that someone would pay for this mistake. It's not a crime to sleep on a park bench. Even in New York, the homeless are treated with respect. When the cold weather settles in, vans are sent throughout the city to take the vagrants to warm shelters where food, water, and beds were available. But here in Las Vegas the police arrest the homeless taking them directly to jail. Maybe it doesn't look nice for a passerby to see a person snoring on a park bench, but that does not make it illegal, it just makes it uncomfortable for the onlooker. True the city thrives on tourism, but it must also address humanism, and the needs of all who live in town. Reflecting on the unfairness of the situation, Kerry would use this arrest as fire to light Spence's case.

Promising to arrive early the next morning, she assured her friend she would be there to get him out. Then she sent a scathing letter to the lawyers in Wyoming. The harassment had to stop. The police were no less relentless in their aggression than the Communist tactics used by the Cubans. Kerry would have Spence send letters, or do something, anything to stop the harassment of this poor pathetic man. Crying herself to sleep, she thanked God for her family, their health, and prayed for speedy outcome of Roberto's case.

Pacing the floor of the tiny cell, Roberto would spend the sleepless night waiting for the sun to awaken the city and allow him to be freed from this hideous jail. Living through the one night without privacy, his self-esteem plummeted to its lowest depths. Without a job, or a home, he was emotionally lost, life had become unstable, and completely insecure. Listening to the snores of the other homeless, he admired their ability to actually sleep in the midst of such inhumane conditions, but for some it was a bed and a toilet they would not ordinarily have access to. Reaching deep into his inner strength, he gathered momentum needed to endure the next few hours until his release. He had to have a plan, a goal that would keep him directed and back on a more positive life. Without a watch, he wasn't aware of the time. He would have to follow the sun's path to estimate when morning would arrive. That was answered quickly as the rattle of the guard's keys unlocked the cell and allowed him and one other vagrant free. Directing them to the clerk's office, they collected their possessions quickly, and quietly departed.

Kerry met him, and gave him a quick peck on the cheek. "I am taking you out for breakfast," she said. And with that, she took his hand, and walked to her car. They drove to a local coffee shop where Roberto ordered a substantial meal of pancakes, bacon and eggs. "I didn't know you were out on the streets," she quietly said. "I wish you would have told me. Jim and I would have made room for you, at least through the holiday."

"I can't always be asking for money," he said. "I would not even ask Juanita. I feel too embarrassed."

Reaching into her pocketbook, Kerry extracted a wad of bills and the IOU. He thankfully took the money, and signed his name. "You know I will pay you back, and with interest," he noted.

Putting the IOU back into her purse, Kerry opted to keep the conversation light. She did not want him to see her anger or her pity. Yet, she did not want to treat him as if he were a child who was incapable of caring for himself. Aware his brittle self-esteem would be easily shattered, she talked about innocuous subjects.

"I will be fine," he assured her. "This money should help me find a place to stay for a while." The usually crowded coffee shop was quiet, as few people got up early to eat a big breakfast the day after Thanksgiving. They had plenty of time and privacy to continue a lengthy conversation. Checking her watch, Kerry, who had a pressing appointment, motioned for the check, and the two departed. The overcast sky reflected Roberto's somber mood, as she dropped him off near his car. Turning around, he pulled off a parking ticket left written by the traffic cops. "Give it to me," Kerry yelled. "I will take care of this."

Friday, he thought, without altering his routine he would meet Alice at the casino for a rousing game of bingo. Patting his shirt pocket, he would use some of the money Kerry had given him to enjoy a night out, and then he would find a place to stay. Collecting his thoughts, he turned over the car engine and slowly drove to Juanita's home. She would welcome him with open arms, and hopefully allow him to take a lengthy shower. Knocking on the door, Alicia opened it with the baby in her arms, "Juanita is at work, " she explained. "But you are free to come in, I am so sorry about your Thanksgiving. Kerry called her late last night and told us what happened, we all feel terrible. Those cops, they just refuse to let you alone."

"Thanks," mumbled Roberto. "Do you mind if I take a shower?"

"Just make yourself at home," Alicia commanded. "I have to take the baby to the doctor. I will see you later."

With the tiny one bedroom apartment to himself, he felt as if he were in a castle. The scattered clothes, dirty dishes piled high in the kitchen sink, and unmade bed, reminded him of his own apartment. Undressing, he pulled clean clothes from one of the plastic bags, stepped into the bathtub, and took a long soapy warm shower. This was the best he had felt in days. Dressing carefully, he left a note for Juanita explaining what had occurred, that he would be going to his usual Friday nightspot and would see her early the next day. But first he would surprise her by cleaning the entire apartment, a job that would keep him busy until it was time to meet Alice. Rolling up the sleeves of the cotton shirt, he turned on the kitchen tap and proceeded to scrub the room from top to bottom. He dusted, mopped, scrubbed the bathroom, changed the sheets, and hung up the clothes. Turning off the lights, he smiled at his handiwork, wondering if the sisters would think they were in the wrong apartment, or a fairy godmother had come to visit.

Refreshed, he fumbled through his pant's pockets locating the car keys, then turned the car north toward the casino. No matter how depressed he felt, walking into the bingo parlor always rejuvenated his spirits. Whether it was the bright flashing lights, the live music, the sounds of people yelling and conversing, or the pretty young waitresses, the carnival atmosphere was enlivening. Walking with his usual hobbling gait, he met Alice wearing a broad smile, and gave him a tender peck on his freshly shaved cheek. Knowing the amount of his ready cash, he opted to purchase two cards tonight instead of the usual four. This would allow the few dollars left to last a bit longer. Seated across from each other they chatted about the past week. But it wasn't until later that evening when Roberto finally told Alice the complete distressing account of his homeless week. Listening intently, she was overwhelmed with pity for her friend; it hurt her to see him so miserable. Excusing herself from the table she said she would return briefly. Taking the oversized purse, she exited the parlor and entered the softly illuminated ladies' room. Oblivious to the noisy surroundings, she extracted her the cell phone and dialed her ex-husband, explaining to him that she was taking over the empty trailer. He had no use for it, he was living with another woman, and if he ever wanted to see any alimony, he would never return to the trailer. Because she was the family breadwinner, running the appliance contracting business, her ex-husband did not feel the need to work. He obtained an excellent lawyer, and Alice got the short end of the stick. She was forced to pay alimony each month. "Such a bum," she would often mutter to herself. It did not surprise her that he quickly agreed to her demands. He had treated her so poorly, and now with the divorce final, and monthly checks arriving, he would do nothing to aggravate the situation. If she could give Roberto a home, that would solve numerous problems. A permanent address, a safe place to eat sleep a mail box, and a place he could truly feel at home would help salvage his life. Elated, she burst out of the bathroom. She walked purposefully toward her companion, grabbed his arm, and dragged him to the coffee shop where she bought his favorite dessert and a cup of coffee

"I wish to offer you my trailer to live in," Alice vivaciously suggested. "It's on the east side of town. It's spacious, needs lots of work, but at least you would have a place to call your home until you get yourself together." She hoped he would take the offer. "This isn't charity. It's just what I wish to do to help out my good friend. Besides, I loved telling my ex-husband what to do. That jerk made me suffer, now it's my turn to see him squirm a little," she heartily joked.

Startled, Roberto hardly knew what to say. Sitting quietly, digesting the offer, he was feeling blessed and speechless. Taking Alice's hand he thanked her. "You are another angel God has sent to save me," he professed. "I will never be able to repay you or thank you enough for your kindness. Of course I would love to live in the trailer."

"Then it's settled. I want you to follow me. It is just one block from my house. As soon as we finish up our bingo cards we will go," she suggested.

Grinning, he simply nodded his head with approval, gobbled down the last bites of the melted ice-cream, and the two departed the café. Hobbling, he pushed his legs to keep up with his tenacious friend as she wound her way through the aisles of gamblers plugging quarters into the slot machines. His mind still reeling from the fact he would have a home, a place to live without worries, he had not really thanked Alice. In the future, he would make sure her kindnesses were matched, but today all he could handle was accepting whatever charity came his way. Entering the smoke-filled bingo hall, they played out the last hands of their cards. Alice had been lucky tonight, winning twenty dollars, while her partner didn't fare as well. Handing Roberto a few dollars, he purchased several more rounds in hope of breaking even. Tonight he would walk away indebted to Alice, not only for her contributions to his losing streak, but providing a place to stay. The animated smile and lilt in her voice expressed her sheer joy at giving a friend a chance at life. The homeless life would devastate Roberto, as it would any human. She was truly blissful for being able to help another person, a person she loved, in such a meaningful way. The saying, "It is better to give than receive," was a huge part of who Alice was, an infinitely good individual whose empathetic heart could respond genuinely to the needs of a close friend. She did not want Roberto to feel as though this was purely charity; she did it out of her love for him, and her passionate soul. She did not wish to see this special man suffer anymore.

"Shall we call it a night?" suggested Alice. "Besides I am anxious to get you into your new home."

"You are the boss," conceded Roberto.

Handing back the bingo cards, they walked to the parking garage. Alice would wait for Roberto to meet her at the exit, and then he would follow her home. He remembered they would be traveling directly east. It was incredibly easy to lose one's sense of direction in the huge circular garages, so she waited until she spied her friend's jalopy in the rear view mirror, and then eased her car onto the congested street. The traffic signals were so long around the strip area, there was plenty of time to catch up if his puttering car should slow down. Heading east on Flamingo, the home of numerous world class restaurants, they convoyed toward the mountains until after miles of traffic signals, she signaled left, and drove north towards the air force base. The distant glitter of the downtown lights marked the vastness of the city. Near the air base, still within the city limits, the landscape had drastically changed from towering buildings to endless, flat, arid desert. The night sky appeared vividly clear, the stars and moon giving off illumination in opposition to the neon lights of downtown. With few streetlights to guide the way, Roberto paid close attention not to lose Alice's car. It was such a long drive; so remote from the lively downtown. Hardly anything was stirring except for the distant calls of the coyotes. Signaling again, he followed her down a gravel road, and parked in front of a metal gate. Reaching into her pocket, she poked a small key into a padlock, opening the chain link fence. Pointing to the large mobile home, she turned toward Roberto announcing, "This is your new home for as long as you care to stay." Handing him the key, she gave him the complete tour. "All the power is on, including the telephone. Garbage pick-up is twice a week, and if you look around there is no grass to water, " she laughed. "Please feel free to fix the place up, it could stand a paint job, and kitchen improvements, and the outside could use some tender loving care. But mostly, enjoy this space, it's your home now, make it comfortable."

Intently examining the large space he was overwhelmed with gratitude, "I don't know when or how I can ever repay you, but I swear I will. It's great, so much room, and a washer and dryer. The place is wonderful. I know I will feel safe and happy here, and will try and fix it up as much as possible," he promised.

Kissing him gently on the cheek she left. She again reminded him that her home was only two blocks away, and if he ever needed anything she would be there quickly. Waving goodnight, he bounded toward his car and pulled out all his bags and stuffing them in the mobile home. Exhausted, he located two quilts, plopped down on the floor and went promptly to sleep. It was too late to call Juanita. He would phone her first thing in the morning and tell her the good news. Even though he was a few miles away from her apartment, they would finally have a place to be together, alone, without interruptions. In his dreams he was visited by an angel, whose identity closely resembled Alice's. He thanked her with flowers, and the sweet smell of bushels of rose petals, then watched as she flew away, disappearing into the cumulus stark white clouds of the morning.

The autumn morning sun snuck into his cozy room through the plastic tinted windows. Rubbing his eyes, he reached for his watch. He was startled that he had slept past nine. Jolting up from the floor he washed up, then called his sweet heart relaying the good news about his newly acquired home. Juanita was overjoyed her lover had a place to stay, and could no longer be considered homeless, although she had a jealous nature tugging at her heartstrings. Wondering why Alice would be so generous, she could only guess that perhaps Alice was in love with Roberto, too. "I am going to pick you up and bring you to my new home," he happily insisted.

Not one to quibble, she was all too happy to see the new place. The animation in his voice marked a much happier man, no longer sleeping on the city streets. His self-esteem had a chance to recover. Unwrapping many of the plastic garbage bags, he carefully arranged the scant possessions throughout the empty mobile home. There was ample space for the few items he had carried from the apartment. Looking at the empty bedroom floor, his first task would be to find a mattress. Remembering a Salvation Army Store nearby, he would inquire if there was a used mattress that would be thrown away. His next thought was to phone Kerry the worry wart. Delighted to hear his voice, she again referred to the empty seat at the Thanksgiving table, how he should have been there enjoying the meal and the family instead of penned up at the local jail. "I promise you," she spoke. "Next year, you will have dinner with us, and it will be wonderful. You will never again see the inside of a jail cell. I have sent letters to Spence making sure this will not happen again. I am thrilled to know you have a place to stay."

"I would like to show it to you shall we meet Monday at the usual coffee shop and then you can follow me over here. I am very happy to live in such a large space, although it is far from the middle of the city. But for now, I am very appreciative for a roof over my head."

Roberto collected his keys, and drove over to pick up Juanita thinking how lucky he was to have all these women shower him with so much love and attention. Turning over the engine, the car sputtered down the gravel road heading south toward Juanita's home. The crisp fall air woke up his senses as he anticipated showing off his new home to his lover and his friends.

Kerry was so relieved that Roberto had made it out of the jail unscathed she requested another drive at the Lutheran Church to help him out. She could readily guess without seeing his new place he would be in need of most everything. The pastor was more than happy to make the announcement, and Kerry was more than happy to cart all the donations over to her friend's new home. After morning services, many parishioners promised to help out, and true to form they did. By the end of the weekend her driveway was teaming with bags dumped off by an endless parade of well-wishers. Remembering the meeting the next day, she filled up the back of the van with the bags, in anticipation of surprising her needy friend. Her heart swelled with love as she stuffed the trunk with bundles of necessities, thinking this would help him survive.

The next afternoon, Kerry, dressed in casual jeans and a soft suede jacket, and met Roberto at the coffee shop. "Kerry," he admitted. "I am truly hungry, hope you don't mind if I order a hamburger."

"Of course not," she answered, "Besides it's much too cold to eat ice-cream. Now, tell me all about your new home. Has Juanita been there? Do you have heat? How about a phone? Where do you do your laundry?"

"Too many questions," he laughed. "You women are all the same. You worry too much."

Voraciously gobbling the burger and fries, Kerry dropped the money on the table, and trailed Roberto out of the café. She carefully followed her friend to his new home. The pitifully long journey made her antsy as they managed to stop at every single intersection, but finally, the sounds of the jets from the nearby air base, marked their eminent arrival. Signaling, he turned onto a gravel road drove three houses down parking in the middle of a vast open lot. Emerging from the car he spread his arms widely proudly showing off his new home.

Kerry was truly impressed, noting how much land; he had a full acre She was thrilled for him. Opening up the door, he toured her through the mobile home. She noted what he needed, and he noted what he had been given. Hugging him, she took his hand, stating that she had a surprise. Walking out to the van, she punched the remote, and opened the large truck loaded with gifts and donations. Holding back tears she demurely stated, "Donations from my church. They all wish you well, and keep you in their prayers. Now come on, lets get this stuff into your new home."

"My goodness," he shouted. "You are going to fill up this place. I thought I had lots of room, but with all this stuff, there may not be any space left. I don't know how to thank you and all your friends at the church."

"We all love you. Anyone who has ever met you loves you. This was from our hearts. All we want is for you to be safe, and stay as far from that jail cell as possible. We understand you are in no position to get a job; you can hardly walk. No one wants to see you sleeping in the streets. You don't deserve to live like that after all you have suffered through." Scrutinizing every nook and cranny she pronounced, " This location truly suits your needs.

It's far away from the bad element downtown. I can see this will be a safe place for you." Opening up her purse, she handed him one hundred dollars in cash, suggesting he use the money to help fill up the refrigerator.

"You know I can't ever repay for your kindness. Maybe some day I can return all the money I have borrowed, but never, not ever, will I be able to give you the care and charity you have given me," he said. Taking her hand he gently brushed her cheek with a kiss.

Overjoyed for her friend, Kerry returned the kiss, and hugged him goodbye. Overcome with emotion she dared not let Roberto see the tears welling up in the corners of her eyes. She needed to be strong. She did not want him to think she cared for him out of pity. This relationship was so difficult, at times she felt she needed to direct him while at other times her heart ached for the horrible suffering he had to endure. She did not want him to think their friendship was based solely upon his neediness. It was symbiotic, he gave her an appreciation of life and caused her to not take all her good fortune for granted. Collecting her purse, she jotted down his phone number, then deftly walked down the metal steps out the front door, yelling out she would return soon. Driving out of the arid treeless lot, she brashly pulled out a handful of tissues and cried profusely into the mound of ruffled white sheets. It hurt her so much to see this man suffer. She loved him as she would of a brother. Searching her soul, she knew there was only so much she could do, so many plans had been set into action, all that could be done was wait. Both she and Roberto were impatient. They wanted the case settled so he could enjoy whatever time he has left on earth.

Picking up the money, he was reverently thankful. But he vacillated how he should spend the sum. While working, he dutifully sent cash home monthly to his mother and eldest sister. Fifty dollars would buy a lot of necessities in the Cuban black market. Or he could use the money to purchase additional necessities for the mobile home Weighing both options, he stuffed half the money into an envelope, addressed it to his mom, and walked out to the mailbox. Out of work for months on end, he hadn't been able to give her anything at all. It was time to take care of the one who had taken care of him. He loved his family dearly and this was the only way he could demonstrate love. Even though he had not earned the money, it enhanced his waning self-esteem to be able to provide for his family. It was more important for him to give to his family, than to spend on himself. He knew Kerry might be angry that he had not used all the money on himself, but she never put restrictions on the money. He was a man. He could make the responsible decisions. He imagined the IOU list stretching out for miles and miles. "How will I ever repay Kerry and Alice back?" was a question for which he could not answer.

# A SHORT JOURNEY
# TO THE MOUNTAINS

Time edged forward with little news of the pending lawsuit. All that was settled thus far was a list of who would not be allowed in the suit, whittling down the defendants to a scant few. He had received letters from time to time apprising him of the appeals, and all the activity occurring on the case, but there were no giant breakthroughs, and no settlements. Faith kept him going, he knew the firm was tenacious, that they would fight for as long as it took to win the case. The battalion of brilliant minds would never allow this precedent to lie in wait, they investigated every legal option, nothing escaped their scrutiny when it came to winning. All he could do was sit and wait, praying for a resolution.

Life was unpredictable, as he found himself living on charity. Because he had no money for rehabilitation for his broken ankle, his ability to walk had become severely limited. Between the affects of aging, diabetes, and improper healing, his gait became progressively unsteady. Unable to obtain a job, he had no means to support himself. When friends arrived with food and money he ate, if they didn't arrive, he went hungry. Roberto and his small band of friends were in constant touch as if it were a telephone chain. One would come to visit, checking the home to see what was needed, then call another friend letting the person know what to bring the next time they visited. This has been ongoing for years, as the community had seen to it that all his basic needs had been met. Seated on his scratched metal folding chair, he looked around his sparsely decorated home. The large living room made the two chairs and card table appear dwarfed. One table light was the only illumination in the entire room. The kitchen, filled with second hand dishes and pots and pans, was adequate, especially since there was rarely food in his refrigerator. The bedroom finally received a mattress, dressed in wrinkled sheets and donated blankets, plus an old television; he had adequate necessities for survival.

There were days he did little, when visiting Juanita or squandering a few dollars at the slots were the only activities. Most of the time he watched television, and waited for the outcome of the case. In his quiet, small, impoverished world, he had no idea the impact this case would have upon the legal system. He saw the case only from his own personal view. The ramifications would lead from the tribulations of one man to changing the fates of thousands of other future defendants. People were watching and waiting for the significant outcome.

The notifications Roberto received from Spence's office meant little. He would read the letters carefully and digest every word, placing them inside a cardboard box. What seemed to be innocuous appeals and legal rhetoric was being closely followed by the media, who understood the significance of each win along the rungs into the federal district court. It was on October 7, 2003, that Anne Gearan of the Associated Press released a headline story, "Supreme Court Allows Former Death Row Inmate to Sue Lawyer," that would spark the surge of news stories reinvigorating the case, making the public aware of the wrongful death penalty suit. Originally, a federal judge threw out the suit, but this was appealed to the

9th U. S. Circuit Court of Appeals and a three-judge panel ruled against the suit. But the court took the unusual step of rehearing the case with an eleven-judge panel, and this time they ruled in favor of allowing suit against Harris, head of the public defender's office as well as Clark County. The six years of appeals had finally come to fruition. Spence's firm won the right to sue the lawyer and the county for inferior legal representation; it was a landmark decision.

Many professed this would open up the flood gates for every convicted criminal to stake a claim back to the courthouse for a retrial, or that it would cause a rift in the intimate relationship between a client and his attorney. Not so. Allowing the case to proceed made those in power accountable for their actions. The oath taken by all lawyers promises conduct of the highest performance. What happened to Roberto was conduct at its poorest performance. For the first time, a suit had come before the Supreme Court where the judges had to judge themselves, where accountability took precedence over all other matters.

The phone calls came frequently, as well wishers congratulated him on the Supreme Court's decision to allow the suit to take place. But one call was disturbing. It was Ron Smythe, who upon hearing the verdict was all too quick to call his friend and refresh his memory as to who would have control of all the money when it started rolling in. Ashen, Roberto hung up the phone. He had not only forgotten about their little deal, he had totally forgotten where the agreement was located. Ron wanted complete control over all his finances, but this had already been taken care of. He had given Kerry this responsibility. Placing the phone unsteadily on the receiver, he replayed the events of their dinner meeting, then began furiously shuffling through the drawers in the bedroom looking for the document. After a frantic half hour, he located the two-page paper at the bottom of his sock drawer. He was terrified he wouldn't be able to get out of this entanglement, but wasn't sure what to do. The only thing he was sure of was that he didn't want anyone handling his money other than Kerry and himself. Folding the papers into his wallet, he would take this to Kerry and get her opinion as to what to do.

Thrilled after all these years of patiently waiting out the system, he had finally won the right to have his day in court. Now it was time for the public defender, the police, and the county to squirm, but all they would lose was money, nothing compared to losing a large portion of a life. His secluded life had been brashly interrupted by the large headlines and his quiet world ruffled with anxiety and anticipation. Antsy, he could not sit around in the confines of the trailer. Thinking about the scant amount of bills tucked inside his wallet, he decided to take a trip up to Wyoming, and pay a visit to his lawyers. Reading the headlines made him wonder when the case would be settled and for how much. He was truly desperate for money, and with his bad leg, he was still unable to work. He thought if he paid them a visit, it would help expedite the settlement, or at the very least, shed more light about the details of the suit. Opening up the worn wallet, he pulled out the agreement he had hurriedly signed with Ron Smythe. He knew if anyone would be able to get him out of this mess it would be Spence. With the possibility of settlement in the near future, he needed to make absolutely sure this unscrupulous man would have no rights to handle the money.

Phoning Juanita, he asked if she could take a few days off to take a ride up to Jackson. Always up for an adventure, she gladly agreed to go, although she would have to get the approval from her boss. Later that day he took the bus down the avenue, meeting her after work so they could discuss plans for the impending trip. Seated in the middle of the bus, one elderly man walked over and asked him if he was Miranda. "I seen your picture in the paper, and we are all rooting for you," he explained.

"Thank you for caring," Roberto shyly replied, as it dawned on him that this case had tentacles outreaching much further than just his case. Celebrity never entered his mind, but the neighborhood was watching and waiting for results. A poor Cuban immigrant going up against all the bureaucracy the city could muster, and winning — this was far better than slaying a thousand dragons. This was a win for the poor. Grinning, he sat mute until the short ride dumped him in front of the rental car shop. Walking into the old work place, he took a seat and waited for Juanita to appear. Out of the dingy manager's office walked his old boss, appearing haggard looking, his shirt wrinkled and spotted, his hair matted down with sweat, and his pants filthy from a large coffee stain. Holding out his hand, he shook Roberto's hand vigorously, showing him great respect and admiration. "I had no idea what you had gone through, and now I understand why you had a fight with one of the workers. By the way, that guy is long gone. Juanita showed me the story in the newspaper. You are quite a hero around here. I told Juanita it was okay to take a couple of days for your little trip. Actually I will pay her. She has earned some vacation time. I am sorry things didn't work out, and I am sorry about what you had to go through." Shaking his hand again, he departed the sales room back to the steamy garage.

Appearing pleasantly surprised, Juanita gave her boyfriend a light kiss, then the two scooted out the side door into her sweltering car. Even as late as October, with the sunrays shining directly into the front seat it would take several minutes to comfortably drive home. Pulling out a bag of maps the sales clerk had given her, they began plotting the trip up to Wyoming. Since neither had driven there, they would have to follow the road signs carefully, charting the trip in advance. Much of the way would be desolate, with no facilities or motels, so they actually had to plan where they would spend the night. "I just hope the old car will make it," he optimistically said. "But if I talk to the car, and tell it this is an important trip she will come through for us."

Laughing, Juanita kissed him deeply, agreeing the old car would make this trip in one piece. Her dry hands and limp hair were potent reminders of the arduous physical labor of detailing cars. It saddened him that she was the one working, not himself. "We go up to see the lawyers, and maybe they will tell us when the money will come in. I don't want you working, at least in a place like this. When the case is settled, you will not have to work anymore. We can buy a nice house and live happy, carefree lives. This is what I want for the both of us. So maybe this trip up to Jackson will give us the answers to our future."

Taking his hand, she kissed him lovingly. "I want whatever you want," she answered. "Please promise me you won't be disappointed if the lawyers can't give you an answer, you remember what your friend Kerry said, that this might take a long time to settle."

He bobbed his head in agreement, but he was sick and tired of constant reminders; that settlements took time, and patience was a virtue. "My God," he ranted." I spent fourteen years in hell, I don't want to have to wait another fourteen years to settle." Gathering up the maps, they headed for his mobile home where solitude would afford them time to scrutinize the best route. As the afternoon breezes cooled off the interior of the car, so too, did the breezes calm Roberto's restless spirit. Opening up the front entrance of the mobile home, Juanita's nose twitched. "What is that awful smell," she asked. Quickly surveying the kitchen, she noticed he had forgotten to throw out the garbage, and in broken

English, she admonished him for being too lazy or forgetful to take care of cleaning.

"You see," he boasted. "This is why I need you home with me, to take care of all these womanly things, Trash, that is not something I think about. But you know what it means to keep a house clean."

"No excuses," she muttered, and grabbed a garbage bag stuffing the remnants of several partially eaten meals. Men."

Organizing his thoughts, he remembered a copy of the contract hastily signed with Ron Smythe. He withdrew the wallet making sure the paper was intact. Inside the car, he pulled out all correspondence from Kerry and Spence, and dropped the pages haphazardly into a weathered tote bag. Grabbing his watch, zipper jacket, and car keys, they were ready for the adventure. His slim wallet foretold the reality they would not be able to afford a motel room. The insides of the car would serve as their room. Ruefully, Juanita accepted her fate, offering to pay for a motel room, but her stubborn boyfriend would not allow that option. She accepted his decision, she had slept on the streets of Las Vegas, and sleeping in a car in the remote Wyoming mountains wouldn't be so bad. Grabbing a blanket she suggested Roberto to do the same. The high altitude and the cold mountain air would mean a chilling night. Listening to her advice, he took an extra quilt and two pillows. At least they would be warm, even if a little uncomfortable.

Packed up, the two commenced the journey. Leaving the warmth and bustle of the city, they soon found quiet and peacefulness in the ever winding uphill route to Jackson. Once again animals and greenery came into view and replaced the starkness of the dried desert floor left from summer heat. After seven hours, she rolled down the windows, and allowed the crisp cool mountain air to wash over her like a new day. And perhaps for the two of them, the trip would prove this to be true; giving them a renewed spirit. Spying a small group of deer, she nudged Roberto, and pointed out the leaping cluster of animals, then opened up her mouth widely as she witnessed a few gigantic buffalo grazing on open field greens. "It's beautiful here," she proclaimed.

"Yes," he agreed. "But, do you see all that white stuff on the tops of those mountains? It snows here, and it's always cold. No thank you, I would never live here." Fidgeting in the driver's seat, he suggested they stop at the next coffee shop for a fill-up and some food. The deserted road seemed lonely, especially after leaving the tumult of the city, but it served to calm their minds, preparing them for the discussions that would ensue with the lawyers. Both knew it was important to have cool heads, to be able to think logically and realistically. Speaking with Roberto, Juanita knew he was anything but a simple man, and she was never one to mix up the difference between having simple needs and having a simple mind. Conversing with a higher level of sophistication than she was capable of often embarrassed her into never missing an evening English class. She knew much of what the lawyers would say would go beyond her comprehension, but just sitting next to her lover, adding support, would prove enough for him. Whatever news they would offer, she would help Roberto internalize and accept, serving as a sounding board for his troubled thoughts as he restated and dissected their messages and advice.

Reaching for his arm, she hugged him, then looked out the window intently reflecting on the true happiness she felt whenever they were together. Both had suffered loves lost, but this time around seemed deeper, more meaningful than any of the others. To love completely, without any ulterior motives, without stating commitments or planning into the future was how they loved. It was the immediacy of the moment that defined their existence, no talk of the future, or even the next week. As a man who had spent fourteen years on death row not knowing which day he would be executed, he learned to live for the moment, because in prison that was all he had.

After hours on the highway, they finally pulled into a truck stop filling up the car with gas, and their stomachs with eggs, over-sized buttermilk pancakes, and large cups of steaming black coffee. Looking around the well-scrubbed restaurant, Juanita felt uncomfortable, as she was the only woman other than the tired worn faces of the three waitresses. After eating voraciously, they used the bathrooms, and jumped back to the car for the continuation of the trip. As they traveled deeper into the mountains, the straining engine could barely make it up the steep inclines. Driving close to the right edge of the road, Roberto was courteous, allowing the speeding trucks and autos the ability to pass him easily. Wincing, Juanita's faith in the haggard car to make the trip wavered. She feared they might be trapped in a snowstorm, or stuck by the side of the road and consumed by vicious, hungry mountain lions. Patting her on the leg, Roberto sensed her anxiety, alluding to stories of how this car had always been a trooper, never letting him down. "She will make it," he soothed. "She has been through worse, and has always come through for me, just have a little faith."

Without uttering a word of disbelief, Juanita sat back, and engulfed her thoughts in the striking beauty of the countryside. Never had she been in this part of the country, so vast and so beautiful, with the splendor of the powerful mountain peaks, the lavishness of the grasslands, and the abundance of flowing streams and lakes. America was truly a magnificent place. If only the people who lived here reflected the quality and the grandeur of the bountiful land. As the sun was resting in the western skies, they began looking for a suitable quiet place to spend the night. With the car as their only shelter, they needed a secluded location that would not call attention to other humans or unwanted wildlife. They pulled into an abandoned campground. Its oversized evergreens and thick brush provided some additional shelter, and the availability of a rustic bathroom. Parking, they emerged unsteadily from the long drive, stretching and walking off hours locked in one position. Although the twilight provided little light, the smell of the pine trees, and the chirp of the birds, erased trepidations of being attacked by wild animals. Calm, quiet, the forest seemed more like a sanctuary than a place to fear. Opening up the trunk, Juanita pulled out a bountiful bag of prepared food. Thinking ahead, she prepared sandwiches, and cookies, then added sodas, a thermos of coffee, and several pieces of fruit. "We will not go hungry," she insisted. "Even though we can't afford a hotel room, it doesn't mean we can't eat."

Hugging her closely, he professed his enduring love. Too cold to picnic outside, they sat in the backseat of the car, eating in silence, listening to the foreign sounds of the woods floating through the cracked window. A hooting owl, some fluttering, a whooshing of wings, the cry of a baby deer, the thrashing of a beaver's tail, filled the emptiness of the evening. "It all sounds friendly enough," she said, "I guess we will make it through the night without being eaten by a hungry bear."

Both stuffed, they arranged the blankets and pillows as comfortably as possible, Roberto taking the front seat, and Juanita the back. Afraid to sleep, they spent the night in silence, anticipating the first glimmer of dawn.

Slowly cracking the car door open, Roberto announced it was safe to leave, as he ran towards the bathrooms. Splashing bitter cold water on his face awakened every sleepy muscle, preparing himself for another long day on the road.

Locating her shoes, Juanita clutched the quilted winter jacket as she found her way to the rustic camp latrines. Although showerheads marked the possibility of feeling clean, she knew the water would be as icy as that with which she washed her hands and face. Startled by the frigid crystal water, this would be as clean and refreshed as she intended. Moving quickly, she darted back to the car, ready for the last day of the journey. Departing the campsite, she was relived they had made it through unscathed, with a hot cup of coffee and some breakfast and they would be good as new.

After two hours on the road, the gas tank was as ready for fuel as the passengers. Pulling into another truck stop, they ordered the same meal as the day before, using the warm, clean facilities of the quiet roadside restaurant. Laying out a map, they plotted the final route, calculating that they would reach Jackson by mid-afternoon. Satiated with the warmth of the food they were energized to plod ahead.


A sleepy town, the clouds painted the sky with a calmness of spirit, a sense of serenity and peacefulness in contrary to the flurry and abundance of brilliant minds at work. Perhaps nature allowed man's mind to think at its best when cocooned within the safety of the mountains and the untouched landscapes, but whatever the reason, Roberto had made this pilgrimage to find answers and restitution. No need to look at the stately buildings to comprehend what work went on inside, it was the symbol of legal minds living out the meaning of the constitution. Pointing to the name on the archway, Roberto explained who owned the practice and the fame Gerry Spence carried in the legal profession. Truly an icon, Spence's books and publications were recited daily throughout the law schools and the media. He was the guru of the legal system, working for human rights as no other attorney had ever done. In this private reclusive city, he had built a small army of disciples, where he daily held court, teaching his unique theory and application of law. Not unlike the reverence of a monk's temple, the walls housed a respect for the teachings and application of the sacredness and purity of the law. Respect and admiration shrouded both the students and clients as they met the geniuses of the law.

A smiling receptionist welcomed the clients and asked their names. Roberto announced his urgency to speak with Spence. Glancing at the computer log, she was unable to find his appointment, " I don't have an appointment, but," shaking Smythe's document and the local newspaper headlines, "I didn't think that would be necessary," spoke Roberto.

Rattled, she hurriedly rang Spence's line, and explained the unanticipated arrival of Mr. Miranda. Would he be able to meet with him? In spite of the attorney's ambitious schedule, he would make the time for a man who had traveled two days for help. Ushering the couple into a warm conference room, the receptionist thoughtfully brought in cups of coffee, scrounging a small plateful of leftover donuts. Even her young eye captured the austere life this couple lead. Her job was to provide comfort, not intimidation, and this she did well.

The clients ate ravenously as they awaited the attorney's appearance. The room was as Juanita had imagined. The walls appeared as though they had been lifted from the neighboring forest then perfectly carved to fit into the heights of the ceiling. The wooden table, rustic in appearance, had been shined to perfection as if to allow papers to slide smoothly from one end to the other, and the chairs boasted a rich tapestry from Indian tribal patterns. Pulling out the document Roberto had signed with Smythe, he was prepared for the meeting. Forcing himself to calm down, he knew it was important to collect his thoughts before spurting out inflammatory statements. Grasping Juanita's sweated hand, he kissed her, thanking her for making the trip, "I am so glad you are here to support me," he uttered. "I want you to know what is going on with this case. You will be the one who shares in all the money. It's important you understand."

Shaking her head, what she truly understood was that he wanted to show the attorneys that someone loved and cared for him, and was watching over his needs. The money, she knew, may never come, or he may never live to enjoy it, but right here, she did all she could do, and that was support the man she dearly, unabashedly loved. Within these hallowed walls everything seemed relevant and important. The vigilant attorneys would attack each document making sure that no stone would go unturned.

As the attorneys paraded in, they cordially smiled, shaking hands with the rigorous strength of lumberjacks. Lying Smythe's document on the conference table, it was quickly snatched up and read with deep contemplation. "We will take care of this, " promised the attorneys. "But," shaking an admonishing finger spoke an attorney. "Don't sign another document unless you consult us first. Now, we are sure you want to know about the progress of your pending lawsuit. At this time, it is still being kicked around the courts. We are still playing the waiting game. The Supreme Court has upheld the case. It's back into the hands of the defendants. The settlement for when and how much we can settle this case for is still being negotiated."

With gentle, uncompromising dignity, the lawyers attended to the unscheduled clients for a long time, answering questions, speculating on outcomes, and offering advice. Although nothing was settled, Roberto's mind was eased that the case was moving along, even if at a snail's pace, and that his lawyers were willing to offer constant help and advice. Their advice was not to placate nor show despondence, but to layout the reality of courtly proceedings. Although everyone was in agreement that time was paramount, they would be forced to be patient so justice could be properly served. A bright glean in Spence's eye, a tip of his head, and Roberto would rest assured knowing his fate lay in the most competent of hands.

Overwhelmed by the quiet interplay, Juanita simply stood by quietly, and shook the hands of all pertinent parties, and then calmly departed the meeting. Feeling as though he had left a meditation meeting rather than a confrontational legal battle, Roberto's anxieties were laid to rest. "Was the environment so imbued by nature that permeated the demeanor of the attorneys, or was it simply their unique styles?" he felt. But however he summed up the experience, he left satisfied that his destiny was in the best of hands. Taking Juanita's arm, he opened the office door, and pensively walked to the car. Extracting his wallet from the back pocket of his khakis, he found just enough cash to pay for the gas home. Ever the positive one, Juanita exclaimed they would make it. The trip to Jackson was uphill, going home it would be a breeze. Rolling down the window, she gathered in the last breaths of refreshing mountain air. "I love this place," admitted Roberto. "But do you have any idea what the winters are like? So cold, and snowy, you can be stuck in the house for days or weeks before its safe to go out. No this place is not for me. Enjoy the scenery. We won't be returning."

With belief in his jalopy, the two made it back to Las Vegas by late Sunday evening which allowed just enough time for Juanita to rest up before another busy week at the rental company. Kissing her lover with deep intensity, she thanked him for taking her along, and for sharing his life, "I love you," she murmured, slipping out the car door and into the busy apartment. The mid-autumn dusk began to cool the air as he proceeded north on the boulevard to his spacious, yet sparse trailer. His thoughts were laden with happiness as he again referred to his list of goals, the most important one having been aptly accomplished; finding a lover. Retribution would come. He would have to wait. There was no option. He only prayed he would be alive to enjoy the fruits of the attorneys' labor.

Returning to the mobile home, he collapsed on the mattress, falling asleep before the first commercial blasted the airwaves on the waning television. Dreams of the past invaded his quiet slumber. Even in sleep, the unconscious beckoned him to relive life in prison; the horrors of seclusion in a tiny airless cell, the pain and anguish when penetrated with a revengeful inmate's knife, and the constant humiliation served up by the sadistic guards. Waking up trembling and disorientated, sleep would not return. Stumbling out of bed, he walked to the window staring at the night sky, "I am free, but why don't I feel free? Please God, save me from these nightmares," he begged. Grabbing a pack of cigarettes, he slid open the living room window and spent the rest of the night smoking away the nightmares.

The loud blare of the telephone shook him out of his daydreams. "It's Kerry," his fast friend announced. "Now tell me about your trip. Was it a success? Did you find out anything? Did they have an idea when it might be settled?"

Kerry's rambling interview caught him unprepared. Without as much as taking a breath, she continued peppering him with questions until he finally interjected a succinct reply. "I found out nothing. They really can't give me an answer. All they told me is that they would take care of that contract with Smythe, and not to sign any documents with anyone unless they approved."

"Well that's reassuring," she responded. "I am sorry that you weren't able to get more information. We will all just have to keep patient and keep the faith in these people. Before I forget, I want you to come for Thanksgiving dinner this year. Remember last year? How you ended up in jail, I want to make it up to you."

"I appreciate the invite, but Alice asked me over. And since it's just up the street, I told her I would come. Sorry, but thank you so much for asking. You know you are my best friend, and I care a lot about you."

"Don't worry," she said. "I truly understand, and besides there is always Christmas, and a million other holidays we can share together. I just don't want you to be alone. You are part of my family and you are always welcome."

Hanging up the phone, Roberto beamed. Even in his miserable life he had come to know wonderful people who loved him dearly, cared for him genuinely, and were willing to share their lives with him. Unable to work, friends were all that would see him through the troubled times. A constant trickle of money, food, clothing, and household goods was continually forthcoming. Although there was no money for cigarettes or luxury items, the refrigerator was kept stocked with food. Kerry was relentless in reminding the church preacher to solicit the congregation. It was almost as if the church had adopted a child who had become the responsibility of the community. Without the ability to collect unemployment or welfare, there was no means of support.

Dressing for Thanksgiving dinner, it sickened him that he had no money with which to buy Alice flowers or purchase a small gift. At times, poverty was incredibly depressing and downright humiliating. The limp of his leg had become more pronounced over the last few weeks, exaggerating his appearance as a weak, powerless, penniless man. Dressing in donated clothes, he spit-shined a pair of black patent loafers, buttoned a frayed

Ralph Lauren pinstriped shirt, and threw on an oversized black tweed jacket. Having just shaved and showered, he examined his reflection in the mirror thinking at this moment, in spite of his poverty, he didn't look that bad. Turning off the lights, he walked the short three blocks to Alice's home and the comforts of her holiday fare.

Although the two were extremely close, she had recently found a boyfriend who was more than willing to allow Roberto into their lives. Opening up the door, Jake offered a smile and hearty handshake to the guest. Both men seemed to tower over Alice's short stocky stature, as they stood in the cozy living room. The fragrant smells drifted through the air, reminding Roberto how hungry he was. In spite of constant charity, there were times, especially around the holidays, when his cupboard was bare. Ironically, he thought Americans would be more generous during holiday season, but the reality was they were more wrapped up in family obligations, having no time or thoughts for outsiders. But here in Alice's home, he would find what the love of a friend meant. Generous beyond his ability to comprehend, she had given him a home, her caring, and most of all, her time. Seated at the welcoming kitchen table, the three enjoyed traditional holiday cuisine as Jake ceremoniously carved the golden brown turkey filled with breadcrumb stuffing. Lifting up the plates, Alice generously heaped on mounds of sweet potatoes, creamed peas, and perfectly mashed potatoes. "You are quite a cook," announced Roberto.

Grabbing a couple of beers, Jake nodded and gestured his arms in agreement as he lightly patted his swelling belly. "This is my favorite meal of the year, and I have to say that Alice, my love, you have done a splendid job." Offering a beer to Roberto, who shook his head. No. He explaining that his father was a drunk and he was terrified to imbibe in any alcoholic beverage.

"My father," elaborated Roberto. "Was mean and violent when he drank and I do want wish to be like him. He beat up my mother and my sister. I swore off drinking when I saw what it did to him. He was like a time bomb exploding after the first gulps of rum. I appreciate your offer though. You are both so kind to have me over, and I really, truly thank you."

Kissing him on the cheek, Alice let Roberto know how happy she was he had joined them. "Just a small dinner between friends," she interjected. "And we are glad you came. We know you don't celebrate this holiday in Cuba."

After consuming the last morsels on the plate, Roberto helped Alice clear the table and clean up the kitchen. "Why don't you join Jake in the living room," she suggested.

"No, I wish to help you. After all the hard work cooking, the least I can do is help you clean up. Besides, I have had plenty of practice doing dishes. I always help out Juanita." Grabbing the sponge, he scraped the pots and pans until they literally shined like new, then filled the dishwasher, and mopped the floor. Yawning, he felt an overwhelming sense of exhaustion. "It must be all the food," he admitted. "But I am so sleepy I can hardly keep my eyes open. I better walk home before I join your snoozing boyfriend on the coach." Turning to his hostess he thanked her again for all the charity she had given him — a home with all utilities paid, use of a telephone, a television, and most of all, constant attention and caring. "There is no way on earth I could ever repay your kindness, but maybe you'll be repaid in heaven. God has a special place for people like you" As tears welled up, he hugged Alice tightly, and slowly walked home. He felt as if he had gained three hundred pounds. His legs barely made it up the six wooden steps into the empty mobile home. Fatigued, he plopped down on the mattress, turned on the television to his favorite Spanish music station, receding into a deep slumber.

Dreams were fitful. There was an unusual numbness overcoming his arm and leg. Tossing and turning, he forced himself to rest out the nightmare, knowing the strange sensation would leave when he woke in the morning. With the first light of day, the sunrays peered into the bedroom and washed the space with a soft yellow light. Sluggishly, he began to awaken, yet his arm and leg remained numb. His mind was confused. He was unable to think. He was terrified. Crawling to the living room, he tried to make it to the kitchen, but was immobile. The phone rang, and it was Kerry. "My God Kerry, I can't move. My arm and leg are numb."

"What do you mean?" she shrieked. "Explain exactly how you feel." In a confused state of mind, he described the numbness. There was no doubt in hers what his problem was. Clearly he had suffered a stroke. "I will be there in a few minutes. Don't worry. You will be fine," she lied. Grabbing her husband, they flew out the door, revving up the large van and heading north towards the airbase. Turning to her husband, Kerry admitted that she didn't want to call an ambulance unless she was sure he needed help, as Roberto and she often miscommunicated because of the language variations. "Let's just wait and see how he is," she cautioned, although in her heart, she was terrified. Driving faster and more carelessly than the law allowed, the two arrived fifteen minutes later. The fence had been latched and locked up. There was no way for her to get in but to climb over the metal fence, something she hadn't done since her teenage years. Tenacity in heart, her husband grabbed her feet and catapulted her over the top. The next barrier was the mobile home. Trying both the front and back doors, she had no choice but to somehow go through the sliding glass window. Hearing his dire screams for help, Kerry yelled back that she was trying to get in.

"I can't move," he cried out. "I can't move. Please help me."

Grabbing several cement blocks, she concocted a make-shift ladder up to the window, then roughly slid it open. With all her strength, she crawled in through the small space. Lying on the floor, Roberto was naked from the waist up. Her beloved friend was completely immobile and freezing cold. Screaming out to her husband to call for an ambulance, she knelt down beside him, placing his head on her lap. "You are going to be just fine." I promise you," she spoke, as tears rolled down her soft cheeks. Forcing a smile, she sensed his thinking was clouded, as his eyes were unable to focus. Thrashing his arm in the air, he kept asking what was happening. Why did he feel so strange? All Kerry could do was offer comfort until the medics arrived. Within three minutes, the blast of the sirens could be heard in the crystal clear November morning air. Gently rocking him, Kerry consoled his terrified mind, speaking of the goodness of God, the love of his many friends, the compassion of Jesus, and faith in the future. Silently praying that God would see fit not to take this man's life tonight, she clutched tightly to his head, holding his hand as if the connection would guarantee her living energy would melt into his.

Crashing through the locked gate, the ambulance sped purposefully to the entrance of the mobile home. Gently placing his head on the floor, Kerry rushed to open the door, allowing the three medics access to the dying patient. Brashly, the men questioned Roberto, forcing him to answer questions. They were searching for lucidity, as they placed a blood pressure wrap snugly on his left arm. Gently pressing on various limbs and muscles, they prodded him with questions, extracting as much information as was possible. Tears flooded Kerry's vision. Her heart was pounding so loudly she thought the sound would shake her friend out of his dazed state. The medics asked for some form of identification. She needed to obtain the information from Roberto. Gently tapping his foot, she asked him where his wallet was, but there was no response. Grabbing his hand, she spoke in a louder, harsher, tone trying to capture his attention, but it seemed impossible. Jim was busy helping the medics lift Roberto onto the stretcher. Torn between leaving him and searching for the wallet, the medics made the choice — she had to locate some form of identification or the hospital might refuse service. Rushing into the bedroom and ransacking the closet, she located his wallet hidden inside a well-worn jacket. Racing back to the living room, she spied her husband helping the medics lift Roberto's lifeless body onto a stretcher. Although not fat, he was a tall man, muscled from shoulder to legs; his lifeless body was too heavy even for the seasoned medics. Jim's help made a difference. Secured on the stretcher, Kerry soothed his fears telling him he would be fine, that he was in excellent hands She told him not to worry, his friends would help him get through this. Praying, she asked God to allow the spirit of life to remain in his mind and soul. He needed to live. The constant flood of tears remained as she cited several passages from the Sunday psalm book. Taking Roberto's hand, she maneuvered around the attendants so he would feel her constant touch. She knew even in his confused state of mind it was important to have a tactile sense of the world. Holding and massaging his hand would help soothe him.

"I must tell you," piped Kerry to the medics, "He is indigent, he has no money, where will you take him?"

"The closest hospital. Probably Lake Mead, just follow the ambulance," he instructed curtly. The three men carefully expanded the stretcher, and cautiously carried the patient out the metal door, down the wooden steps. Unable to roll the gurney over the rough terrain, the three lugged Roberto to the opened back of the ambulance.

"We will follow you," Kerry yelled, still weeping beyond control. Unable to drive, she clutched her husband's arm, asking him to follow the ambulance. Glancing around the property, she ran back to the home and turned off all the lights, slammed the door shut, then wildly raced back to the van. Although they couldn't run the red lights, Kerry knew where the ambulance was going. They would arrive within minutes. They would not lose track of their friend. Unable to capture some form of composure, Jim demanded she be strong at least until Roberto's fate was known.

"He needs you to be strong for him. You might have to make important decisions. you need to be able to think clearly," he cautioned. Handing his wife a wad of tissues, she dried her eyes, her face, and neck. "This is such a shock, we both need to be able to help him, and to do that we must both be able to think logically. Now, do you have any of the telephone numbers of his friends?" Jim asked.

Pulling out her cell phone, she began scrolling down the address book, but before she had an opportunity to make the first call, the medics announced there was a change of plans. It seemed as though the hospital would not accept indigent patients, even in dire need of resuscitation. With an IV dangling from his arm, the medics reloaded the patient back into the ambulance, screaming out that they would be headed to University Medical Center. Blasting the sirens as if to spite the emergency room intake personnel, they sped directly southward. Calling ahead, the ambulance alerted the emergency room of the urgent problem, asking for specialists to be prepared for the incoming patient. Vigilantly checking vital signs, everyone prayed Roberto would make it to the hospital alive. The medics chatted, joked, and stimulated their patient into some type of response, but none could be detected. Lying comatose, his limp body held no sign of life except for laborious shallow breathing. Shaking his head, the attendant was worried Roberto wouldn't make it to the next hospital. "Those bastards," he muttered under his breath, "How dare they refuse a patient." Angry and agitated, he realized that no amount of medical training could help a patient when emergency rooms refused immediate care. The medics were aware that the sooner a diagnosis was made and administered the more likely the patient would recover. The attendant cast grave doubts on the prognosis of the man lying in his care. His experience with stroke victims had taught him immediate care meant the difference between life and death.

The driver adroitly snaked through the congested street with the expertise of a race car driver, arriving minutes later at the emergency entrance. Hoisting the gurney, they slowly lowered it to the ground, then sprung it up to hospital bed height. Rolling the lifeless patient into the bustling entrance, two attendants grabbed the gurney, and raced into a room prepared for stroke victims. With forthright professionalism, the nurses and doctors worked at lightning speed, replacing the IV line with a new one filled with medication to offset further brain damage. Removing his clothes, the nurse hooked up a heart monitor and another IV line allowing needed medication to easily flow. One doctor yelled out orders for an immediate CAT scan enabling them to assess the amount of damage. Waiting until the patient's vital signs were stable, two nurses rolled him down to the imaging room, with orders to scan just his head. Roberto still unconscious, two muscular orderlies gently, yet instantly transferred Roberto to the imaging table, strapping him down tightly in case he would awaken during the procedure. Within minutes, the x-rays had been completed and were ready to be read. Calling up to the attending doctor in the emergency room, the radiologist related the results, that in fact the patient had suffered a stroke with severe trauma to the brain. Prognosis at this juncture was not predictable since no one knew when he had actually suffered the stroke, but the doctors continued with treatment giving him medications to allay additional damage.

Edgily pacing in the crowded waiting room, Kerry was completely distraught. Although anxious to contact his friends, she decided to wait until the doctors had agreed on a prognosis. Worried, she didn't want anyone else to needlessly suffer unless she was able to fully explain the nature and seriousness of her friend's illness. Hair stringing down her face, cheeks blackened from smudged mascara, and bright red eyes portrayed inner misery. She loved this man, as did so many. She had put so much of her time and energy into making his life as comfortable as possible. And then God came along and further destroyed a man who had already suffered intensely. Clutching a clump of tissues, losing the last tears, she walked to the window searching the star-filled skies for an answer.

With a strong quickened pace, the on-call resident, dressed in wrinkled hospital scrubs, motioned to Kerry and her husband as the doctor rounded up three chairs for an informal conference. Seated in a quiet corner of the waiting room the young female doctor asked the couple their relationship to the patient, as privacy was well guarded in patient care. Offering up a brief explanation, the attendant was satisfied with Kerry and Jim's relationship with the patient. The doctor continued a detailed explanation of the extent of the damage. Holding up an x-ray, she pinpointed the portion of the brain affected by the stroke. "All we know at this time, is that he has suffered a traumatic stroke partially paralyzing the left side of his body. They are taking him to an intensive care unit, and we will monitor his vital signs. It is impossible to know the long term affects, because we don't know when he suffered the stroke. I promise you he will get the best care, and we will do all we can do for him. He has slipped into a coma caused from the brain trauma, but we are treating him with drugs that break up blood clots, allowing the blood to move smoothly through his arteries. The clot in his brain should begin to break apart and will take the pressure off the affected areas. Once the drugs begin to work, there should be an improvement. I will have to ask you to be patient. It is hard to predict, but he is a strong man, in good shape. So right now, we should look forward with some optimism. Do you have any questions?" the doctor asked.

"When can we see him?" asked a teary-eyed Kerry.

"I suggest you come back in the morning," answered the doctor. "He will be sleeping the rest of the night, and you will need strength to help him. We are putting him the intensive care unit, but you can come and spend the day. They are very liberal with visiting hours in this hospital."

Both shook the doctor's hand. The worried couple somberly departed the hospital. Kerry began flipping through the address file on her cell phone; she called Juanita, and Alice, and alerted them of Roberto's problem. Sadly, she realized there was no one else to call; his family lived in Cuba, and contacting them might be next to impossible. Alice's phone seemed to ring incessantly until a groggy voice answered.

"Alice, it's Kerry, I wanted to let you know that your friend Roberto is in the hospital," she rambled. Relaying the events of the day, she tearfully asked if Alice could go to his home, locating telephone numbers or addresses of his Cuban family. She felt it was important for his siblings and mom to know what had happened, and to pray for his recovery.

"Sure," Alice answered. "What do they know? How severe is this? Will he recover? He is such a strong man, I just can't believe this could happen. Just yesterday we all sat together eating

Thanksgiving dinner. He was joking, laughing, and seemed to be very happy. Why did this have to happen to him? Hasn't he suffered enough?' Sobbing, Alice couldn't utter another word. Clinging onto the phone, her tears dripped down her face. She was so shaken, she could hardly move. Recalling the last time they were together she again spoke up.

"Kerry, I do remember he kept saying that he was exhausted, and that his ankle was bothering him making it harder to walk. When he left the house, he constantly remarked how sleepy he felt and that it must have been all the delicious home made food making him so tired. Maybe he was beginning to have the stroke then and I didn't have a clue. If only I would have called him the next morning. But I got so involved in my work, I forgot."

"Please do not feel guilty. I just need you to help contact his family, and to check on the home. We left in such a hurry, no one checked on all the lights being turned off or doors locked."

"Sure, I will go over there first thing in the morning. Now please give me your cell number. When can we visit Roberto?" Copiously jotting down all the information the women promised to keep in close contact during the coming critical days. They both were keenly aware of the grave nature a stroke. Although neither spoke the word, death was an imminent reality. The late hour forced the conversation to halt quickly, as they both needed ample rest to mollify Roberto's life.

It was imperative to many that this man should live, and maintain a strong rational psyche. The lawyers did not wish to bring a lawsuit posthumously; his death would surely weaken their ability to negotiate the pending suit. It seemed crushingly unjust that Roberto could die, never tasting the fruits of his arduous climb for exoneration and justice. Although money certainly was a major factor, the salience of the impending suit would mark his life as meaningful. It was Roberto's opportunity to represent the salvation of the poor and indigent émigré; he needed to be in court the day judgment was decreed.

Still rattled from the shock of Roberto's illness, Kerry began dialing Juanita's number. She knew she would catch her sound asleep but this matter couldn't wait until morning. Struggling to keep her voice clear, she began relaying the events of the evening to Roberto's lover. "I didn't mean to wake you," Kerry hesitated. "But I thought you should know Roberto is in the hospital. He has suffered a stroke. The doctors can't tell us at this moment how severe it is. We just have to pray he will be fine. Don't rush out to the hospital tonight; he is sound asleep," Kerry lied. "He should feel much better in the morning." Torn between admitting the truth and sugarcoating the stroke, she took the middle ground. There was no sense in rushing to the hospital. There was nothing she or anyone could do but wait. "Look," Juanita, Kerry suggested. "I will meet you tomorrow, at the intensive care unit, by then, hopefully we will all know more. Now just get some rest."

Trembling, Kerry placed the cell phone in the accessible section of her stuffed pocket book, hoping it would not ring before the night ended. Although she usually drove, her husband chauffeured them back home safely. The couple rode home in silence. They were both deep in contemplation over the health of their beloved friend. Pushing the garage door opener, they heard the familiar bark of their two mutts scrambling out the doggie door, licking and jumping buoyantly. Annoyed at the loud sounds, Kerry uncharacteristically brushed them aside, lumbered up the tile steps, stripped off her sweated clothes, showered and plopped into bed. There was no use in surmising that sleep would come, but at least she could stretch out on the king bed, pray, hope and plan for whatever God would see fit to render unto her dearest friend. What she did know was that he was a fighter. He would not give up easily. In his comatose state, she trusted that fighter in him would force itself to the surface, shaking off the threat of death. Slowly closing her eyes, sheer exhaustion wrapped itself around her spirit, allowing sleep to come quickly.

Sleep did not come to Juanita, and by midnight she had dressed and was out the door. Waiting until morning to know the fate of her lover would seem an eternity. She needed to be with him. Walking brusquely past the evening guards, she slipped into an awaiting elevator taking it to the intensive care ward. Juanita bid good evening to the nurses on staff, as they readily pointed the direction of the newest patient's bed. Unaccustomed to hospitals, she apprehensively tip-toed to the bed, fearful to touch his hand. Standing silently, concentrating on each breath, the gravity of his illness became painfully clear. Each contraction of his lungs was so labored, she was frantic he would stop breathing. His skin, usually dry, was damp and clammy. His eyes showed no sign of movement below the bronze lids. His parched lips and lifeless limbs terrified Juanita into the realization of eminent death. Completely unresponsive to her soft words and gentle touch, she hunched over and wept quietly, silently, for fear of making a commotion and being thrown out. She spent the night, and stayed by the bedside until he awakened. She wanted him to know she was there, waiting, watching, and caring. A night nurse, observing the visitor thoughtfully brought over a small cushioned chair. The nurse whispered it would be fine if she spent the night, and if she needed anything to simply push a tiny red button. Nodding, Juanita pulled the chair closer to the bed and tenderly held her lover's hand. She sat motionless until her head dropped in exhaustion at the edge of the hospital bed.

Before the sun could weave its golden glow into Kerry's bedroom, she awoke startled with the reality of her friend's sudden illness. Tripping out of the warmth of the king size bed, her mind raced assessing the duties she needed to fulfill on behalf of Roberto. The memory sunk in that he had assigned her total control over his life if he should die or become incapacitated. Sorting through a labyrinth of documents, she extracted the power of attorney, along with various other legal instructions, and placed them in her briefcase. Then she phoned the Spence attorneys to apprise them of his dire situation. The aroma from the rich coffee that Jim had prepared, sharpened her wits and helped her gather some semblance of order to the hectic unpredictable situation. "Roberto has suffered a severe stroke, " she instructed the lawyers. "And the doctors cannot say how badly it will affect him. Currently he is in a deep coma. We are waiting for him to wake up, and once he does, everyone will know a lot more. I just wanted you to be aware of the circumstances, as we are all extremely upset and worried. I will call you when we know more, and I wish to thank you for all your help. You have given him so much, and I pray to God it won't be wasted." Tears streamed down her face. Her voice became hoarse as she listened to the empathetic advice of the lawyer. Barely able to coax another thank you out of her throat, she hung up the phone, ran to the bathroom, and quickly dressed for the impending hospital visit.

"I can't see," Roberto suddenly screamed out. At the base of his bed four friends, Juanita, Alice, Jim and Kerry, had begun a vigil, hoping and praying he would awaken from his deep coma. Now early Saturday afternoon, he had finally spoken a few incoherent words to his unknown audience. "Where am I? What has happened to me? I can't see," he repeated.

Juanita began the reply explaining in Spanish what had transpired. Then Alice, Jim, and Kerry took their turns, speaking in low soothing voices. Each reassured him he would recover, that he would be fine but he would need much rest. While Kerry was in mid-sentence, the patient collapsed back into his coma. Ringing for the attending nurse, Alice explained what had occurred, describing his sudden wakening and incoherence. Jotting down the information on his chart, the nurse elucidated that this was common in stroke patients. Pointing to the IV drip, the nurse explained the types of medications and the impending tests the doctors had prescribed. "But mainly," the soft spoken nurse admitted. "It's a waiting game. We do not know anything about his history, so it is impossible to predict how he will respond to the medication. The tests will give us a pretty fair idea of the amount of damage, and the prognosis."

Surrounded by loved ones, the unaware patient remained motionless for hours, while the visitors solemnly chatted among themselves. At this juncture, everyone feared the worst. As minutes turned to hours, they knew the prognosis could only go from bad to worse. Kissing Juanita and Alice good by, Kerry departed the miserable scene unable to stand by uselessly. "Call me if there is any change," she asked.

Alice shared endless evenings with him and developed an intense friendship She was laden with grief. A valuable human being might be taken away from this earth well before his time. Not a religious woman, she prayed harder than she had ever prayed for Roberto's life to be spared. Looking up from the bed, she and Juanita noticed an orderly bringing in a small bright bouquet of flowers. Taking the card, Alice read the words of encouragement from the Lutheran Church. "Incredibly thoughtful, " sighed Juanita. Both women were keenly aware that the hospital provided the poverty stricken man with what he had considered luxuries: three meals a day, color cable television, a private phone, clean sheets, and a bath. By any standards, he was being taking care of meticulously, and thoroughly.

Although University Medical Center was the only place in

Las Vegas for the indigent, one would never know it from the high quality of care from both the doctors and the nursing staff. Juanita noticed that all the nurses continually conversed with the patients, even though there was no possibility they would respond. "Why do you talk to him so much?" questioned Juanita.

"You know," the young Mulatto nurse responded. "The patients might be playing hooky, and want to hear what we really think of them," she winked. "But truly, it helps keep them in touch with reality, keeping their mind going by creating stimuli. Keep talking to him. Take his hand, play music, anything to grab his attention so he comes back to us real soon."

"Thank you, I will do as you suggested," she said, as she took her lover's hand and began a slow massage.

Fatigued, Alice announced her departure and promised to return early the next day. Hugging Juanita, Alice reminded her she needed rest, as there would be more difficult times ahead. Because of the tiny shared space, there was no room for a cot, or even a comfortable chair. Spending the night would prove impossible. Smiling in agreement, Juanita looked at her watch, stating she would stay another hour. "I want to be here if he wakes up," she explained. "When he was up for just a few moments, he was so completely disorientated. My being here should help him. I know you are right. I do need rest. I can't tell you how much your generosity has meant to Roberto. He always says to me how lucky he is to have found such a loving devoted friend and how he could never ever repay you for all your kindnesses. Sometimes I think I should be jealous, but then he reminds me that you have a great boyfriend, and that Roberto loves you in a totally different way. I hope when the settlement from his case comes through he will have the chance to give back some of what you have given him" Choking on her words, she said "I do not know what will happen if he dies. I do not know if the suit will continue. The money is no good to him if he is gone."

Unable to respond, Alice quickly ventured into the dim of the corridor. Lost in thought, she bumped into an orderly pushing an elderly man on a gurney. Apologizing for her clumsiness, she clutched her pocketbook, and almost ran out of the hospital. Using a wide stride, she sat unsteadily behind the wheel of her pick-up truck and turned over the engine, heading home. So blinded by the continuous flow of tears, she barely made the trip home safely. Unlike Kerry and Juanita, her agnostic theology found no solace in seeking God's explanation. Her dearest friend's illness needed some form of logic. If the doctors could explain the stroke, then they should surely be able to fix the problem, she surmised. "He can't die. He must not die. There is too much living in his heart. It just would not be fair, " she postulated, "I know he must live. It's just not his time." And with those dogmatic thoughts, she pulled hastily into her dusty, weed-filled driveway, and opened the truck door, screaming out to the foreman that they were late, to grab the box of tools, they were heading to the southwest project.

Hearing a loud grunt, Juanita was shaken from her sleep. Instantly opening her large brown eyes, she woke up to the sounds of her lover restlessly moving about the bed. He appeared dazed, frightened and confused. Looking directly at Juanita, he tilted his head, asking who she was, and then turned and looked around the room, asking where he was, and what had happened. Running out to snare the attending nurse, the two returned quickly to see the patient half way out of the bed. "I am going home," he announced. "This isn't my home. I don't know anyone here. This isn't my bed. Those aren't my clothes. My name, what is my name?" he uttered as the orderlies placed him securely back into the bed and raised the side rails.

Hysterical, Juanita screamed out that he didn't know who she was. Patting her hand the nurse explained the side affects of the stroke, and the problems it can cause. She told Juanita to be patient, that time and medication had a way of reversing much of the initial damage. The nurse instructed assuredly, "He will begin to do better, he will know who you are." Adjusting the IV, rechecking the medication and vital signs, the nurse jotted down notes on the medical chart, reminding Juanita the doctor would arrive shortly. Juanita redirected her attention back to Roberto, and scrutinized every movement and sound he projected, praying his mind would focus on reality. For hours, he thrashed about the bed, twice losing balance until finally the orderlies tied his hands to the metal bars to keep him from further inadvertently harming himself. Rather than cry, Juanita remembered the importance of talking and touching. Strutting purposefully to the nurse's station, she obtained a newspaper, and an assortment of well-worn magazines, and carried them back to the crowded room. She pulled up the sole chair and commenced reading with forthright energy. She had no intention of losing the man she loved; she would pull him back to reality. She would force him to live.

In Roberto's mind's eye he could not explain the inherent brain frenzy he was suffering, but the voice reading unfamiliar text seemed familiar. As glimpses of reality flickered in and out of his consciousness, he slowly began returning back to life. His sleepy mind began shaking off the cobwebs of certain death; he began to fight. Stimuli entered his brain filling the empty void with fragments of meaning. Blinking his eyelids, he tried to move his hands, but they were immobile. Frightened he cried out, "My hands. Where are my hands?"

Instantly putting down the newspaper, Juanita stood up, and covered his face with hers. "Its me. It's Juanita," she spoke sternly. "Your hands are tied to the bed to keep you safe. If you promise not to fall out, I will untie them. I love you. You have been very sick. We are all waiting for you to return to us." Tears raced down her tired cheeks bones. She untied the bandages, allowing freedom of movement. Sitting up in the bed, he gazed around the room, again asking where he was and what had happened. Ascertaining his level of comprehension, Juanita badgered her lover with humorous simple questions. "And just who do you think I am? What on earth are you wearing? Who is that stranger lying next to you? What is on your breakfast plate?"

"Do you think I am crazy?" he joked. "Juanita, you are my lover, and I am hungry, please get me some real food."

Fleeing the room, she ran to the nurse's station and reported the recovery, begging for someone to help her. Grabbing the nurse's arm, Juanita literally raced back to the cubicle. The nurse and Juanita were stunned to see the patient sitting up, completely lucid.

"Juanita," Roberto cried out. "Please tell me what has happened, where am I?"

The astute nurse whose worn face wore a constant serious expression, treaded tentatively in releasing knowledge of the stroke to her charge. She gingerly approached the topic, aware the Mulatto man may not have full grasp of the English language. She left the technical information and prognosis to the doctor, and just explained what had occurred. Congratulating him on his sudden spurt of lucidity, the nurse maneuvered the pillow and the bed sheets, observing neurological damage to his limbs. Considering the intensity of the coma, and the unknown time of the stroke, he appeared to be recuperating at an unprecedented rate. Replacing her sardonic expressions with a smile, she turned her eyes to Juanita, pronouncing the patient vastly improved from his arrival. Juanita, convinced that the endless hours of reading had helped his recovery, continued an endless tirade of chatter, changing from Spanish to English. Although she never missed an English class, there were many words she had yet to be able to translate. Besides she knew it annoyed Roberto she used Spanish; he would stop her mid-stream and force her to use the correct word. Right now, she believed, his mind needed to be jolted, annoyed, whatever it took to bring him back to her. Using a rudimentary Spanish expression for sickness, dolor en la cabeza, she was interrupted.

"No," he explained. "It's headache, that's the correct English word."

Smiling, she knew he was on the mend; the angels were returning him back to the living. It wasn't time to go.

As the seemingly endless hours passed, he would vacillate between lucidity and semi-consciousness, uttering logical conversation, then lapsing back into a foreign gibberish. When friends would come to visit, they stood at the base of the bed. Roberto's responses would be unpredictable. "Who are you? "he would utter. When the visitors answered back, he would shake his head in exasperation, "I know you. You are my friend." Much to the relief of Juanita, he always knew her name, but played games, thinking it humorous to elaborate his precipitous state of mind. But when Kerry arrived, she did not find Roberto's mocking so funny. Still shaken from his comatose state, she did not appreciate his humor.

On Sunday afternoon, a colorful flower bouquet arrived from the attorneys in Jackson. Brightening the room, everyone remarked how incredibly thoughtful Spence's firm was making each client feel important. Nobody felt guilty about the lackluster purchase of quintessential hospital gifts. Roberto's friends spent their hard earned money to meet basic necessities. There would be ample years ahead where his troop would rally around him making sure he would never go hungry, or wander the streets homeless.

By Monday afternoon, there was a marked improvement in his health. Joking with the nurses, complaining about the small food portions, and fighting with his roommate for television selections, revealed his ability to function almost as normal. Other than losing a portion of eyesight, all other physical problems disintegrated. He was ready to leave the hospital. Institutions controlling freedom were reminiscent of jail life, a life he did not wish to be reminded of. In spite of the excellent care by the doctors and nursing staff, the cloud of loss of freedom shrouded his every moment. It was like a silent suffocation of his senses. Fearing he would become sicker if he remained, he plotted his departure. Wrapping the light-weight cotton robe loosely around his stomach, he made his way to the end of the hall, chiseled some change from a elderly man in the starkly lit waiting room, and called Juanita.

"They are releasing me in the morning," he lied. "I would love it if you could pick me up." He knew she would readily acquiesce, that it would never cross her mind that he had checked out on his own accord. Wryly grinning, he sauntered slowly back to the tiny room, which was filled with the snores of a young Mexican man suffering from a severe hangover.

Bright Wednesday morning, he shed the hospital gown, donned street clothes, packed the few possessions clustered on the night table, called Juanita, and exited the hospital. The late fall air was chilly, as he paced impatiently in the glare of the sun waiting for the car to arrive. Still unsettled, his mind wandered between reality and the distorted world of brain damage. Consorting with his ego. Roberto complacently relented to the fact there would be bad times ahead, and he would just learn to cope. Another day or week in the confinement of the hospital would not alter the prognosis. Armed with prescriptions, and various bottles of medications, he would endure the illness in the freedom of his mobile home, not locked into the bed or the routine of the hospital staff. It was quite easy for him to escape. he simply walked to the elevator, forced a purposeful stance, and slowly exited through the sliding glass doors. Not a question or odd look flashed his way.

"Ah," he sighed gently kissing Juanita on her lips. "It feels good to be outside, to breathe fresh air again."

Quickly taking over, she insisted he hand her the prescriptions and various bottles of pills. She would presume the responsibility of the nursing staff. Reading the labels, she praised the day she had entered night school to learn English. Although she was not social, and felt uncomfortable, if not somewhat inferior to Roberto's charitable friends, this time she decided to call them for additional help. Taking care of the man she loved would be a full time job for an uncertain amount of time, yet she still had to make a living supporting both herself, and her sister's family. Driving cautiously, the conversation was sparse, fraught with a hesitancy; neither one knew what to expect.

The stroke had entered his life like a lightening bolt. Both feared it could happen again, with fatal results. Clutching his hand, she squeezed it hard as visions of his coma weighed heavily on her memory. Saying a silent prayer, Juanita reminded her lover to show continued faith in God, that it would help him get through the bad times. Shaking his head, he just wanted simple peace of mind, and to regain back lost vision. "We are home," she announced, cautiously opening the passenger door. Pulling his arm over her shoulder, he leaned into her thin frame as the two struggled to the front door. The impairment to his vision, left him in a constant state of imbalance, and as he wobbled unsurely up the wooden steps. Bracing his strong hands against the metal walls, entering the dim of the home, he felt completely disorientated. He screamed out, "Where is the bathroom?"

Juanita tearfully reminded him, that she was at his side, there was nothing to worry about, she would be there forever. Clinging tightly to the stronger right arm, she coaxed him into the bedroom, fluffed up the pillows, and straightened the sheets, and blanket, while he found his way to the mattress. The mood swings caught Juanita off guard as he wavered between loving thankfulness to annoyance to disorientation. Pulling off the well-worn sneakers from his swollen feet, she turned on the television, prepared coffee, and comforted him in every way possible. An instant snore marked his exhaustion from the simple trip home. His body needed rest to recoup from the trauma suffered. In sleep he would commence the arduous task of healing. There was no denying the terror and overwhelming responsibility handed to her. Reflecting, she began a personal running thought of, "one day at a time."

Assembling the plethora of medicine bottles in a long row, she maneuvered them around until they were ordered by time and dosage, then vigilantly composed a schedule which her patient would religiously follow. Glancing at the worn Timex watch, she was reminded it was time to go back to work. Reluctantly kissing Roberto goodbye, she reminded him to stay in bed with the covers pulled tightly. It was winter, and it was cold.

Although not a generous man, Juanita's boss had allowed her three days off with pay to stay with Roberto in the hospital. Hating to leave him in such a precarious state, there was no alternative but return to the rental company, detailing cars. She hesitantly drove out the gravel front yard, and careened her head out the window yelling, "I love you." She warned him to behave.

Before Juanita reentered the streets, she held the car at the edge of the property, then unhinged the license plate on his decaying jalopy, hiding the keys deep inside her pocketbook. This would guarantee that if he decided he felt better, there would be no unexpected joy rides.

Sleep came easily and in great abundance as Roberto's body began the lengthy healing process. Lucidity became more prominent than disorientation as the sullen cold winter days dragged on. Questioning why he had returned to Las Vegas after the city had treated him cruelly lay heavily on his mind. Between the police force, the public defender's office and the district attorney, it seemed as if the entire legal system was against him, yet the moment he left the county jail, he reentered the streets, and claimed them as his own. It could have been destiny, or the incomparable beauty of the land that captivated and captured his heart, or the obsession of retracing the case in hopes of finding evidence that would finally affect exoneration, that held the attraction. The cloudless sunsets of rose-colored shades melting into midnight blue, opened up the starlit heavens each night, giving off an illusion of endless space. Perhaps it was the unrestricted eternal sky serving as a metaphor for the way he wished to live out the remainder of his days on earth. Closing his eyes, falling back into another deep sleep, dreams reverted back to childhood, and the comfort doting from mom and grandparents.

# PROMISES KEPT

Seated on a dented metal folding chair Roberto gazed out the window and spent endless hours doting on cars passing by, watching the neighbors walk their motley canines, and perusing the beckoning sky which turned from brilliant shades of orange and yellow to cool midnight blue. Life had become monotonous, almost one-dimensional. With the loss of most of his eyesight, and no training in coping with the new disability, freedom had again escaped his reach. Unable to drive, or balance his step for short distance walking, he had become trapped in the mobile home. Bitterly complaining about his blindness to Kerry, she began investigating alternatives offered by social services and Medicaid. Always positive and hopeful, Kerry was a welcome intervention into Roberto's limited life.

Smartly dressed in a deep burgundy gabardine pantsuit, her smile reflected love and caring for a man who needed more than just a hug and a few dollars. "I am going to call Spence's office, tell them your problems. Let us see what they might be able to do. They have been so kind, so thoughtful, perhaps they have a way to help you," she optimistically suggested.

Puttering around the messy kitchen, she swept the floor, washed the dishes, and warmed up a bag of fried chicken and French fries. Pouring two large glasses of diet soda, she placed them on the rickety card table. She gently guided his arm as she handed him small pieces from the plate. "At least my taste buds aren't blind," he joked gobbling up every morsel on the plate.

Glancing at her gold watch every five minutes, Kerry impatiently, yet remorsefully announced she was late for an appointment. It was very difficult for her to sit still, and with a potential client waiting she excused herself.

"Don't feel like you have to baby-sit me," he wheedled "I will be fine."

Giving her friend a hefty bear hug, and a lingered kiss on the cheek, she darted out the front door, and restated her promise to contact the law office as soon as was possible.

Left alone, the balance of life came to haunt him. Yes, he was blessed with friends, and he probably would never go without the necessities of life, but so much time had escaped his living. Fourteen years was a lifetime for many, a lifetime he was not allowed to live, and now almost blind, the overwhelming sense of unfairness, of not being considered as worthy of a successful life, chided and irritated his psyche. The stroke was a painful reminder that life was running away from him; his time was beginning to run out.

The next time, if there were a next time, he might not be so lucky, as to cheat death. Or worse, the stroke could leave him totally incapacitated. No longer patient, platitudes couldn't console his spirit. He was a needy man. Unable to hold a job, all his support came from charitable friends. He hated living such a dependent life. Every time Juanita pecked him a kiss goodbye it served as a reminder of his degenerating mental and physical condition. Closing his eyes, drifting into a fitful sleep, he prayed Kerry's promise to entreat the Jackson lawyers to expedite the case would come to fruition.

Two weeks of rest and care bode well for the patient as he began claiming back a portion of his health. A stronger walk, slower even breathing, and a return of his taste buds, marked the initiation of the healing process. Sprawled out on the disheveled covers, the ringing phone jarred him out of an afternoon siesta.

"It's, Kerry. How are you feeling? And I have good news for you," she rattled on. "Spence is aware of your situation and has planned a meeting with you and the defendant's lawyers next month. He told me he would be calling you soon to begin preparing you for the important meeting. I think you should see some light at the end of the tunnel. Spence sounded very determined to wrap up this case."

Hardly believing his ears, he asked Kerry to repeat the conversation. "Perhaps the other side is ready to settle, I sure am," he tooted. "Maybe the waiting game is over. Kerry, I can't thank you enough for helping me. I owe you so much. There is no way I can begin to thank you, but when I finally get the money I can pay you back for the endless times you have taken care of me. I really truly appreciate all that you have done for me and all that you have given me. You are a true friend, and I feel so lucky to have known you," he said.

"Please stop," she insisted. "You will need your strength to face their battalion of lawyers, to stand up for your rights and take back what belongs to you. I will come over and check on you tomorrow. What would you like me to bring you?"

Shyly he asked for a pack of cigarettes, and diet soda.

"If that makes you happy," she acquiesced. "Then that is what I shall bring you."

With a smug smile, he hung up the phone, and daydreamed how to spend the millions of dollars he would be rewarded from the lawsuit. As if counting sheep to deepen his senses into an intense sleep, he counted dollars, and how he would spend each and every one. First a house for Juanita, money for his mother and sisters, a new car, a garden of fruits and flowers, a refrigerator overflowing with ice-cream, a pantry filled with cigarettes...

Lying restlessly on the mattress, he fought with the reality of his situation. Ironically, his body had betrayed him, creating a new and unyielding prison. He was no longer free to come and go as he wished. His eyes were so damaged by the stroke, driving was an impossibility. The trailer had become his new jail cell. It had been over four months since he had suffered the stroke. Venturing outside without accompaniment was impossible. "I must try," he pushed. "I must try and allow myself freedom."

Picking up the phone, he called Juanita and hoped to convince her to take him down to the strip, allowing him the freedom to walk by himself, enjoy an outing without constraints. But instead, her sister answered the phone, explaining Juanita had gone out for a short walk. Upon hearing Roberto's earnest request, she offered to take him herself. Elated at the prospect of being on his own, he carefully dressed, brushed his yellowing teeth, shaved the partially grown in beard, dabbed on cologne, and stood anxiously at the front door. His ride arrived within minutes and they hastily sped to the base of the Las Vegas strip. "There is no place on earth like this," Roberto said, "I bet there are millions of lights down here. The streets are never cold just from the heat given off from all these light bulbs."

Dropping him off near a park bench, she drove off as quickly as she arrived, leaving Roberto as he wished. Alone to wander the streets. The sudden revelation of being on his own sent shock waves through his psyche, causing him to become completely and utterly disorientated. With limited vision, things became unclear. He was unable to discern reality from fantasy; he became terrified, as he began walking in concentric circles. Spotting the man, two bicycle policemen approached and offered to help. In rambling sentences, he explained he was lost, then he pulled out his wallet searching for a name and number of a friend. Tumbling out of the wallet was Kerry's number jotted on a piece of rumpled notepaper. Handing it to the policemen, they immediately dialed the number and explained the circumstances of the call, asking if she could possibility come and collect the disorientated man. "Yes, of course," she cried. "I will be there in twenty minutes."

For once Roberto experienced the goodness of police officers. Waiting for Kerry to arrive, the youthful officers joked, and eased his confused stated of mind. Looking up, the three men could not help but notice the shiny white car screeching up to the sidewalk. Kerry bolted out, grabbed Roberto's arm as if claiming a piece of meat. "This guy is my friend," she pointedly stated to the officers. "And I will be taking him home right now."

Introducing Kerry to the young men, she thanked them profusely for taking such good care of her friend promising this would never happen again. She apologized for being so gruff, but she explained how frightened the call had made her. "He has recently suffered a stroke and gets confused sometimes."

"Oh boy," Roberto grumbled, "She is going to let me have it."

Once safely seated in the car, Kerry toned down her voice as she began quizzing her friend, trying to ascertain his state of mind. Strokes can play tricks on the body and mind, can come back, or cause unexplained behavior. Not that much time had passed since he suffered the trauma. Perhaps there was damage or symptoms that were just now surfacing. Wavering with thought, Roberto relayed the story of what had occurred. Kerry was utterly seething when she found out that Juanita's sister had literally dumped him in the middle of the strip. Even at his own request, she should have known better. It's as if common sense and decency had totally escaped her grasp. Nonetheless,

Roberto was safe and sound, as he promised he would never ever do this again.

"If only I could see better," he complained scornfully. "Then I would know where I was and wouldn't become so confused."

Squeezing his hand as if to acknowledge his latest revelation, she astutely pulled the car into the local Burger King, ordering the super sized meal. She knew he hadn't eaten in hours, and was too proud to admit he was starving. Sensitive to the health of a diabetic, Kerry's conscience would not fail to make sure her friend was well fed before she dropped him off for the night. Handing him the paper bag, he smelled the French fries wafting into the car, He dug into the fast food, thanking Kerry profusely. At the verge of tears, she controlled her emotions until after Roberto was safely tucked into the mattress on the floor. There was no reason to admonish him, this evening had served as a painful learning experience, he had been terrified and humiliated, suffering the aftershocks caused by the stroke. No longer was he in control of his body, rather he was at the mercy of the damage inflicted by the disease.

Carefully examining the house, and making sure he had plenty of fluids and a late night snack laid out beside the bed, she locked the door, letting herself out the back entrance. "I will call you in the morning," she said. Retrieving her keys, she allowed the sound of the engine to drown out the spontaneous outpouring of tears. She wondered what would have happened if Roberto hadn't found her telephone number in his wallet? In the morning, she would buy him a telephone book that would fit in his pocket, so this would never happen again.

Opening up the large envelope that Kerry had dumped off at Roberto's front door, Juanita carefully read the letter from the

Spence firm which set a date for final negotiations. They would be meeting in February at a resort located on the western side of the city, and he was welcome to bring a couple of friends, who could stay at the hotel as guests of the law firm. "Well, I hope I am one of your welcome guests," she teased.

"Yes, and I think I will ask Alice. She could surely use a couple of relaxing days."

Continuing on, the letter detailed the time and location, promising to wrap up years of bargaining. Settlement was clearly in sight. Additionally the firm would be paying to have both eyes operated on, giving him a better quality of life. Tears of joy ran down Juanita's face as she jubilantly read her lover's fate. The packet contained copies of the proposed settlements and the suit. "I feel like there is light at the end of the tunnel," he announced.

Hearing the phone ring, Juanita uncharacteristically answered, handing it to Roberto. "It's Kerry."

"Well good afternoon. Have you been reading the packet I dropped off?" she questioned. "Because I got a phone call from the Jackson office and they asked me to find you a home. They told me about the meeting coming up, and that I should be there, but Jim and I will be out of town. Remember? My son is getting married. Even though I would love to be there, I am already committed to my son's big wedding day. But, from where I sit, you could not be in better hands. It looks like settlement is on its way. I think we should all go out to dinner and celebrate. I will pick you up tomorrow evening."

Happily, he relayed the contents of the letter, forgoing the part where he would take Juanita and Alice to the resort, not wanting her to feel slighted even though Kerry would be out of town. Hanging up the phone, shaking his head, he admitted Kerry was as jubilant as he; it was almost impossible to believe all these years of waiting were approaching the finale, and restitution would be imminent. At last an important goal would be achieved — the chance to live out whatever life was left, in comfort. A safe place to live, money for siblings and mother, payback to the friends who charitably dolled out funds, were primary on the list. Perusing the simple entrapments of the mobile home, he projected how wonderful it would be to have a clean home, filled refrigerator, stocked pantry, the smell of fresh flowers decorating an intimate dining table, and perhaps even a mutt to stand guard at the vestibule.

Alice met Roberto and Juanita early on an overcast February morning, two days before Valentine's, heading directly westward to the designated resort. Driving up the valet ramp, they collected their gear, and walked towards the front desk announcing they were with the Spence firm. Handing over three room keys, the bellhop respectively showed them to the adjoining rooms. Luxurious beyond anything Roberto had ever known, he joked it would be difficult to leave. Juanita and Alice just giggled, pointing out the lavish bathroom filled with fragrant soaps, shampoos, plush towels, enormous bathtub, and marble floor. "Hell," suggested Alice. "Let's make this a party and order room service." Still giggling, Juanita nodded in agreement, motioning to the menu. With the finesse of a highly seasoned traveler, Alice selected a gala spread complete with wine, and of course a giant bowl of chocolate ice-cream for the hero. "There are times when we just have to enjoy," Alice winked. "I want to make sure our friend here has his favorite food on earth, and plenty of it."

Noting the message light was flashing, Alice picked up the phone and jotted down the information; the meeting would commence in the morning shortly after breakfast, in the seclusion of a private conference room. But Roberto was to come alone. Juanita would walk him down, leaving as soon as he was comfortably seated. Miffed she was not welcome at the meeting. Alice suggested it would give them ample time to investigate the resort and have a little fun. As they played with every gadget in the room, laughed and talked, the day sped by rapidly. Glancing at her watch, Alice announced she was turning in for the night as she was planning a lengthy soak in the giant marble tub.

Checking his appearance, Juanita escorted her lover to the conference room, surreptitiously departing the meeting. Seated nearest the window was the prestigious bank of lawyers representing the Spence firm. Dressed in simple tailored clothing, Gerry Spence took quick command of the room, introducing his client, and protégés. Without undue pomp and circumstance, he quickly cut to the chase, elaborating that they had traveled a long and arduous distance to come to this table, and his client should be given his due share. Silence filled the room as each contemplated the best way to reach an agreement. Although the original claim asked for fourteen million dollars, one for each year in prison, the figure was whittled down to be digestible for both sides. The courts had spoken, and Roberto was to receive fair and adequate compensation for negligence, undue pain and suffering.

On the opposite side of the rectangular table sat the defending attorneys for the State of Nevada, on behalf of the District Attorney's office, the Public Defender's office, and the police force. The State's lawyers did not wish the press to splash the names of his clients over the front pages. They all had lovely homes, mortgages to pay, young mouths to feed, and reputations to protect. It was in the best interest to make this case slide into oblivion. The simple question was how much would it cost? The State had lost in court and was ordered to cough up the settlement. Although it was painful to bite the bullet and pay Mr. Miranda, the State's lawyers were keenly aware of the alterna-

tive, not abiding by the Judge's decision meant negative publicity. It was clear from the plethora of local and national news articles, the press was on the plaintiff's side. Everyone was cheering
for Roberto. To not pay him for the State's mistake would provide fodder for a story that would negatively impact the city of
Las Vegas and the state of Nevada.

Chatting and negotiating, a euphemism for stalling, the
annoyed Mr. Spence rose, and methodically quoted an ultima-
tum, a bottom line figure, turned to his troop and announced
they had said what they wanted to say, and they were departing.
He intimated the press would surely love to know how the case
was finalized. The remaining lawyers put their heads together as
if in a Sunday football huddle, and declared the terms would be
settled expeditiously. Bidding them good day, the Jackson
entourage stiffly departed the conference room, overhearing a
cackle of bickering amongst the exasperated State's attorneys,
still shuddering from the dramatic display of candor and expertise. There was no doubt in anyone's mind of the power, bril-
liance, and knowledge the Spence firm brought to the negotiating table, he was truly a legend in his own time. For once, the
scale of justice tipped heavily in Roberto's favor He would get a
settlement, perhaps not every penny, but plenty.

Selecting the youngest member of the Spence team, she took
her client's arm and ushered him back to the room. Explaining
the delicate art of resolution, she clarified Mr. Spence would
contact him as soon as he heard from the opposition. Sitting list-
lessly in the opulent room mindlessly watching cable television,
Roberto retrieved the bellowing phone from the night stand.
The younger protégé explained that an agreement had been
made but the details needed to be documented. Not wanting to
commit to a specific figure, it was inferred it would be substantial sum of money.

That evening, the three celebrated by ordering room service: a fine gourmet meal including steaks, wine, and a selection of desserts. Satiated, Roberto put his head on the pillow. "So now I know what it is like to be rich, to have money and spend it anyway I wanted." Turning to Juanita, taking her hand, he said, "You will not have to work any more, you will stay with me in a beautiful and safe home. We will have food to eat, buy a new car, go to the movies, drive to the ocean. We will be free and live life the way we want."

Throwing her arms around his neck she hugged him warmly. Plumping up the pillows, she suggested he get some rest. So much had taken place. Kissing her friends good night, Alice departed, reminding them she would be driving back early the next morning, "You two might be on vacation, but I have a business to run. There are over thirty installation orders. Thank goodness every home needs a refrigerator," Alice said.

The mobile home tilted from the whipping winds of a late spring sandstorm, as tiny stones pelted the roof, and windows. Alone, Roberto barely heard the ringing from the brown plastic phone. "Hello, who is calling?" he asked. In spite of the blustering winds, the voice was familiar. It was Mr. Mc Cullough, the attorney from Jackson announcing the settlement. "Please speak louder," Roberto yelled into the phone. It's hard to hear."

Adjusting his voice, the attorney relayed how much money Roberto would be receiving, that the checks were being processed, and the package would be delivered directly to him. The attorney explained how the money would be allocated; what portion the firm would be keeping and what Roberto's check would be.

Two days later there was a bang on the metal door. An unfamiliar voice announcing she had an urgent package. Throwing on a shirt, and zipping up a pair of wrinkled jeans, Roberto hobbled through the hall unlatching the rusted lock. Opening up the door, he squinted at the stranger. "I am here to take you to a quiet place to receive your money," she spoke. "Would you like to take Juanita with you?"

"Yes," Roberto responded. "Wherever I go, so does she. You have my money? Cause I do not see a wheel barrel filled with green bills."

"Not to worry, you will have your wheel barrel in a few hours," the stranger replied.

Taking Roberto's arm, they walked to the long sleek limousine. Juanita was already comfortably seated in the back. She handing him a glass of Coke and announced, We are on our way to paradise." Neither one ever turned their heads to look back.

Seated in the comfort of a luxury car, he rolled down the window feeling the warm spring breezes cross his brow. He looked up to see a flock of sparrows flying northward. Now, I can be free as those birds, I can do what I want, go where I want. I am finally free.

*The End*